Social Construction in Context

D1078459

WITHDRAWN

Social Construction in Context

Kenneth J. Gergen

U.W.E.L.
LEARNING RESOURCES

ACC No. 2285893   CLASS 312

CONTROL
0761965440

DATE
-9. JAN 2003

301
GER

SAGE Publications
London • Thousand Oaks • New Delhi

© Kenneth J. Gergen and 2001

First published 2001

All rights reserved. No part of this publication may be
reproduced, stored in a retrieval system, transmitted or
utilized in any form or by any means, electronic, mechanical,
photocopying, recording or otherwise, without permission in
writing from the Publishers.

 SAGE Publications Ltd
6 Bonhill Street
London EC2A 4PU

SAGE Publications Inc
2455 Teller Road
Thousand Oaks, California 91320

SAGE Publications India Pvt Ltd
32, M-Block Market
Greater Kailash – I
New Delhi 110 048

British Library Cataloguing in Publication Data

A catalogue record for this book is
available from the British Library

ISBN 0 7619 6544 0
ISBN 0 7619 6545 9 (pbk)

Library of Congress catalog card number 0000000

Typeset by Keystroke, Jacaranda Lodge, Wolverhampton
Printed and bound in Great Britain by Athenaeum Press, Gateshead

CONTENTS

ACKNOWLEDGEMENTS

Chapter 1 a revision of 'Constructionism and realism: how are we to go on?' In I. Parker (Ed.) (1998) *Social construction, discourse and realism*. London: Sage.

Chapter 2 revision of a paper by the same name in *Theory and Psychology*, (1997), 7, 31–36.

Chapter 3 a revision of a paper by the same name. In H. Simons & M. Billig (Eds.). (1994). *After postmodernism*. London: Sage.

Chapter 4 a revision of an article by the same name, in *History of the Human Sciences* (1997), *10*, 151–173.

Chapter 5 revision of 'History and psychology: three weddings and a future'. In P.N. Stearns & J. Lewis (Eds.), *An emotional history of the United States* (pp. 14–32). New York: New York University Press.

Chapter 6 original paper

Chapter 7 original paper

Chapter 8 a revision of 'Global organization: From imperialism to ethical vision. *Organization* (1995), 2, 519–532.

Chapter 9 revision of an article by the same name in *Journal of Applied Behavioral Science* (1997), *32*, 356–377.

Chapter 10 a revision of an article of the same name. In L. Holzman & J. Morss (Eds.). (2000). *Postmodern psychologies, societal practice, and political life*. New York: Routledge.

Chapter 11 a revision of an article by the same name. In J.E. Davis (Ed.), *Identity and social change* (pp. 135–154). New Brunswick, NJ: Transaction Books.

To dialogic companions who unceasingly beckoned beyond the borders: Kurt Back, Michael Billig, Jerome Bruner, Mary Gergen, Harold Goulishian, Rom Harré, Edward Sampson and John Shotter.

PREFACE

It was over 15 years ago that John Shotter and I began to discuss the need for an intellectual sinew that might bind together the sweeping dialogues of discontent in the social sciences. Could we locate a theme that might give common shape to the restless quests for alternatives to the pervasive naturalization of the human sciences? There were exciting developments in ethnomethodology, feminist social science, ethogenic psychology, labelling theory, symbolic anthropology, critical theory, dialectical psychology, power/knowledge theory, and historical psychology among them. And these developments seemed importantly linked to the demise of foundationalist science and its replacement by historical and social accounts of knowledge. At least one way of tying these various movements together was captured by the term *social construction*. Although drawn from the annals of the sociology of knowledge, the concept was now secreting itself into numerous discussions across the disciplines. Most importantly, to the extent that the genesis of knowledge can be traced to communal life, the sciences cease to be the arbiters of the real. No longer can scientists remove themselves from responsibility to the human project with knowledge claims simply demanded by what there is. With knowledge thus denaturalized and reenculturated, the vast repositories of the taken for granted – accumulating at least since the period of the Enlightenment – are opened for fresh reassessment. The implications seemed enormous.

John and I shared our hopes of fostering dialogue and further development of constructionist endeavours with the editors of Sage in London. The heady mixture of enthusiasm and wise counsel with which editorial director Ziyad Marar responded were essential to what followed: the birth of the Sage book series, *Inquiries in Social Construction*. In the years since, John and I – later joined by Sue Widdicombe – assisted an enormously talented group of scholars from across the human sciences in generating 21 volumes of work in a constructionist vein.

The Social Construction of Lesbianism (1987) Celia Kitzinger
Texts of Identity (1988) John Shotter & Kenneth Gergen (Eds)
Rhetoric in the Human Sciences (1988) Herbert Simons (Ed.)
Collective Remembering (1990) David Middleton & Derek Edwards (Eds)

Everyday Understanding (1990) Gun Semin & Kenneth Gergen, K (Eds)
Research and Reflexivity (1991) Fred Steier F (Ed.)
Constructing Knowledge (1991) Lorraine Nencel & Peter Pels (Eds)
Therapy as Social Construction (1992) Sheila McNamee & Kenneth Gergen
    (Eds)
Discursive Psychology (1992) Derek Edwards & Jonathan Potter *Psychology
    & Postmodernism* (1992) Steiner Kvale (Ed.)
Constructing the Social (1993) Theodore Sarbin & John Kitsuse (Eds)
    Conversational Realities (1993) John Shotter
Power and Gender (1994) Lorraine Radtke & Hendrikus Stam H (Eds)
After Postmodernism (1994) Herbert Simons H & Michael Billig (Eds) *The
    Social Self* (1995) David Bakhurst & Christine Sypnowich C (Eds)
Reconstructing the Psychological Subject (1997) Betty Bayer & John Shotter
    (Eds)
Re-imagining Therapy (1997) Eero Riikonen & Gregory Smith *Constructing the
    Mediated Self* (1996) Deborah Grodin & Thomas Lindlof (Eds)
Pathology and the Postmodern (1999) Dwight Fee (Ed.)
Social Constructionism, Discourse & Realism (1998) Ian Parker (Ed.)
The Social Construction of Anorexia Nervosa (1999) Julia Hepworth

We look back with delight at these offerings – wonderfully rich,
intellectually bracing, and often daring. At the same time the present work
will serve as a marker: it represents the closing contribution to the series.
This is not at all because interest in the subject matter has drawn to a close.
Rather it is because the dialogues on social construction have become so
widespread and richly variegated that the concept of a circumscribed series
is no longer viable. To suggest that there is a particular series of books that
expresses the essence of current inquiry is wholly misleading. In certain
corners of the scholarly world a constructionist sensibility is now so fully
engrained that it even ceases to require a specific denotation. The series has
been successful in contributing to a common consciousness, but at this
point the consciousness requires little more from an effort such as this.

My hope is that this book will serve as a worthy conclusion to the series.
In important degree the content of these chapters has been provoked or
stimulated by these offerings. In this sense the present work may be viewed
as a tribute to the authors and editors with whom we have worked – both
a complement and compliment. At the same time, my debts here are far
more extended. The voices of so many – near and far, now and in the past
– are echoed in these pages that a proper recounting is impossible. I close,
then, with only a single moment of particular gratitude to symbolize the
greater debt. This is to Cynthia Holt, my administrative assistant, whose
effective interventions at every phase of the project were essential to its
successful conclusion. Thank you for joining me in this endeavour.

INTRODUCTION

Deliberations on the social construction of the real and the good have burst across the sundry disciplines of science and the humanities. They have stirred enormous controversy concerning such long-revered concepts as truth, objectivity, knowledge, reason, authority and progress. They have fuelled what we have come to see as 'the culture wars', and 'the science wars'. As many see it, we can no longer return to the comfortable assumptions of traditional scholarly and scientific work, and a host of related institutions such as mental health, education, the justice system, organizational life and politics. Ferment and change are everywhere in evidence. For almost two decades I have been deeply immersed in these deliberations. I have cast a critical eye on much that I once held dear, searched for syntheses of the developing dialogues and struggled toward visions of promising alternatives. Much of this work is contained in two previous volumes, *Realities and Relationships* and *An Invitation to Social Construction*.

Largely owing to my immersion in this work, I have been invited into a variety of new domains of discussion. Both allies and antagonists have challenged me to extend my thinking across disciplinary boundaries, to come to grips with the complexities of societal practice and to speak out on various cultural issues. I have been exposed to a variety of conceptual, critical and practical challenges, and asked to explore the potentials and limitations of constructionist thought as it extends into new territories. In certain respects these have not been easy times. It is far more comfortable to remain within a single trajectory, where favourite ideas continue to recombine in various self-satisfying forms. It is also comforting to sustain the old battles against an outworn positivism, secure that one occupies the intellectual and moral high ground. But, alas, there is a close relationship between comfort and decay – the eternal return of the same. If I heed the criticisms, take on the challenges, accept the invitations, I am precariously destabilized. Yet I have come to feel that within these vertiginous moments lie invaluable potentials. In the present volume I would like, then, to share some of the outcomes of these various challenges, specifically as related to the worlds of the academy, societal practice and cultural life.

The costs of a flourishing paradigm

To be sure, these essays are highly disparate in their specific concerns. At the same time, however, there is an underlying unity and it is this unity that is evoked in the title of the work: *Social Construction in Context*. Some background is required in order to appreciate what is at stake. At the outset, dialogues on social construction draw from numerous sources across the sciences and humanities – sociology, literary study, history, anthropology, women's studies, psychology, communication, cultural studies, and more. As I see it, these dialogues largely function in three significant ways – as *metatheory*, as *social theory* and as societal *practice*. As a metatheory (or theory about theory), social constructionism not only challenges empiricist accounts of knowledge, but indeed stands as an impediment to all first philosophies of knowledge. For the constructionist, all claims to knowledge, truth, objectivity or insight are founded within communities of meaning making – including the claims of constructionists themselves. Constructionism in this sense is not concerned with truth beyond community, but with what might be called providential intelligibilities. At the level of metatheory, most constructionist scholarship has been critical. Authoritative claims about the nature of the world are everywhere challenged; demonstrations of 'the social construction of . . . ' everywhere emphasize the cultural and historical lodgement of the otherwise taken for granted. Slowly, however, the possibilities for a 'positive programme' of social constructionist science and scholarship are beginning to emerge.

At this level of metatheory, nothing specific is demanded in the way of substantive inquiry. The metatheory contains no specific requirements for theory, method or practice. Rather, constructionism asks a new set of questions – often evaluative, political and pragmatic – regarding the choices one makes in these domains. It also invites a dramatic expansion of what may counted as legitimate inquiry and expression. At the same time, however, many social scientists have been moved to expand on social constructionism as an empirically viable theory of social life. If a plausible case can be made for the social constitution of scientific knowledge on the metatheoretical level, then such a case can also be made for the generation of knowledge in all domains – in government, the justice system, the business world, medicine, religion, communities, the family, therapy, and so on. Further, such assumptions can be extended to account for cultural process more generally, the character of 'the rational', the genesis of memory, the circulation of meaning, the nature of social power, and more. The descriptive and explanatory literature is rich and ever expanding.

Finally, many scholars and practitioners draw from constructionist ideas to fashion new forms of practice. In the social sciences, for example, both the focus of research and the methodological tools are affected. Mounting research into discourse practices, rhetorical efficacy, popular culture, the subtleties of ideology, colonialist influences and media representation among them all tend to manifest constructionist assumptions. Further, constructionist dialogues are triggering dramatic developments in methodology; what is now referenced as the 'revolution in qualitative research' can be traced directly to constructionist lines of thought. Narrative methods, collaborative methods, auto-ethnography and performance methods are illustrative. These developments within the scholarly world parallel substantial transformations in practice outside the academic world. Notable are new developments within such communities as organizational development, family therapy, social work, counselling, education and mediation. As practices emphasizing dialogue, co-construction, collaboration, community building, narrative and positive visioning expand, so do they typically carry constructionist assumptions.

I find these developments in metatheory, theory and practice enormously exciting and worthy of continued dedication. At the same time, however, these developments are bought at a certain cost – that of growing isolation. These various dialogues and practices have brought constructionism into a productive self-consciousness, but simultaneously tended to create constructionism as a domain unto itself. One enters the arena to find it so fully engaging and productive that it becomes a world apart. This tendency toward isolation is also coupled with a certain self-congratulatory element – as if such investments were conceptually, ideologically and practically superior to all that has preceded. Slowly a shield of containment is erected – possibly essential to the development of constructionism – but which ultimately leads to redundancy, rigidity and enervation.

As a group these essays attempt, then, to sustain the constructionist connection to context – to those cultural texts from which constructionism emerged, but that ultimately supplied the grounds of difference from which constructionism drew its very identity and meaning. At present this con/text is largely composed of domains of meaning and practice that either exist independent of constructionism (the vast domain of that which is 'not constructionist'), or that are actively set against constructionist endeavors. In the former case, most of the world's population carries on without consciousness of construction, nor are constructionists altogether curious about that which is 'out of the dialogue'. Many scientists and scholars outside the dialogue indeed have come to see constructionist ideas as menacing. Many find that constructionism undermines warrants for truth claims, seeming to render science equivalent to mythology. Hence 'the science wars'. Others find constructionism's moral and political relativism pallid if not reprehensible. And still others find that constructionism has been all too occupied with critique, and its substantive contribution to social understanding too narrow. It is the challenge of crossing these and other bridges to context that furnishes the backdrop for much of the present volume.

Engaging with the con/text

As I have realized in this writing, my response to the challenge of context crossing takes three primary but overlapping forms. First there is the attempt to elaborate the relevance of constructionist ideas for various contextual domains. Specifically I have selected two academic undertakings – historical psychology and organizational science – and three areas of practice – therapy, education and organizational ethics. These elaborations are scarcely monologic; the move is not to extend the perimeters of constructionist thought indefinitely. Rather the hope is to extend the dialogues in such a way that new clearings are opened and new practices invited. Yet, I am also concerned with various groups often antagonistic to constructionism: realists, ethical foundationalists and social activists. Can these voices be addressed in such a way that hostility can give way to productive dialogue? This concern opens to the second means of context crossing.

In this case I engage in a certain critical self-reflection. I sense that constructionist arguments (even my own) have too often functioned as a sword, with the elimination of empirical study, ethical foundationalism, realism and so on as its seeming goal. In my view there is nothing about constructionism that is so nihilistic. The arguments have too often been overdrawn, insufficient attention has been given to overlapping investments, and the advantages of these otherwise 'bankrupt' traditions overlooked. Thus, in several chapters – especially those treating realism, the limits of pure critique and organizational science – I try to reflect critically on constructionist endeavours. Just possibly such reflexivity can encourage the antagonists to free up the voices of doubt they too inherit. Surely if we speak in multiple tongues we shall find certain venues in which productive conversation can emerge and the prevailing animus can be assuaged.

Finally, the attempt to replace the bareness of alienation with cross-pollinating potentials takes the form of substantive conceptualization and practice. Here the attempt is not so much to initiate dialogue through elaboration and self-reflection, but to generate resources that non-constructionists might also find useful. One need not be religious to appreciate the beauty of a medieval cathedral, or grow up in Japan to enjoy sushi. In the same way, if the constructionist dialogues give rise to engaging ideas and useful practices, they may be readily appropriated by others. Again the boundaries begin to blur. Chapters on therapeutic and educational practices are especially sensitive to this possibility, and the chapters that close the book – on identity politics and on technology and the moral self – actively chart ways of understanding and practising of broad relevance.

Organization of this book

Perhaps the archetype of the Trinity is in ascendence, as I have also chosen
to divide the contents of the book into three sections. The initial set of
five chapters treats constructionist ideas within the context of ongoing
deliberations on social scientific knowledge. Under the rubric of 'Social
Construction and the Human Sciences' I take up a variety of critical issues
confronting constructionist ideas as they concatenate across this intellectual terrain. Here the focus is first on major tensions encountered when
constructionist ideas enter a domain of study. In Chapter 1 I treat the
ongoing antagonism between constructionist scholars and realists. My
concern here is not only the relationship between constructionism and the
empiricist tradition; I am especially concerned with 'realists to the left',
those who otherwise join constructionists in their critique of traditional
empiricism but who resist constructionist relativism on political issues.
The major question is whether such antagonisms must be sustained, or are
there more productive possibilities? Similar issues arise in Chapter 2, where
I try to move beyond the scholarship of deconstruction in psychology.
Volumes of scholarship now illuminate the socially constructed character
of psychological conceptions – both in science and daily life. Does such
scholarship mean the termination of psychological science, or are there
more promising alternatives? In Chapter 3, I move from these more pointed
explorations to a more general concern with the function of critique. Here
I inquire into the limits of constructionist critique as commonly practised
and open discussion into more collaborative means of deliberation.

This reflection on critique sets the stage for the two final chapters of
the section, both of which attempt to elaborate various implications
of the preceding analyses. In Chapter 4 I explore the forms of voice that
are employed within human science writings – both traditional and
experimental. The analysis thus equalizes the rhetorics of romanticism,
modernism and postmodernism in the sciences, and enables us to pose
questions concerning their situated utility. Finally in Chapter 5 I examine
the relationship between historical and psychological scholarship, both in
terms of their traditional antagonism and in light of more recent constructionist scholarship. I employ the latter to develop positive programmes of
collaboration between the disciplines.

In Part II, 'Social Construction and Societal Practice', the focus moves
from academic issues to social practice. In Chapter 6 Lisa Warhus joins me
in using constructionist ideas to reflect on broad-ranging initiatives in the
therapeutic world to understand therapy as movement in meaning. Here
constructionism not only serves as an ordering and integrating device, but
as a means of pressing for the development of new practices. In Chapter 7,
educational specialist Stanton Wortham joins in a similar effort, this time
directed to developments in pedagogy. This chapter also foregrounds a
continuing concern in this book with relational theory and practice. The
two remaining chapters in this section of the book are concerned with life

in organizations. In Chapter 8, I take up the challenge of organizational ethics and the broad concern with the ethical insensitivity of global organization. Although globalism is typically seen as a threat to human welfare, I try to spell out ways in which a relational orientation to organizational life can actually thrust the global organization into a position of moral leadership. Finally, in Chapter 9 Tojo Thatchenkery joins me in considering how the practices of organizational science can be enhanced by the kind of postmodern thought embodied in constructionism. Much as in the case of therapy and pedagogy, we make use of emerging practices to vivify the potentials.

In Part III, 'Social Construction and Cultural Context', I turn to issues of broad cultural significance. The attempt is to place constructionist ideas in the service of societal understanding – to bring critical analysis to bear, to appreciate wherever possible and to work generatively toward alternative futures. The two sites of focal interest are identity politics and communication technology. In the USA the identity politics movement arguably represents the most significant change in political patterning of the past thirty years. Eschewing the traditional two-party system, political affiliations are aligned with one's social identity – African American, woman, gay, Hispanic, and so on. Chapter 10 treats both the affinity and the tension between this movement and social constructionism, with the aim of moving beyond identity politics to more viable forms of political engagement. In the final chapter, my concern is with the implications of twentieth-century communications technology for sustaining the moral order. In my view such technology threatens any hope of lodging moral action within individual minds or social groups. As in the preceding chapter, I search for a transcendent move toward relational action.

In a broad sense these final essays attempt to bring into practice some of the arguments developed in preceding chapters – especially those within Part I. The point of these inquiries is neither to 'tell the truth' about societal life nor to establish some new foundation of reason or value. Rather, the hope is to incite dialogue on our contemporary condition, to generate discursive resources with which we can critically and appreciatively reflect and to open spaces for new forms of coordinated action.

PART I

SOCIAL CONSTRUCTION AND THE HUMAN SCIENCES

1

CONSTRUCTIONISM AND REALISM: A NECESSARY COLLISION?

> In order to enact a transformative politics, one must identify correctly the source of the problem – but from a relativist perspective, there can be no such thing as a correct analysis.
>
> Dana L. Cloud, in *After Postmodernism*

> The saints are gathering at the real places, trying tough skin on sharp conscience . . . you can hear them yelping.
>
> A. R. Ammons, *The Confirmers*

In important respects the drama of social constructionism was born of opposition. Constructionist writings drew their principal energy from their multi-dimensional critique of the longstanding tradition of positivist/ empiricist science. Long reigning was the view that scientific claims to knowledge were effectively uncontaminated by culture, history and ideology – that indeed empirical science was the crowning achievement in the human attempt to understand nature and self. Constructionist critique – emanating from the history of science and sociology of knowledge, gaining breadth and depth through contributions from critical theory, feminism, literary theory, rhetoric, and more, and then spilling across the disciplines – flew in the face of the acceptable. The capacity of science to generate transcendent truths – beyond history and culture – or by dint of rigorous methodology to 'carve nature at the joint', was thrown into jeopardy. And hence the drama – often called 'the science wars – that

continues to pervade the scholarly and scientific world. For constructionists, all claims to 'the real' are traced to processes of relationship, and
there is no extra-cultural means of ultimately privileging one construction
of reality over another. Realism is on the run, and the response has been
aggressive and acrimonious.

Constructionist critique was enormously appealing to many groups
whose voices had been marginalized by science, and to all those whose
pursuits of social equality and justice were otherwise thwarted by existing
authorities of truth. Constructionist arguments not only served to level the
playing field, but also opened the door to broadscale political and moral
critique. As later chapters will detail, constructionism and culture critique
walked hand in hand. Slowly, however, those engaged in social change
began to find that the constructionist axe turned back to gash the hand
of the user. There was no critique of the power structure, oppression or
injustice that could lay claim to truth beyond construction – that was itself
not 'one way of understanding' among many, as opposed to 'the correct
way'. A new schism emerged, one in which culture critics found constructionist ideas inimical to their ends – insufficiently passionate, confident or
cantankerous. While their targets live in constructed worlds, culture critics
have not wished to jettison the privilege of truth claims. Constructionist
ideas thus came under attack from both 'right' and 'left', with both
antagonists sharing a commitment to realism.[1]

The complexity of the conflict has further intensified: first, many
enamoured with social constructionist ideas have wished to document
their implications. Research has been mounted, for example, into processes
of conversation, the media and identity construction. And such research
is often accompanied by an investment in precisely those claims to 'truth
through method' that constructionism has been at pains to subvert. If
conversation is a major means by which we secure the sense of truth,
constructionists ask, how can one 'get it right' about the nature of discourse
or conversation? Further, humanists, phenomenologists and cognitive
constructivists – who welcomed the constructionist emphasis on meaning
making and its critical challenge to positivist hegemony – soon found that
many of their own icons – intentionality, agency, experience, and cognitive
construals – were thrown into question. While largely willing to see the
material world as a construction, they wished to hold fast to certain to the
realities of the mind. The relationship to constructionism resultingly
cooled.[2] In effect, the scholarly atmosphere is striated with conflict – realism
and constructionism are everywhere in conflict. How, then, are we to
go on?

Conflict in cultural context

It is useful to situate this form of academic conflict within the broader
context of society. Conceptual conflicts are virtually endemic to scholarly

life, and in significant respects bear a similarity to altercations within the broader society – for example, between political parties, religious factions, unions and management, and so on. In virtually all cases we confront differing conceptions of the real, the rational and the good, along with commitments to integral patterns of action and particular arrangements of material. As many commentators have also noted, societal conflict has become an increasingly commanding feature of the contemporary cultural landscape. We not only confront increasingly prevalent cleavages in terms of racial, economic and gender differences, but also on issues of sexual preference, the environment, abortion, pornography, religion, social justice, and more. Elsewhere (Gergen, 1991) I have attempted to link this explosion of grass roots activism to the emerging technologies of communication. As such technologies enable persons of like disposition to locate similar others, to declare group consciousness and to generate agendas of change, so do we find an increasing profusion of value-based sub-cultures. I shall return to this expanding domain of difference in the final chapter.

In what follows I wish to treat the realism/constructionism antinomy within this broader context of societal conflict – viewing our present controversy as tissued to the society, and in turn, possibly bearing on its future. If we have created a sea of struggle within the academic sphere, how are we to proceed? Is there anything in our mode of comportment in this case that bears on broader societal potentials? Are there any insights to be garnered from our interactions that harbour promise of broader implication? My particular way of treating these questions is informed by social constructionist dialogues. My specific hope is to step out of the agonistic and ingurgitating modes of argument that have separated realists and constructionists, and inquire into our collective actions themselves. From a broader historical or cultural standpoint, why we are at logger-heads, what is at stake for us and what alternatives exist or could be created?

The present analysis is composed of four parts. First I address the constructionist resistance to realism, what is at stake in the avoidance of ultimate claims to the real. I then turn to consider the potentials of solving the realism/constructionism dispute through reasoned argument. My conclusion here is not optimistic. In an attempt to move forward, I then raise questions concerning the ways in which we as scholars and practitioners situate ourselves within the competing discourses of realism and constructionism. What is it to employ these discourses in our various relations? In addressing these questions we begin to locate a space for reconciliation, what my Irish colleagues call a 'Fourth Province' – a domain of neutrality outside the borders of conflict. Finally, given the potential for softening differences, I turn to broader implications and applications.

Resistance to realism: the case of the missing body

As a précis to the more general analysis of conflict, it is useful to address those many colleagues who have joined in the critique of traditional science – often employing constructionist arguments – but who wish to hold to remnants of an unconstructed world. Constructionists are variously scolded for 'throwing out the baby with the bath-water', and entreated to remain firm on certain matters. I have considerable sympathy with these responses, but at the same time strong reservations. It is this resistance that deserves preliminary attention. Perhaps the two domains of the real most strongly embraced by my colleagues are *power* and the *body* – the former especially significant to cultural critics and the latter to the helping professions. I will treat issues of power more fully in Chapter 7. Here let us consider the 'problem of embodiment' in more detail. An article by John Lannamann (1998) provides a convenient textual forum. Speaking primarily to an audience of therapists, Lannamann begins with a personal story: his parents were Christian Scientists and did not believe in practices of modern medicine. As a result Lannamann suffered the needless death of his brother. The denial of bodily reality by Christian Scientists, and the resulting agony, seemed for Lannamann to bear a resemblance to the conditions created by social constructionism. Constructionists, too, seem to deny the reality of a body outside discourse. It is in the material body, suggests Lannamann, that we confront 'the limits' of construction, a reality that must necessarily inform and correct the all too 'playful' peregrinations of the constructionist. To neglect the material body is to replicate the myopia of Christian Science – where the myth of the spirit masks the realities of disease and death.

This is surely a significant charge and one with which I am deeply sympathetic. To be sure, I live in much the same world as Lannamann; we both take bodies, disease and death very seriously. When my children were physically ill I sought medical attention as opposed to a spiritual advisor. And I will readily talk about my pain and pleasure, seek annual medical check-ups and donate funds to famine relief and clothing to the Purple Heart. However, it is at precisely this point of 'sure knowledge' – where bodies just are what they are, where we know very well what we experience and we can clearly distinguish between health and illness – that constructionism becomes a most valuable asset. A constructionist intelligibility opens what can be a precious space for reflection, reconsideration and possible reconstruction. Herein lies an enormous emancipatory potential, granting us a capacity to step outside the taken-for-granted and to break loose from the sometimes strangulating grip of the commonplace. And herein lies the possibility for new futures as we are invited to consider possibilities for reconstruction. We are prompted to explore alternative understandings of 'what is the case', and to locate meanings that enable us to go on in more adequate ways. For those who live in complex societal circumstances, the potential for creative reconstruction is a continuous treasure; for lives despondent, tormented or tortured such resources may be essential.

It is in this vein that analysts have taken a keen and critical interest in 'bodily inscription', or the ways in which the body is variously constructed in contemporary society (Featherstone, Hepworth, & Turner, 1991). Here the attempt is typically critical, attempting to question taken-for-granted assumptions in hopes of liberation. For example, critics question the presumption of gender differences (Butler, 1990; Kessler & McKenna, 1978), the common construction of beauty and the female body (Suleiman, 1986), the concept of the diseased body (Hepworth, 1999; Martin, 1994), and so on. So too there have been active attempts to blur the traditional distinction between the human body and the machine. Beginning with Donna Haraway's (1985) classic analysis of the cyborg, theorists have been keen to explore the political potentials of breaking the human/technology metaphor (Driscoll & Brahn, 1995; Gray, 1995).

A constructionist sensibility also opens a new domain of dialogue on health and disease. For the constructionist, 'health' and 'illness' are terms that acquire their meaning within particular traditions of relationship. We may agree that 'something is going on', in what we call my body, but such agreement places no necessary demands on the configuration of phonemes we use in description or explanation, or how and whether we treat it. In Nelson Goodman's (1978) terms: 'If I ask about the world, you can offer to tell me how it is under one or more frames of reference; but if I insist that you tell me how it is apart from all frames, what can you say?' In this vein Kleinman (1988) and Young (1997) challenge the existing conceptions of the body in contemporary medicine. And relevant to treatment possibilities, Arthur Frank's volume, *The Wounded Storyteller* (1995) offers a major opening. If illness is simply illness, then we might consign our bodies to the care of the medical professions and be done with it. Yet, as Frank demonstrates, there are other stories to be told under such conditions. In particular, he points to the advantages of a 'quest narrative', in which the individual uses the occasion of the illness to embark on a quest – a movement eventuating in a deeper understanding of self and society. One may see the possibility for a change of character through suffering, an opportunity to speak for those who suffer, to bear testimony and thereby contribute to the greater wisdom of the community. In the same way, if material death is simply material death, and that's the end of it, what an impoverished world of meaning we inhabit! If death can also be a rejoining with lost loved ones, a place at the right hand of God, a movement in an endless cycle of becoming or an ultimate tranquillity, our world is enriched: cultural life is more inhabitable.

There are further reasons for resistance to unconstructed bodies: if there simply are material bodies in the world – full stop – then what else should we add to the ontology of the undeniable? I am informed by my colleagues in sociology about the reality of social structure; economists tell me about the hard realities of the economy; political scientists speak of *realpolitik*; for many anthropologists culture is certainly undeniable; and for most of my colleagues in psychology there is no denying the existence of cognitive process. On what grounds shall we accept material bodies into the realm of the undeniably real and prohibit these further entries? And if we cannot deny these additional realities, what else will be offered as real beyond culture and history? As we add all the obvious realities of the world to the compendium of the undeniable, are we not ultimately driven into a reproduction of common convention, to living in worlds of meaning constituted without respect to the emerging conditions of our lives? And what then of constructionist hopes for emancipation and reconstruction? As we increase the domain of the obviously real so do we foster social paralysis.

To bring the point home, what is to prevent us from adding to our concerns with physical illness the reality of mental illness – for most of my clinical colleagues simply 'there' prior to and regardless of one's discursive community? Surely, they say, we confront the brutal reality of depression, attention deficit disorder, schizophrenia and the like. Or do we? We may all agree that there is something unusual about an individual's behaviour, but why should we suppose that the community of clinicians and psychiatrists are correct in calling it a 'mental illness', and that DSM categories are maps of this world?[3] Why should we agree that the 'disease of depression' – which was never 'discovered' until the present century – now inflicts one in ten persons in our culture? And why should we acquiesce to wholesale prescription of pharmaceuticals such as Prozac, Ridilin and lithium? If we give up our capacity to question the callings – the all-too-obvious realities of sub-cultures or societies – then we become the victims.

The constructionist resistance continues: such terms as 'real,' 'true,' 'rational' and 'objective' possess deadly potentials. To be sure, they are enormously useful within particular communities for affirming traditions, facilitating mutual trust, ensuring forms of coordination and generating collective enthusiasm. However, they are fraught with danger when participants in such communities extend what is local to the plane of the universal – real for all people, transcendentally true, fundamentally rational, indisputably objective. When the obvious reality of the local is thus protracted, so is the groundwork laid for the obliteration of other traditions – those who 'don't see things for what they are', dwell in 'false consciousness', 'reason imperfectly' or are 'hopelessly subjective'. Nor are the denizens of such cultures likely to gain voice, for theirs is obviously ignorant, mere folklore, mythical, mystical, or worse (also see Edwards, Ashmore, & Potter, 1995). It is just this arrogance of the local that stoked the Western colonialist fires – and the subsequent devastation of traditions throughout the world. I can readily appreciate Lannamann's reaction to the needless loss of life he attributes to Christian Science beliefs. I'm sure I would feel much the same. The danger lies not in the grief and anger but in the derogation of Christian Science for not recognizing the truth of material bodies. And should we extend this plain truth indefinitely, we should eradicate the tradition – and possibly all other traditions holding the truth of the spirit to be more primary than the reality of material.

Animating animus: the pleasures of eradication

While these arguments are clear enough, they have not been everywhere compelling. Attacks continue from both conservative and radical directions. In major respects the course of development in such debates is quite familiar. It largely recapitulates the form of academic conflict serving as the mainstay of scholarly life. There is high drama to be derived in championing an ideal or a value against an infidel opposition. This is no less so in the case of defending scientific objectivity against the ravages of charlatanism, mysticism, ideologism or fundamentalism than it is in condemning oppression, racism or injustice, or championing a humanist vision of the person. Failure to participate in this drama of good-over-evil is to miss out on one of the most acute pleasures of scholarly life. Nor did we have to await participation in scholarly careers to indulge in this cultural ritual. It was long in place – as we defended our sandcastles against wicked intruders, an intimate friend from calumnious gossip or a beleaguered minority group against unjust policies. In a certain sense, we are all 'Christian soldiers . . . armies of liberty, at the barricades, marching to Pretoria . . . ', and, surely, 'we shall overcome'. Given the glories of championing the good in the face of evil, what are the central options deposited by our traditions at the doorstep of the present?[4]

In the main the most congenial option is (and has been) isolation and subterranean warfare. It is simple enough to divide ourselves into fragmented, hostile and self-satisfied enclaves. We enter our minuscule groups of the like-minded, declare the intellectual and moral high ground, circulate our truths within the journals and conferences protected by our kind, and locate ways of undermining the investments of colleagues and institutions outside the fold. Such a condition largely characterizes the relationship now existing between empiricists and constructionists. It is an emerging state among those groups set against empiricism – feminist standpoint theorists, Marxists, culture critics and humanists among them. It is a state that now threatens to divide all those who otherwise search for alternatives to what we perhaps misleadingly characterize as 'the dominant discourse'.

How can we view this state of subterranean warfare as anything but unfortunate? It is not simply that we thus invite a condition of all against all. It is also a condition that ultimately deadens those within the contentious enclaves. Because this option thrives on separation – on processes of solipsistic self-gratification – there is little means of resolving conflict, no catalytic confrontation that might press the issues forward or offer new insights and potentials. Further, the signifying process within the separate circles continues to feed upon itself, endlessly re-formulating the world in ways that increasingly impede the possibility of critical reflexivity. In this way meaning is essentially frozen in the community of knowledge makers, with concomitant estrangement from the surrounding culture. Not only does the community's framework of knowledge seem increasingly remote, obscure and irrelevant, but from within the community the culture at large seems increasingly ignorant.[5]

Further, we must ask, what are the societal implications of this self-satisfying and self-affirming option? If we are concerned with what is communicated by the scholarly profession to the society concerning the nature of difference, we should do well to close our doors. Not only has the anguish of political correctness, for example, suggested that scholars are little more than bickering backbiters, but we in turn suggest to society that where culture wars are concerned, we have little to offer.

There is a second option animated by the existing animus: argumentative confrontation. Again as scholars we are fully prepared for this ritual, and in certain respects our mode of conduct contributes to the society at large. We demonstrate the potential for replacing armed combat with an exchange of words, extending the resources for peaceful resolution of conflict. Thus, we can pursue rational debate, drawing the battle lines more sharply and clearly in hopes that, over time, the superior paradigm will win. We avoid the torpor of solidification and move toward a superior level of comprehension – or so it is supposed. I have severe doubts about the potential of traditional argumentation to yield compelling solutions in such cases. In Chapter 3 I shall take up several principled problems inhering in argumentation as a mode of resolving differences. However, there is one major flaw in the process of argumentation specific to the present case: both realism and constructionism are lodged within differing presumptions about the nature of knowledge, reason and value. Resultingly the positions are inherently incommensurable. They cannot properly be compared within the terms of either position, because the very presumptions from which each argues automatically foreclose on the alternative intelligibility. For example, the realist cannot convince the constructionist by pointing to evidence of, let us say, 'a real material nature', for such evidence has no currency within a constructionist ontology. The very use of a realist rhetoric would itself appear ideologically problematic. Further, the constructionist cannot use rhetorical pyrotechnics to compel the realist, because the recognition of 'mere rhetoric' would disqualify the arguments. Similarly, constructionist charges of ideological bias prove thin, as realists presume the possibility of objective or ideology-free readings of the world. Good reasons in one camp are fallaciously misleading in the other.

At the same time, for constructionists to argue on grounds that might convince the realist, they would violate the assumptions of constructionism, thus lapsing into self-contradiction. The same would hold true if realists plumped for the superiority of their position on grounds of its linguistic felicity or more fetching textual tropes. One might be moved at this point to defer to a third, more neutral standpoint from which adjudication might issue. However, this would be to insert yet a third ontology, one standing at odds with both protagonists. Would either the constructionist or the realist, for example, wish the outcome of debate to be decided by a spiritual fundamentalist or a Zen master?

In terms of the broader society, argumentation may be a significant improvement over isolated antipathy. However, there is little hope that argumentation can ever reduce the intensity of the struggle. From the present standpoint, we might anticipate just the opposite, with argument essentially galvanizing opposition and intensifying antagonism. This is certainly the typical case within the academy. Unless there is strong agreement on the grounds of differences, and what counts as rationality and evidence, arguments are seldom settled through argumentation. As Thomas Kuhn (1970) remarked, too often such struggles are dissolved only through the expiration of the opposition.

Realism and constructionism as cultural resources

Given the problems inhering in both passive and active modes of antagonism, what options remain? One promising possibility is to search for common ground, to locate at least one significant assumption congenial to both realist and constructionist accounts. For example, although differing in underlying suppositions, both realists and constructionists – and indeed almost anyone participating in the Western tradition of sense making – will find it unremarkable to say that language is used by persons in coordinating their daily activities. The use of requests, commands, commendations, corrections, greetings, and so on, all have practical consequences in cultural life. If this view is reasonable, then we may also agree that, whatever else they may be, both realist and constructionist arguments are forms of discourse. However else they may function, both are used (primarily by scholars) in carrying out forms of cultural life. Rather than viewing realist and constructionist intelligibilities as expressions of individual minds, as transcendental logics or as truth posits, for the present we might agree to consider them as forms of speaking or writing – composites of words and phrases used by people on various occasions with certain consequences. To the extent that such discourses are useful for various groups, we are also positioned to see them as cultural resources, modes of intelligibility developed within certain cultural traditions and now adding to the contemporary cultural repertoire. In this frame we can explore more pointedly the situated utility of both such discourses. This analysis, in turn, may yield a new range of options for going on together.

To begin, let us suppose that all the protagonists in the realist/ constructionist debate possess both of the discourses ready to hand. Both intelligibilities are available to the protagonists. We might presume this dual capacity simply by virtue of willingness to engage in debate; one would scarcely wish to plump for one side of the argument without familiarity with its contrasting number. Given the broad availability of these discursive resources to the debating parties, let us further suppose that there are occasions on which the various protagonists are likely to use each of these idioms in earnest. The users would wish to have others treat these words seriously – that is, treated within the common conventions of practice. Thus, for example, the most ardent constructionists will rely on the realist tradition to teach their children 'This is a dog' and 'that is a cat'. And if the constructionist saw his house was on fire and screamed 'Run, there's a fire!' he or she would not wish the family to look with suspicion and reply 'Oh, that's just your construction'. The constructionist would wish the warning to be treated within realist conventions. Likewise, those who embrace tenets of realism will often draw arrows from the quiver of constructionism. Would the most committed realist wish to delete from his/her repertoire such conversational moves as 'That's just your story', 'This is a cultural myth', 'They are making it up', 'This news report is slanted in favour of the government' and 'The way you are putting that is oppressive'. Even the unreconstructed empiricist, blind to constructionist theory, might wish to say, 'Given their theoretical commitment, I can see why they would draw that conclusion', or 'Physics, biology and psychology constitute different ways of conceptualizing the world'.

Whether the possession of these dual vocabularies poses a dilemma for the individuals involved is moot; however, in light of the work of Billig and his colleagues (1988) we might well suspect that for most people these potentially opposing discourses rest unproblematically side by side along with a host of alternatives (e.g. spiritual, romantic, mythical). To host multiple discourse potentials is akin to having the capacity for playing multiple games. The capacity to perform well at chess does not necessitate the exclusion of bridge or poker.

Given the capacity of all protagonists in the debate to employ both realist and constructionist discourses, we might also suppose that there are occasions when virtually all would agree on which of the discourses is applicable or appropriate. That is to say, on certain occasions most of those engaged in realist/constructionist debates would join together in the harmonious use of a similar vernacular. Because most of us share a cultural history, and because we have been exposed to similar systems of education and occupy similar positions of privilege, we will tend to converge in preferences and conventions – from tastes in food and drink to standards of scholarly excellence. I suspect under these conditions that almost all of us would stand fast against neo-Nazis, the Mafia, Islamic terrorism, smuggling heroine, torture and murder. Using a compelling discourse of realism, we would point to multiple failings and immoralities. Further, in fine constructionist form, protagonists from both sides of the aisle would be happy to demonstrate how the National Socialist party – through the rationalization, glamourization and circulation of discourse within German culture – created the conditions leading to the Holocaust. By the same token, most of us would fight fiercely against the dissemination of such discourses today.

With ample agreement among protagonists on discourse use let us press the case to its ironic conclusion: those who typically champion constructionism might well employ a realist discourse to throttle the realist, and the realist might willingly adopt constructionist arguments to subvert constructionism. While this may seem improbable, closer inspection suggests that such tactics are not uncommon. It has long been recognized in the social studies of science that scholars attempting to demonstrate the constructed character of scientific knowledge will employ empirical evidence (case material, photographs, documents) to secure the case. Without precisely this kind of reference to the real world construction of laboratory realities, the social studies of science would scarcely have gained entry into scholarly dialogues. On the other hand, how often have constructionists been confronted by realists clamouring to point out that constructionist arguments are themselves constructed. Here, the realist essentially embraces constructionist arguments in order to subdue constructionism. In the USA, the charge of 'political correctness' is typically employed by realist conservatives to defend their traditions against constructionist forms of attack. As they claim, such critiques are simply ideological biases posing as reason, and are oppressive to their traditions. Yet, this form of argument is essentially borrowed from the constructionist critics who have placed them in jeopardy. Demonstrating the ideological saturation of the taken for granted is essentially a rhetorical mainstay of constructionist criticism of the dominant order.

In one significant variation on these ironies of inversion, realists are often given to criticizing constructionists for being realists, and vice versa. As realists point out, constructionists employ realist presumptions in describing bodies of knowledge as constructed. For constructionists, 'discourse' is treated as real, as are narratives, metaphors and relationships. Yet, if the constructionist is actually a realist, as such a critique suggests, then why should the realist necessarily object? Of course, most construc- tionists deny the reality of what they seem to be describing, arguing that they are forced into a realist language by virtue of our conventions of writing. The language does not permit a split screen in which one simul- taneously both says and unsays. Yet, to be sure, such deconstructionist apologetics also employ a realist motif. By the same token, constructionists accuse realists of constructing their worlds. But, why should this necessarily be an accusation? How else can one make the world intelligible outside of conventions of construction?

As we find, both those who represent themselves as constructionists and those who make realist arguments within the academic sphere draw from the discourse of the opposing position – often within these debates and certainly outside them. In this respect, we might view these discourses as cultural resources, ways of talking and writing born of particular traditions and available to all for carrying out the practices of daily life, both professional and otherwise. If this conclusion seems reasonable, then our attention is drawn to the particular functions or purposes served by such discourses. How are they used, and what are the societal repercussions?

Of particular concern is how do these discourses play out in the context of various cultural practices. Here it seems clear that realist discourse is essential to the achievement of complex forms of human coordination. The pilot attempting to land an aircraft must share a common language with the traffic controller, and a common practice of indexing this language, or disaster is invited. For all intents and purposes, the 'aircraft', the 'altitude', the 'runway', the 'airspeed' and the like are very much real. Here it may be said that realist discourse is a language of mutual trust; it unites participants in a way that promotes order and predictability. At the same time, such discourse also functions as an instrument of control. It cordons the domain of possibility and thus favours forces of conservatism and the institutional status quo. It promotes distrust of all those who do not share the conventions of understanding. Constructionist discourse often functions in the reverse: it is a liberating agent, challenging the taken-for-granted and opening new realms of comprehension and action. Yet, in doing so it also undermines the legitimacy of precious traditions, along with practices of complex coordination and dispositions of mutual trust. In a Bakhtinian sense we might say that realism operates centripetally – favouring unity and solidarity – while constructionism functions centrifugally – unsettling and creating. In this light we see that both discourses may be vital to our future well-being.

Beyond debate: confronting conflicts of practice

As we find, viewing constructionist discourses as cultural resources – not unlike our democratic and legal institutions, educational systems, science, the arts and spiritual practices – permits us to open new and less combative spaces of conversation. It is important, however, that we do not terminate discussion of differences at this point. Rather, we arrive now at the threshold of a new problem. At least one significant way in which the discourses of realism and constructionism function is to support particular forms of action. Thus, even if we abandon the search for the transcendentally superior discourse, we still confront ranges of actions rationalized by these discourses. Further, there are many activities favoured by each of these discourses that are viewed with suspicion – even contempt – by the other. For example, traditional realists in the social sciences often favour hypothesis testing, experimental manipulation, neutral observation, statistical analyses, universalizing explanation and the avoidance of ideological discussion. Critical realists eschew all these activities and opt for unmitigated critique of the dominant and oppressive orders of society. For many constructionists, there are important problems inhering in both forms of activity – for example, problems of inhumanity, dominance, naivety and imperialism in the case of empiricism and unfettered antagonism in the case of critical realism. At the same time the explorations in qualitative research, historical and cultural analysis and theoretical innovation favoured by constructionists are viewed as all too liberal and loose by both empirical and critical realists. Again, how are we to go on together? Is warfare – either subterranean or overt – the answer? Are we thrust again into postures of annihilation?

These are important questions, rendered all the more profound in terms of the broader cultural context in which they occur. For these kinds of antagonisms are prevalent – both within the culture and throughout the world. Whether or not we can locate means of co-existence within the academy has a bearing on life beyond the tower. If we cannot discover alternatives to mutual annihilation within, then we must ask whether our activities do not provide models for societal conflict. In contrast, if we can locate modes of mutuality these may serve as significant resources for the culture. In certain respects it may be our concrete forms of relationship – as opposed to our philosophies of knowledge and value – that have the greatest potential for the culture more generally.[7]

The magnitude of the challenge here cannot be overestimated, and at this juncture I can do little more than open discussion on options issuing from a constructionist consciousness. Such discussion commences with this chapter, but pervades many of subsequent chapters of the book. In a later treatment of relational politics (Chapter 10) I will attempt to draw together some of the central results of these discussions. For now, however, it will be useful to return to the preceding analysis. In particular, can we locate within this approach to the realist/constructionist antinomy conceptual tools or self-exemplifying practices that might provide promising departures for the future? What, if anything, can the analysis thus far contribute to the problematics of conflicting practices? In my view there are four significant implications.

Shifting the discursive register

Although much of my writing over the past decade has been critical of realism and concomitantly positive toward the potentials of constructionism, the present chapter has moved in a different direction. I have attempted to relinquish the adversarial/advocacy posture, and searched rather for a means of deliberating on the antinomy itself. More broadly, we may see this as a shift in the discursive register, moving from a position within the conflict to one that problematizes the conflict itself. The reader will have to judge the efficacy of this move in reducing the annihilative impulse. However, as a linguistic performative there would seem to be considerable advantage in such shifts. No longer am I thrusting the defender into the position of the evil other, but rather I am inviting him/her to consider with me our common condition. If this invitation is accepted, then we embark on a new form of relationship, one with a potentially productive as opposed to destructive telos.[8] One might question this attempt to shift discursive registers, inasmuch as the proposed grounds for deliberation may seem too congenial with constructionist arguments themselves. To speak of realism and constructionism as discursive resources already seems to accept tenets of much constructionist writing. To me, such a conclusion is unwarranted. As I pointed out, the view of language as a pragmatic resource is both constructionist and realist. It is to propose constructionalism as a realism. There is no intrinsic and exclusive relation between assumptions of linguistic pragmatics and social construction.

The shift in discursive register resonates with practices developed in family therapy. When a couple or family are moving in a destructive direction (e.g abuse, violence, life risk), a significant option developed by family therapists is that of shifting to a meta-level of discussion. Rather than a husband responding to harsh criticism with an angry counter-attack, he might ask, for example, 'Why are we doing this', 'Is this really what we want' or 'Is there another way we might handle this?' In each case, movement into the meta-discussion essentially terminates the pattern of mutual assault in which the participants are otherwise engaged. In some cases it may be less important to answer such meta-questions than the fact that the new deliberation constitutes an alternative mode or relating – typically far less destructive than otherwise. This shift of registers also suggests that we might ultimately broaden our queries to include other factors that might help us sidestep patterns of mutual blame.[9] There may be many other means of suspending the ongoing rituals of antagonism, interrupting and reorienting in ways that might sustain as opposed to terminate relationships.

Separating expression from personal essence

Following the proposal that all participants in the debates on realism vs. constructionism employ both realist and constructionist discourses in various conditions – either in concert or antagonistically – we may profit from distinguishing between speaker and speech, identity and discourse. In this sense we may say that there are no realists or constructionists per se – no individuals whose essence is stamped indelibly with one mode of expression or another. Rather, we are all cultural participants who adopt these and other discourses on various conversational occasions. In this sense our writings about these issues as scholars may have little to do with our discursive habits in other locales – speaking with children or our parents, with bus drivers or priests. Rather, the very placing of the realist and constructionist discourses at odds with each other is an activity situated largely within the academic domain. We enter as polyvocal participants, but on this occasion agree to represent ourselves monovocally in opposition to each other.

One important outcome of separating words from persons is that we reduce tendencies toward the *psychological essentializing of evil*. If we are confronted with actions we view as inhumane, unjust or oppressive the tendency to presume that such acts reflect an inhumane, unjust or oppressive desire or state of mind is thwarted. The actions do not define the essence of the person; they are simply that which he/she does on a particular occasion. In the same way, one may see one's own actions – whether they are commentaries on realism or constructionism, culture critique or qualitative research – as 'what I do' but not 'what I am'. With this separation a way is cleared for productive interchange among colleagues or fellow citizens. One is encouraged to see the way in which the other's activities are situated for him or her and how they function within their particular context – how it is that an otherwise normal (as opposed to morally tainted) individual might engage in these actions. Again this is not to say that the critical edge will be lost; rather, the way of approaching the other shifts in tenor. As a result fresh options may emerge.

Exploring polyvocal potentials

As proposed earlier, all protagonists within the realist/constructionist debate have the potential of voicing each other's position and, in fact, often do so. Indeed, in the present chapter I have given voice to both positions, and simultaneously to a third, carried within my more epistemologically blurred proposals. Am I thus truly a constructionist? What would 'truly' mean in this case? Yet, it is not simply our cognizance of discursive potentials that is at stake here. Lives are typically constituted by a rich and ever-shifting array of activity. To condemn a person for a particular form of conduct is to overlook this broader range of action. When the condemned activity is cut away from this broader range of life investments, the person loses dimension; he or she is reduced to a loathsome singularity – one voice alone. In contrast, to explore the full range of the other's actions in the world will typically complexify the judgment. The other is a multitude, not one, and many of these voices are ours as well. For example, the constructionist may condemn what seems an enormous waste of resources in the laboratory testing of circular and politically offensive hypotheses. However, when the accuser is sensitized to 'the culprit' as a loving parent, who devotes time to a local food kitchen, sends money to the environmentalist movement, and is responsible for the well-being of a paraplegic brother, the character of the offending differences is transformed. Not only are we likely to find ourselves within the other, but as well to realize the other's value on many significant issues. The conjoining of certain feminists and religious fundamentalists against pornography is a case in point. However the conflict is ultimately resolved and should ideally take into account these mutualities. This latter point bears closely on a final issue.

Recognizing relationship

There is a final, more subtle implication of the preceding analysis, one that will be amplified as the volume unfolds. Consider again the interdependent character of constructionism and realist discourses. As we found, not only do these discourses require each other for their intelligibility but, moreover, each employs elements of the other in its attempt to subdue the other. In effect, the intelligibilities cannot stand alone; their logics are intimately interwoven. Does this condition of interlocking discourses have analogues in the more general domain of conflicting practices? This is a significant question with broad theoretical and practical implications. If we may view discourse as a form of action, then we might anticipate that the binary basis of meaning characteristic of discourse may also undergird the meaning of action more generally. Thus, like discourse, anything that we recognize as a culturally intelligible action gains its significance as such by virtue of what it is not (i.e. alternative patterns of action). In this sense actions are neither intelligible nor valuable in themselves; they acquire such meaning through the existence of difference. Thus, for example, to carry out qualitative inquiry gains its significance by virtue of its contrast with quantitative research; universalizing hypotheses acquire their intelligibility in their contrast to historicizing; and so on. The activities are inseparably related. There are also many instances in which a given activity requires remnants of its contrast in order to secure its intelligibility. At least traditionally, for example, both qualitative and quantitative research have presumed an independent world which they attempt to reveal, both employ distinctions to delineate the contours of this world and both embrace a continuum of more/less.[10] They are united in certain conceptions of inquiry.

More broadly, we are led to inquire into the more general condition of interrelationship of otherwise conflicting practices. How are practices that we condemn related to those we embrace? Do our commitments to a certain form of life automatically lay the groundwork for a class of the alienated other? To opt for a smoke-free environment, for example, is to create smokers as a class of undesirables; without the preference the class would be unremarkable. And to what extent do otherwise conflictual activities draw from the same tradition, thus rendering implicit support for each other? When a militia movement bomb destroyed the municipal building in Oklahoma City, taking the lives of over 130 people, outrage was pervasive. For most of us justice seemed well served when the bomber, Timothy McVeigh, was sentenced to death. Yet, if we examine the ideological commitments of the militia movement we find them firmly rooted in the proud American traditions of freedom and justice. If the federal government is believed to be destroying individual rights and squeezing dry the common citizen, an armed defence is justified. And drawing importantly from the same tradition, so are we justified in putting McVeigh to death. The grand tradition is sustained in both instances.

In conclusion

Constructionist and realist discourses can be set against each other. However, combative argumentation is only one option available to us in the case of differences. As I have tried to demonstrate here, there are other, less 'natural' options that lead us into in more promising territories. Nor do these options entail synthesis – the emergence of some novel position that contains elements of both. Rather, by casting these discourses as cultural resources, we are positioned to appreciate their positive powers along with their possible limitations. In the present case I have also attempted to show how this orientation opens up possibilities for treating conflicting traditions both in the academy and the society. Shifting the discursive register, separating expression from person, emphasizing polyphonic expression and exploring relationship are all ways of reducing the annhilative impulse and lend themselves to richer and more sustainable forms of communal life.

Notes

1 For examples of culture critiques of constructionism, see Cloud (1994) and Parker (1998).

2 See, for example, Freeman (1999) and Martin and Sugarman (1999).

3 Constructionist critiques of mental illness now form a substantial genre. For an extended bibliography, see http://www.swarthmore.edu/SocSci/kgergen1/

4 The extent to which issues of 'the good' are conjoined with epistemological conflict is nicely treated in Natter, Schatzki, and Jones's (1995) edited work, *Objectivity and its Other*.

5 As many now believe, economic science has largely drifted into this estranged condition. Economic theory and research is largely self-referential, its assumptions are seldom challenged from within the field, there is little dialogue with scholars outside economics and the work is little understood or appreciated by other scholars.

6 An excellent illustration of the self-conscious use of both realist and constructionist discourses is provided in Bohan and Russell's (1999) *Conversations about Psychology and Sexual Orientation*. In this instance each discourse is found to carry a certain kind of rhetorical weight, and the combination is far more powerful than either discourse alone.

7 A strict separation of theory from practice is unwarranted, as theory itself represents a form of practice and all forms of inquiry are constituted in part by theoretical modes of indexing. However, for purposes of expanding the range of relevant considerations it is useful here to sustain the traditional distinction.

8 For an analogous treatment of constructionist vs. essentialist approaches to sexual orientation, see Bohan and Russell (1999).

9 See Merttens (1998) for a variation on discursive shifting in the realism/constructionist debate. Rather than a frontal engagement – argument as war – she makes her argument in terms of a first-person narrative; through this form of storytelling the 'matter of principle' is removed as the central feature of exchange. We are invited to consider her life conditions and the place of theory in this context.

10 In recent years qualitative research has taken a distinct 'postmodern turn', with numerous researchers now eschewing the realist presumptions of the past, as well as some of these traditional tendencies. See especially Denzin and Lincoln (2000).

2

THE PLACE OF THE PSYCHE IN A CONSTRUCTED WORLD

Dialogues on social construction now span the range of inquiry in the sciences, humanities and professional schools. Constructionist scholarship has been devoted to understanding the generation, transformation and suppression of what we take to be objective knowledge; exploring the literary and rhetorical devices by which meaning is achieved and rendered compelling; illuminating the ideological and valuational freighting of the unremarkable or taken for granted; documenting the implications of world construction for the distribution of power; gaining an appreciation of the processes of relationship from which senses of the real and the good are achieved; comprehending the historical roots and vicissitudes of various forms of understanding; exploring the range and variability in human intelligibility across cultures; and more.[1] Yet, while serving a broad generative function, psychologists have been singularly resistant to joining the constructionist dialogues. Social constructionism is a rare topic in common discussions of mental functioning and dysfunction.

There are many reasons for the general insularity of psychological science from this intellectual watershed. Certainly among the most important is what many take to be a fundamental antagonism between the psychological and constructionist projects. Within traditional psychology, mental processes are not only the chief subject of inquiry, but serve as the critical fulcrum for explaining human action. In contrast, for constructionist theorists the chief locus of understanding is not in 'the psyche' but in processes of relationship. All that psychology traces to mental origins constructionists might wish to explain through micro-social process. If the psychological project were fully vindicated, there would be no explanatory remainder, a world of human action for which social constructionism would be a necessary adjunct. The reverse seems equally as plausible: the vindication of constructionism would portend the end of psychology.

However, this dolorous conclusion is not inevitable. It is favoured primarily by a realist metaphysics and a correspondence view of language, both of which sustain a view of science in which there is a single, knowable reality and in which theories compete for explanatory and predictive superiority. It is this view of science that has fostered a recurring pattern of internecine antagonism in psychology, with behaviourism eradicating mentalism, and cognitivism then silencing behaviourist voices. However, as illustrated in the preceding chapter, constructionist scholars are not typically drawn either to a realist metaphysics or a correspondence theory of language. For the constructionist there is little justification for foundational enunciations of the real; whatever we take to be essential is an outcome of social interchange. Theories cannot be falsified by virtue of their correspondence with something else called 'the real', but only within the conventions of particular enclaves of meaning. Thus constructionists establish no transcendent grounds for eliminating any theoretical formulation. From this standpoint, to eradicate a theoretical perspective would not only be tantamount to losing a mode of human intelligibility (along with related social practices), but to silence a community of meaning making. Within a constructionist metaphysics it would be virtually impossible to locate grounds for such suppression, and indeed many would argue that there is implicit in constructionism a strong pluralist ethic (see, for example, Sampson, 1993a).

Given a constructionist metatheory, how are we then to view professional investments in psychological research, as well as mental health practices, public policy advisories and other practices based on ontologies of mental process? If not eradication, what role is the ontology of the mind to play in a constructionist orientation to human action? Or conversely, what place is there in psychology for social constructionism? It is here that the constructionist concern with the pragmatics of language usage becomes paramount. For the constructionist language serves neither as a picture nor as a map of what is the case; rather (following Wittgenstein, 1953), it acquires its meaning from its use within human interchange (which usages may also include a 'game of describing reality'). From this standpoint, any analysis of scientific or scholarly accounts of the world would primarily (though not exclusively) be concerned with the uses to which such languages are put. Within what kinds of relationships do they play an important role, and what are the repercussions of particular forms of language use for those who directly or indirectly participate in these relationships? There can be no canonical slate of criteria for evaluating such appraisals, as various communities will share different concerns, which may themselves change with time and circumstance. Furthermore, the way such questions are addressed and answered must itself be viewed as a byproduct of a community, neither lodged within nor answered with respect to 'the real', but reflecting community investments and conventions of the time. This is scarcely to discredit such inquiry; one can scarcely do more than raise questions of the real and the good within particular traditions. Rather, it is to open scholarly and scientific discourse to the full range of relevant communities (see also Feyerabend, 1978), without granting any community an ultimate 'grounds of assessment' by virtue of which other voices may be silenced.

Within this context I wish to consider in this chapter three major orientations to psychological inquiry as informed by constructionist meta-theory. The first of these orientations, which emphasizes *denaturalization and democratization*, is at once the most fully developed within the constructionist arena and the most fully critical of existing psychological scholarship. At the same time its positive potentials for psychology have not been sufficiently addressed. The second orientation, *revitalization and enrichment*, is far more positive in its orientation to psychological inquiry. Although it is the least developed, its elaboration seems critical to the future of the discipline. Finally, I wish to explore constructionist efforts to remove certain problematic features from the compendium of mental predicates, and to reconstruct the discourse in more promising ways. In particular we will be concerned with attempts to refigure the psyche as socio-cultural. This *social reconstructive* effort has dramatically accelerated in recent years, but its internal tensions and broader ramifications have not heretofore been addressed. Through this analysis we may emerge with a more variegated understanding of the relationship between psychological and constructionist endeavours, an appreciation of affinities and interdependencies of traditional and constructionist approaches to psychology, and an enhanced sense of humility regarding all adventures in making meaning.

Denaturalization and democratization

There are reasons other than hegemonic threat for the failure of most psychologists to join the broader dialogues on the social constitution of knowledge. Among them is surely the critical posture of much construc-tionist scholarship to date – an impulse that seems aimed at dismantling the authority of psychological science. Further, because of the restricted forms of argumentation within the empirical wing of psychology, with rare exception (cf. Held, 1996), its denizens have been at a loss to answer these assaults. Neither insights into methodology and statistics, nor recourse to 'established fact' – favoured moves within traditional empiricist argumentation – count as legitimate rejoinders to forms of constructionist critique. Yet, critical constructionism is not 'all of a piece'; differing arguments are at stake. In order to appreciate the force of these critical efforts, along with their potentials and shortcomings, it is important to distinguish among them. Although convergent, they rest on three distinct lines of reasoning: *ideological unmasking, rhetorical deconstruction* and *social analysis*.

In the case of ideological unmasking, constructionist critics point to the societal ramifications of psychology's modes of describing and explaining human action. As professional accounts are disseminated within the culture, bearing the stamp of scientific authority, so do they inform people's actions and instruct social policy. In Foucault's (1980) terms, there is a close relationship between claims to knowledge and cultural power. Given the capacity of the profession to generate multiple and diverse accounts of the person, choices in description and explanation are thus matters of moral and political consequence. Within this context professional psychology becomes a prime target of critique, criticism that is exacerbated further by the profession's seemingly disingenuous claims to value neutrality. Thus, constructionist scholars have variously set out to demonstrate the ways in which existing psychological accounts (and the practices which they sustain) lend themselves to broadening governmental control (Rose, 1990); destroying democratic foundations (1984); promoting narcissism (Wallach and Wallach, 1983); championing individualist ideology (Fowers and Richardson, 1996; Sampson, 1977); eroding community (Bellah et al., 1985; Sampson, 1977); sustaining the patriarchal order (M. Gergen, 1988; Hare-Mustin and Marecek, 1988; Morawski, 1994); contributing to Western colonialism (Gergen, Gulerce, Lock, and Misra, 1996); and more.

This form of critique contrasts sharply with literary and rhetorical deconstruction. Representing a convergence of developments within Continental semiotics, poststructural literary theory and rhetorical studies, it is reasoned in this case that all sensible propositions about persons are lodged within broader systems of meaning. In large measure, the intelligibility of any proposition is derived from its placement within this system as opposed to its referential relationship to non-linguistic occurrences (e.g. my ability to construct intelligible sentences about the nature of 'love' depends primarily on a textual history as opposed to observations of 'the phenomenon itself'). Rhetoricians add importantly to this concern with the textually driven character of psychological intelligibility by demonstrating the manner in which such discourse is fashioned for social effect. Here it is argued that descriptions and explanations of mental life depend importantly on the ability of the rhetor to achieve intelligibility with ('to persuade') a particular audience (to explain or express 'love' to a child, as opposed to a romantic partner, a priest or a New Guinea tribesman would require radically different word choices). For rhetoricians, intelligibility is often traced to various rhetorical tropes, such as narrative or metaphor. For example, regardless of 'the data', accounts of human development cannot escape the demands of 'proper storytelling'.

In this context, the problem of professional psychology does not lie in its discursive commitments per se, but in its claims to objective grounding for such commitments. Truth claims, it is reasoned, operate to silence competing voices; the discourse of objectivity and political totalitarianism are allied. The constructionist critic thus functions to unmask the literary and rhetorical strategies responsible for the sensibility (objectivity, intelligibility, felicity) of propositions about the mental world. An early example of such unmasking is provided by Smedslund's (1978) attempt to demonstrate that most experimental hypotheses in psychology are non-falsifiable inasmuch as falsifications would be linguistically incoherent. Similarly, I have argued that all propositions relating mental predicates to an external world (either stimulus or response) are circular; their intelligibility rests on implicit tautologies (Gergen, 1987; see also Wallach and Wallach, 1994). More broadly, scholars have variously argued that theories of the mind grow not from observation (inductively) but are derived from prevailing metaphors (see, for example, Gigerenzer, 1996; Soyland, 1994), and from conventions of narrative or storytelling (Gergen and Gergen, 1986; Sarbin, 1986). Constructionists have variously explored how 'the facts' of cognitive dysfunction ('irrationality') are created through rhetorical tropes (Lopes, 1991), how the *APA Publication Manual* sustains implicit assumptions about human action (Bazerman, 1988), and how such manuals circumscribe forms of communication and relationships – both within the profession and between the profession and the culture at large (Budge and Katz, 1995).

A third logic of constructionist critique, the social analytic, is stimulated by significant developments within the sociology of knowledge and the history of science. Here scholars have been particularly concerned with the ways in which social processes shape the profession's assumptions about its subject-matter, its methodologies and ultimately its conclusions regarding the nature of the world (see, for example, Kuhn, 1962; Latour and Woolgar, 1979). For psychology, the significant argument is that it is through social negotiation that investigators determine the grounding assumptions (ontology, epistemology) within which research will occur. Once the grounding assumptions (paradigms) have gained consensus, then all interpretations of evidence will necessarily serve as support; paradigms are not thus 'tested' against fact, rather they determine what will be counted as fact. Informed by these developments, the critical analyst points to the unwarranted and totalitarian claims of scientific psychology to accurate and objective readings of the mind. Unmasking the social processes intrinsic to the production of truth also serves to challenge longstanding boundaries within the discipline. Because of traditional commitments to truth through specialized methods there are strong tendencies for the disciplines to become insulated and self-serving, thus absenting themselves from broader dialogic engagement – both within the academy and society more generally. Social critique thus serves as a catalyst for broader interchange.

The social critique in psychology gained early support from ethnomethodological explorations of the social negotiation of factuality – for example, of suicide (Garfinkel, 1967) and gender (Kessler and McKenna, 1978) – and from labelling theories of deviance (Spector and Kitsuse, 1977). Investigators have since gone on to explore the social construction of the mind, including cognitive processes (Coulter, 1979), anger (Averill, 1982), emotion (Harré, 1986), schizophrenia (Sarbin and Mancuso, 1980), child development (Bradley, 1989), sexuality (Tiefer, 1992), anorexia and bulimia (Hepworth, 1999) and depression (Wiener and Marcus, 1994).

This line of exploration has also been augmented by studies of the historical and cultural contexts of belief about psychological processes.

In the case of historical work, scholars have variously been concerned with the social origins of people's constructions of foul and fragrant smells (Corbin, 1986), mental development (Kirschner, 1996), multiple personality disorder (Hacking, 1995), boredom (Spacks, 1995) and 'the human subject' in psychological research (Danziger, 1997).[2] Cultural anthropologists have also explored the cultural embeddedness of various conceptions of the mind (see, for example, Bruner, 1990; Heelas and Lock, 1981; Lutz, 1988). In effect, by tracing taken for granted beliefs about the mind to local circumstances, the traditional presumption of a 'universal subject-matter', is placed in jeopardy.

At the outset, these three lines of critical scholarship (often working together) pose a formidable threat to traditional empirical psychology. With the empirical grounding for professional truth claims undermined, so is the rationale for traditional research, along with the profession's claims to authority within the culture more generally. Further, the critics themselves have often contributed to the sense of an impending elimination of psychological inquiry. The titles of works edited by Ian Parker and his colleagues, for example *Deconstructing social psychology* (Parker and Shotter, 1990) and *Deconstructing psychopathology* (Parker et al., 1995), are apposite. However, such a funereal conclusion is without warrant. As earlier proposed, there is nothing within constructionist premises that necessarily argues for the elimination of any form of discourse. While constructionist critiques may often appear nihilistic, there are no means by which they themselves can be grounded or legitimated. They too fall victim to their own modes of critique; their accounts are inevitably freighted with ethical and ideological implications, forged within the conventions of writing, designed for rhetorical advantage, and their 'objects of criticism' constructed within and for a particular community. The objects of their criticism are no less constructed than the traditional objects of research, nor do their moral claims rest on transcendental foundations.

There is more. Even by constructionist standards, a rationale for empirical research can be generated. One of the central arguments within constructionist metatheory is that language is not mimetic: that is, it fails to function as a picture or map of an independent world. Rather, it is proposed, language functions performatively and constitutively; it is employed by communities of interlocutors for purposes of carrying out their relationships – including the local constitution of the real and the good. As I have argued elsewhere (Gergen, 1994a), such a view does not obliterate empirical science; it simply removes its privilege of claiming truth beyond community. There is nothing in constructionist arguments, for example, that would call for an end to medical research. The constructionist would simply point out that its ontological categories along with the identification of 'sickness' and 'cure' must not be viewed as transcendentally accurate, but as byproducts of historically and culturally located, ideologically invested aims. In the same way, psychologists may properly employ conceptions of mental process in empirical research, and indeed such research may be used to supplement processes of prediction within other sectors of the culture (for example, the prediction of voting patterns, jurors' preferences, or the rate of suicide). The constructionist claim is chiefly that there is no foundation for the addendum 'is true' to the language use in these endeavours.

As we find, the critical voice of the constructionist should not be viewed as liquidating. Rather, these lines of critical scholarship serve the useful functions of denaturalization and democratization. In their denaturalizing the 'objects of research', along with methodologies, research reports, statistics and resulting practices, critical inquiry first invites an appropriate humility. It functions to curb the presumptuous claims to unbridled generality, truth beyond culture and history, and fact without interpretation which have generated broad scepticism within the culture more generally, and yielded scorn more globally from those failing to share the premises. Simultaneously, such critiques function as a continuous invitation to the psychologist to avoid the blinders of the singular explanation, and to expand the range of interpretive possibilities available to the profession and the culture. All that seems 'clearly the case' could be otherwise. We shall return to this issue shortly.

In addition to the advantages of denaturalization, these forms of critique also favour a pluralist politics, both within the profession and with respect to the profession's relationship to its many publics. Within the profession they invite suspension of the lethal conflicts among competing schools, and a broadening of the dialogic base of the field. Constructionists would be opposed to a disciplinary 'mainstream' as such a condition would signify intellectual constriction and ossification. Humanist, phenomenologists, feminists and the spiritually oriented, for example, would share reason and results with behaviourists and cognitivists. No longer would other cultures be viewed primarily as sites for extending one's parochial model of the mind, but as rich repositories of alternative intelligibility. Constructionist critique also opens the profession to multiple voices from the culture more generally. Where psychology had largely been deaf to ethical and ideological misgivings concerning its practices, critical scholarship welcomes such inquiry into the professional forum. This pluralization of voices is especially important, inasmuch as the assumptions of empirical psychology offer no means of self-examination save through their own premises. Finally, efforts to denaturalize and democratize invite a dialogic relationship between the profession and its many publics, forms of interchange that should not only serve to render professional work more intelligible, but enhance the applicability of professional work for the public good. In effect, when its threatening rhetoric is removed, we find constructionist critique can vitally expand our capacities for reasoned deliberation and societal engagement.

Revitalization and enrichment

As proposed, there is nothing within a constructionist metatheory that necessarily militates against empirical work in psychology. By the same token, constructionism itself does not prohibit the entry of any term into the lexicon of mental life. In this sense, critics of constructionism who complain of its tendencies to denigrate or obliterate the self (Harré and Krausz, 1996; Osbeck, 1993), or agency and uniqueness (Fisher, 1995), or to privilege the social over the material (Michael, 1996) mistake the metatheoretical orientation for a foundational ontology. Constructionist metatheory neither denies nor affirms the existence of any mental 'entities' or 'processes'. The constructionist question is not whether the mind 'really' exists; constructionism obviates issues of fundamental ontology in favour of questions about the pragmatics of interpretation within communities. In the same way, psychology's traditional discourses of cognition, emotion, motivation and mental disorder and the like are not antagonistic to constructionist metatheory. Rather, for the constructionist, such discourses are simply forms of constructing the person within an evolving professional community, forms that may bear a close and interdependent relationship with common modes of speech and action within the culture (see, for example, Cushman, 1995).

For the professional psychologist, mental discourses have a high degree of communicative utility. Indeed, without shared discourses of this kind there would be nothing to intelligibly call 'a profession'. However, given a valued tradition of discourse and practice, constructionist metatheory does invite a range of provocative deliberations. Among them, what forms of psychological discourse are to be favoured and for what purposes? For whom are these languages useful and for what kinds of projects? Do current investments primarily benefit the constituents of the professional community; in what way do they help or hurt the recipients of such designations? To the extent that professional discourse is appropriated by the culture, what kinds of policies, institutions or individual actions are favoured? What forms of cultural life are rendered invisible or obliterated? And, given the potential of such discourses to contribute to societal trans-formation, what new or revived forms of discourse are invited?

It is in this domain of dialogue that we locate a second major orientation to psychological inquiry favoured by a constructionist standpoint. While deliberations on the utility of current pursuits is essential, constructionism also frees the investigator to suspend the taken for granted ontologies of the profession. The impetus toward consensus ('unified psychology') is modulated, and the scholar is invited to explore the penumbra of emerging intelligibility, forms of possible but unrealized articulation. I am not speaking here of a myopic accumulation of 'psychobabble', but, rather, of the careful and caring development of psychological discourse keyed to specific cultural (moral/political) ends. If psychological language is used by persons for carrying on cultural life, then new forms of language invite alternative futures. Alternative conceptions of mental functioning may favour forms of life more promising to many people than the currently obvious and unquestioned. In this case the scholar abandons the problematic role of describing 'what is the case' and sets out to forge languages favouring what may become. Detached observation gives way to what we may view as a *poetic activism*.

Yet, while constructionism removes the weight of existing ontologies, movement into meaning can scarcely proceed outside the traditions of any community. A discourse created outside the textual histories of any culture would not only fail to communicate, there would be no practices to which it was relevant. No cultural work would be achieved. It is in this respect that so much of the discourse generated within isolated academic enclaves is elsewhere discredited as 'mere jargon'. In effect, the construction of new meanings must draw from extant traditions without duplicating them. It is useful here to consider the potentials for discursive enrichment as drawing, first, on traditions within the home culture (historical archeology) and, second, on alterior traditions (cultural exegesis).

In the case of historical representation, the challenge of discursive enrichment places a premium on sustaining psychological traditions that have otherwise been suppressed by the dominant discourses. For example, the humanist tradition has been largely ignored within the major texts of the profession. Yet, while problematic in certain respects, the demise of the humanist discourse of individual intention serves as a threat to cherished cultural institutions (e.g. democracy, ethics). Similarly, while phenomenological theory was virtually obliterated with the early rise of behaviourism, abandoning the language of subjective experience removes from the culture a significant reason for valuing human life. The resuscitation of these languages in terms of contemporary theoretical and cultural dialogues – humanist on the one hand (see, for example, Rychlak, 1988) and phenomenological on the other (see, for example, Polkinghorne, 1988) – seems a highly valuable undertaking. Similarly, a vital enrichment of resources is represented in the attempt to revive the hermeneutical tradition (cf. Addison and Packer, 1989; Martin and Sugarman, 1999; Messer, Sass, and Woolfolk, 1988), once essential to the very concept of psychology as a *Geisteswissenschaft*. Hermeneutical deliberations serve the valuable function of thwarting the modes of depersonalization so common to the empirical research tradition.

I find much to be credited, as well, in work that draws from our traditions in such a way as to expand the range of 'valuing discourse'. The psychological profession has been so captivated by the instrumentalist ethos and its emphasis on problem solving that its primary offering to the culture has been a discourse of deficit (Gergen, 1994a, Chapter 6). The massive and ever-expanding terminologies of mental illness, for example, all function as means of placing social identity at risk. As the discourse is placed into action, it discredits, divides and distances. Vitally needed, then, are discourses inviting people into more valued modes of being, ways of constructing self and others that add to the sense of well-being and human welfare. Among the important contributions of this kind I would place early attempts to reconstruct women's psychology in a more empowering register (Belenky et al. 1986; Gilligan, 1982), Lifton's (1993) conception of the protean self as a source of resilience, Csikszentmihalyi's (1990) construction of the 'flow' experience and the emerging interest in wisdom (Sternberg, 1990). Much to be welcomed are the recent attempts to establish a positive psychology to compensate for the deficit orientation so dominating the field to date. (See especially the January, 2000 issue of *The American Psychologist*.) In spite of their realist predilections, in each case the theorists sustain and enrich languages that invest persons with special gifts, potentials and powers.

Other work in the positive register is more directly informed by constructionist metatheory. Here scholars are less likely to 'describe existing states' than to opt for expanding possibilities of constructing the self. For example, Averill and Nunley (1992), argue for the possibility of leading an 'emotionally creative' life, one that goes beyond conventional emotional expressions and understandings. In their book *Constructing the Life Course*, Gubrium, Holstein, and Buckholdt (1994) abandon the traditional view of epigenetic trajectories of development, and explore the possibilities for collaborative construction of individual futures. This same orientation towards the creative use of construction now pervades a large domain of therapeutic theory and practice (see, for example, Anderson, 1997; McNamee and Gergen, 1992; Weingarten, 1991; White and Epston, 1990).

These are but a sampling of illustrations of the way in which scholars can draw from existing cultural dialogues to crystallize ontologies of the person, intelligibilities that are often more 'actionable' than the formalisms of the academy, and which explicitly carry with them implications for cultural transformation. The potentials for such poetic activism have scarcely been explored. Spiritual traditions, for example, are enormously important within the culture, but have been generally eliminated from the psychologist's vocabulary. The reappropriation of history must be complemented as well by opening the field to alternative cultural conceptions. Slowly we begin to realize the potentials of Indian writings on the mind (see, for example, Paranjpe, 1998), Asian social psychology (Sugiman et al., 1999), Confucianist conceptions of self (Tu Wei-ming, 1985) and Mestizo concepts of the person and mental health (Ramirez, 1983). This process of cross-fertilization is but in a fledgling state and much to be encouraged.

As I am proposing, constructionism stresses the resuscitation, creation and appropriation of psychological intelligibilities; herein the discipline augments the discursive resources of the culture. The attempt, then, is to enrich psychology in ways that may favour positive transformations of society. Yet, a reflexive moment is required in the present case. Three issues demand particular attention. At the outset, this proposal may smack of the disingenuous. If constructionism abolishes all foundations or ultimate warrants for propositions about persons, the critic may advance, then wouldn't subsequent attempts to 'describe and explain' – as in the above – stand empty ('mere words') or, worse, operate as forms of propaganda? Why should the psychologist engage in such efforts? And what difference would there be between the psychologist's pronouncements on 'flow', 'protean potentials', 'wisdom' and the like and the priest's accounts of god or the spiritual life? In reply, there is little reason for the constructionist scholar to plump for these intelligibilities on any foundational grounds. The accounts of the person would not be favoured because they 'are true', but, rather, because they offer significant options for action. In speaking of psychological processes the theorist need not suffer a loss of confidence, or guilt over duplicity, any more than in calling a 'foul ball' at a baseball game, or declaring child molesting evil within his/her community. Confidence and the sense of authenticity are born of communal participation as opposed to grounding in 'the true', 'the real', or the 'universally ethical'. In this sense psychological theory is no more or less true than spiritualism or physics. Cultural intelligibilities sprout in many soils. However, the tradition of mental accounting is a rich and significant one, in many ways pivotal for the major institutions of the West. The importance of considered, creative and communal attention to its further elaboration can scarcely be overestimated.

The second problem concerns the form of pragmatism implied by the present arguments, and most pointedly the instrumentalist interpretation of pragmatism. As I have argued, constructionism invites the scholar to consider the societal utility of psychological theory and bring into being conceptions favouring certain cultural or world futures as opposed to others. At the same time this view would seem to thrust the theorist into the role of grand strategist, tinkering with the world on his/her terms. Such a conclusion would be unfortunate. In this sense, while allying itself with the pragmatist tradition, the instrumentalist conception of the pragmatic is not a congenial companion to constructionism. The instrumentalist view is largely an outgrowth of individualism and, most particularly, the assumption that individuals are rational and autonomous decision-makers operating to achieve their personal goals. However, constructionism not only fails to objectify the person as an autonomous agent, but when its conceptual implications are extended it favours a view of human action quite at odds with the traditional view. Although we shall treat this view shortly, the important point in this context is to appreciate the difference between a constructionist and an instrumentalist concept of the pragmatic. Constructionism's particular emphasis is on meaningful action embedded within extended patterns of interchange. Thus, meaningful action is always consequential in the sense of bearing an interdependent relationship between what preceded and what follows. By virtue of convention, one's actions thus sustain and/or suppress that which has been and simultaneously function to create a present with future ramifications. Precisely what these 'ramifications' are is open to continuous negotiation, which negotiation itself functions pragmatically in this more relational sense (see also Botschner, 1995).

Finally, the critic might locate within these proposals a 'transformationist bias', that is, a continuous championing of the new, the expanded and the revolutionary as opposed to the accepted, the traditional and secure. Surely this is the dominant sub-text of the above. However, this bias must be seen against the backdrop of the current context, both intellectual and cultural. To the extent that Western psychology is largely a child of cultural modernism (Gergen, 1991), and cultural modernism has achieved broad ascendance (its premises now rationalizing most of the culture's major institutions), then a psychology that simply contributes to the status quo has little to offer the culture. It functions as an elfin voice in a mighty chorus. Constructionism itself is not antithetical to tradition; indeed, tradition is essential to the construction of all meaning. However, to the extent that one wishes to participate in a profession that plays a significant role in expanding the culture's resources, constructionist arguments can lend strong support. In effect, there seems less to be gained in the present era through duplication of longstanding intelligibilities than through catalytic conceptualization.

The social reconstruction of the mind

There is a third orientation to 'the psyche' advanced by constructionist writings, an orientation to which the preceding arguments serve as important antecedents. As we have seen, significant criticism has been directed toward traditional psychology for its implicit support of individualist ideology and institutions. As it is variously reasoned, tracing human action to psychological sources sustains a view of persons as fundamentally isolated, self-gratifying and self-sufficient. From the traditional standpoint, human relationships are artificial byproducts of otherwise autonomously functioning individuals; the social is secondary to and derivative of the personal. As such conceptions are played out in cultural life, critics argue, they naturalize alienation (each of us alone in our own experience), self-absorption or narcissism and a conflict of all against all (each individual for him/herself). Coupled with this critique, however, is the second logic developed above, namely that a major aim of scholarship from the constructionist standpoint should be the enrichment of cultural resources. In particular, through the development of new ontologies, alternative and possibly more promising avenues of action within the culture may be opened. As these lines of argument are compounded, they conduce to investments in reconceptualizing the individual in other than individualistic terms.

There are many forms which such reconceptualization might take – ecological, social structural and social evolutionary among them. However, specifically invited by constructionist metatheory, is the *social* reconstitution of the individual. That is, within the many dialogues making up the constructionist movement, the social is given primacy over the individual. Significant attention is given, for example, to language, dialogue, negotiation, social pragmatics, conversational positioning, ritual, cultural practice and the distribution of power. As earlier advanced, constructionist theorists are scarcely obliged to reinstantiate a constructionist metatheory in their scientific/scholarly accounts of the world or persons. In this respect the metatheory dictates nothing. However, because constructionist metatheory implies an alternative to the individualized conception of human action, there is good reason for exploring its potentials in developing more social or relational accounts of the person. In effect, the third constructionist orientation to the psychological world is to reconstitute it as a domain of the social.

Of course, attempts to conceptualize the individual as a social actor have long been fixtures on the intellectual landscape (see Burkitt's 1991 review). Current constructionist attempts must be viewed as extensions of this tradition. At the same time, there are important differences among current theorists, differences with respect to their affinity to central constructionist tenets. For analytic purposes it is useful to consider a continuum of conceptualizations, varying in terms of their congeniality with traditional individualism (and its close alliance with empiricism) as opposed to the primacy of relationship implicit within constructionist writings. Let us first consider the more conservative pole. Characterized by a deep respect for existing traditions, we find conceptualizations of the social self which 1) place a strong emphasis on specifically psychological states or processes; 2) presume the reality of their subject matter (beyond cultural construction); 3) rely on or attempt to establish foundations for further research; 4) treat the language of analysis as correspondent with nature, and the concomitant role of the scientist/scholar as informant to the culture; and 5) treat the scientific/scholarly effort as politically/ideologically neutral. For purposes of comparison and evaluation, let us first consider social reconceptualizations emphasizing such traditional tendencies.

Individuals as cultural carriers

The nativist–environmentalist binary, around which most of the major debates in psychology have revolved over the last century, furnishes the germinating context for one of the most important attempts at socially reconstituting the self. That persons are influenced by their cultural surrounds has virtually served as a theoretical truism for psychology. This was most obviously the case during the hegemony of behaviourism, but even the nativistically oriented cognitivists have been unable – lest they sink on the shoals of solipsism – to abandon this conceptual mooring. Yet, the manner in which social reconstructions of the individual have now extended this tradition form a dramatic disjunction with both behaviourist and cognitivist formulations. For both behaviourists and cognitivists the strong presumption prevails that the individual is endowed with certain psychological structures or processes. For the behaviourist the environment may stimulate or inform the internal conditions; for cognitivists, environmental conditions provide raw resources for cognitive appropriation. In neither case is the mental fundament itself produced, extinguished or transformed. It is precisely this move that characterizes a range of recent attempts at social reconstitution. As it is variously reasoned, it is not the self-contained individual who precedes culture, but the culture that establishes the basic character of psychological functioning.

Not only does this family of attempts benefit from the environmentalist tradition, but in most cases significant linkages are forged with theories from psychology's past. For example, Bruner's highly influential work (1990) draws sustenance from Vygotsky, Bartlett, Mead and a host of other significant psychological figures in proposing that 'it is culture, not biology, that shapes human life and the human mind, that gives meaning to action by situating its underlying intentional states in an interpretive system' (p. 34). In contrast, James Gee (1992) squeezes support from myriad linguistic and cognitive contributions to argue that 'the individual interprets experience by forming "folk theories", which together with nonlinguistic modules of the mind, cause the person to talk and act in certain ways . . . ' (p. 104). Related attempts to 'socialize' the self have drawn significantly from George Kelly (Neimeyer and Neimeyer, 1985), Freud (Freeman, 1993) and object relations theory (Mitchell, 1993).

For illustrative purposes, let us consider Harré and Gillett's (1994) comprehensive account of the individual as cultural carrier. Although specifically disavowing dualism, the hypothetico-deductive programme and laboratory experimentation, the book rapidly moves on to discuss the nature of psychological states and conditions. 'Concepts,' we learn, are 'the basis of thinking, and are expressed by words' (p.21). Further, 'we must learn to see the mind as the meeting point of a wide range of structuring influences . . . ' (p. 22). The authors then proceed to describe processes of thought, 'cognitive systems that can cope with the complexity and variety of real-world experiences . . . ' (p. 79), the individual as an agent of his/her actions, experience and perception. The reality of these various processes is never in question, nor is their function in dealing with 'the world as it really is . . . not just as one might wish it to be' (p. 49). Further, a full chapter ('Discourse and the Brain') is devoted to linking these mental processes to neural networks. Discussion of brain function serves the additional function of lodging the analysis in 'established knowledge', that is, giving it foundations. It is the avowed effort of the book to establish the basis for a 'second cognitive revolution'. That the analysis is attempting to illuminate the truth of human functioning is a supposition never subjected to reflective scrutiny. Throughout, the authors position their own discourse as truth carrying, with the reader interpellated as unenlightened audience. Nor is the book viewed as ideologically invested. Its primary aim is to inform the reader of the nature of human action, to 'make the main tenets and some of the research results of discursive psychology easily available' (p. viii).

These varying attempts to conceptualize mental process as derivative of social process represent an important step toward refiguring psychology's conception of the person. And, while many constructionists find this explanatory orientation still too conservative, its very resonance with the preceding tradition may serve as its most important rhetorical asset. The views are innovative, but not radically disruptive; they invite existing intelligibilities and skills into dialogue rather than undermining them; they are collaborative rather than condemning. Is there reason, then, for seeking alternatives to the metaphor of individual as cultural carrier? Many would argue affirmatively. By their very familiarity, such orientations run the risk of full absorption into the existing traditions. They too easily become candidates for empirical evaluation, with such assessment implicitly reinforcing a dualist metaphysics that must, in the end, eschew these very conceptions. The metaphysics of empirical assessment presumes the existence of a scientist who can claim truth beyond culture, comprehension beyond 'folk psychology', universality rather than historicity. If these theories of mind as cultural carrier are candidates for truth, then in the end they must necessarily be falsified.

This is not the only reason for pressing the boundaries of intelligibility past the view of persons as cultural carriers. On the conceptual level, these views leave difficult problems unanswered. In my view, the paramount question, how cultural understandings can be acquired by the individual, remains theoretically intractable. As I have argued (Gergen, 1994a, Chapter 5), the problem is insoluble in principle. If mental process reflects social process, then the acquisition of the social must proceed without benefit of mental processing. If mental process is required in order to understand the social, then the mental must precede the social. The social view of the individual collapses. Further, many constructionists find such accounts insufficiently reflexive, not only by virtue of the hierarchies created in their claims to authority, but in their insensitivity to the ethical and political implications of their work. Alternative revisionings of the person are thus invited.

Individuals as culturally immersed

A second and smaller family of theories is less obviously linked to the traditional assumptions of the field. Focal attention shifts in this case from expositions of psychological process informed by culture to social process from which individual functioning cannot be extricated. In such accounts, the self–other (individual–culture) binary is virtually destroyed. For theorists of this stripe, traditional psychology offers few conceptual resources (selected offerings of Harry Stack Sullivan and Vygotsky notwithstanding); other traditions must be located. For example, Edward Sampson (1993a) draws significantly from both Wittgenstein (1953) and

Bakhtin (1981, 1986) in arguing that 'all meaning, including the meaning of one's self, is rooted in the social process and must be seen as an ongoing accomplishment of that process. Neither meaning nor the individual mind is a precondition for social interaction; rather, these emerge from and are sustained by conversations occurring between people' (p. 99). In his development of a 'rhetorically responsive' view of human action, Shotter (1993a) expands the range of relevant contributions to include Vico, Valosinov and Garfinkel. Shotter is concerned with the way 'responsive meanings are always first "sensed" or "felt" from within a conversation, . . . and amenable to yet further responsive (sensible) development' (p. 180).

In this context, Hermans and Kempen's (1993) volume, *The dialogical self: meaning as movement*, provides an instructive contrast to the Harré and Gillett analysis. The extensive accounts of mental process in the latter work can be compared with the *sotto voce* analysis of mind in Hermans and Kempen. For example, for these authors, emotions are 'rhetorical actions' and agency is a byproduct of participation in a dialogic relationship. This more sparing account of mental process is a congenial companion to muted realism. The authors are also sensitized to the function of metaphor in guiding their theoretical account (pp. 8–10), acknowledging that their discussion of mental process is based on the metaphor of the narrative. Eschewing the attempt to furnish foundations, they propose that 'The main purpose of this work is to bring together two familiar concepts, dialogue and self, and combine them in such a way that a more extended view of the possibilities of the mind becomes visible' (p. xx). And, while occasionally weaving data into their analysis, their use of evidence is not intended to fix the conclusion. Rather, 'we want to present some empirical explorations that serve as illustration of our more extensive theoretical and conceptual discussions' (p. xx).

Hermans and Kempen do little to articulate the social/political consequences of their account; they are far more invested in the contribution their work makes to the academic community than to the more general ethos of politics. More political in their theorizing are Sampson's (1993b) and Shotter's (1993a) contributions to this view. Sampson's analysis is specifically dedicated to a 'celebration of the other', and the potential of such a formulation for undermining power and reducing suppression. Shotter (1993a) is deeply concerned with the political dimension of everyday interaction, and with using psychology to give marginal voices a broader space of expression.

The relational constitution of self

There is a third more radical reconceptualization of the mental, and the most congenial with constructionist metatheory. As indicated, such metatheory traces ontological posits to language and language to processes of relationship. By implication all that may be said about mental process is derived from relational process. If this view is pressed to its extreme, one is invited explore a terrain of theoretical intelligibility in which mental predicates never function referentially and social process serves as the essential fulcrum of explanation. That is, we may envision the elimination of psychological states and conditions as explanations for action and the reconstitution of psychological predicates within the sphere of social process.

One important opening to a socialized psychology has emerged from contemporary discourse analysis. Such analysis typically focuses on the pragmatics of discourse, with issues of reference (semantics) bracketed. In the case of mental discourse, then, the analyst is less concerned with the mental phenomena to which such discourse may or may not refer than with the way such discourse functions within relationships. For example, in Potter and Wetherell's (1987) ground-breaking work, the concept of 'attitude' is shorn of mental referents and, as they see it, serves to index positional claims within social intercourse. An attitude, then, is essentially a social claim ('I feel . . . ', 'My view is . . . ', 'I prefer . . . ') and not an external expression of an internal impulse. Billig's (1990) essay on memory focuses on the way in which people negotiate the past, thus defining memory not as a mental event but a relational achievement. Or as Shotter (1990) proposes, memory is a 'social institution'. Edwards and Potter's (1992) *Discursive Psychology* represents a significant attempt to replace cognitive with discursive processes in explaining human interchange. Stenner and Eccleston's (1994) account of the 'textualization of being' also resonates with this line of argument.

Much of my own work in this domain grows from the soil of discursive psychology. However, while focally concerned with discourse, the attempt is to include (1) more fully enriched patterns of performance and (2) the patterns of relationship among participants. In the former case, while discourse is often central to the analysis, spoken and written language do not exhaust the spectrum of concerns. Ideally one would wish to include the bodily activities of the participants, along with various objects, ornaments and physical settings necessary to render these performances intelligible. With respect to relational pattern, the focus is on recurring patterns of interaction. To clarify, consider the case of emotion. Emotion terms (e.g. anger, love, depression) may serve as key elements of conversation and the attribution of emotions to self and others of primary significance in social interchange. I have found it more useful, however, to consider emotional performances more fully embodied (Gergen, 1994a, pp. 210–35). This means viewing linguistic expressions as possible but not essential components of actions that may require patterns of gesture, gaze, bodily orientation (and possibly physical artifacts or a locale) to achieve their intelligibility. Here my initial debt is largely to Averill's (1982) work on emotional performances. However, the attempt is to press beyond the individual performance to consider the patterns of interchange within which the performance is embedded and without which it would constitute cultural nonsense.

I use the term 'relational scenario' to index reiterative patterns of inter-change (*lived narratives*) in which 'psychological performances' play an integral role. Thus, for example, the performance of *anger* (complete with discourse, facial expressions, postural configurations) is typically embedded within a scenario in which a preceding *affront* may be required for its expression to acquire meaning; the performance of anger also sets the stage for the subsequent occurrence of an *apology* or a *defence*; and if an apology is offered a favoured response within the Western scenario is *forgiveness*. At that point the scenario may be terminated. All the actions making up the sequence, from affront to forgiveness, require each other to achieve legitimacy. This form of analysis also applies to other forms of psychological performance (see, for example, Gergen, 1994b, for a relational account of memory).

Unlike much discourse analysis (and the bulk of conversation analysis) this account does not place a strong emphasis on evidential grounds. The goal of truth is replaced with intelligibility. This does not eliminate my positioning of the reader as 'unknowing', but it does render my account vulnerable as 'knowing'. In effect, the intelligibility of the account cannot be achieved without the assent of the reader. Further, consistent with constructionist metatheory and its emphasis on the use-value of language, my attempt has been increasingly to press past the printed page to locate or develop relevant cultural practices. For example, if certain emotional scenarios are inimical to the participants' well-being, how can they intelligibly alter the familiar course of action? The attempt, then, is to extend the use-value of the theoretical discourse to patterns of daily life (see, for example, McNamee and Gergen, 1999). And while much (but not all) discursive work is politically neutral, the present account is explicitly set against individualist ideology and related practices.

While these attempts to reconstitute the self as relational are more radical than the preceding alternatives, in the end we must also recognize their limitations. On the one hand, many scholars find them sufficiently dislocating that grafting them to more recognized (and professionally acceptable) pursuits is prohibited. On the other extreme, the more socio-logically inclined argue that such accounts are far too micro-social. One may indeed reinscribe 'the mind' more collectively, arguing that reason, memory and the like are broadly distributed within organizations or cultures (see, for example, Douglas, 1986). Still others will find these orientations far too elitist. The analyses are intelligible only to the academically privileged. Finally, the strong emphasis on relationships is viewed as inimical to the important values inherent in the individualist tradition (e.g. democracy, humanism, equality). Insufficient attention has been given to the positive character of the tradition that is otherwise placed in jeopardy.

In conclusion

As we find, far from eliminating psychological inquiry, social constructionism functions generatively to expand and enrich its potentials. At the outset, the constructionist impetus toward denaturalization and democratization invites the scholar not only to see how his/her work contributes to the moral and political fabric of the culture, but also opens the field to a broader range of dialogue. Favoured in particular are forms of dialogue that can link the discipline with its cultural surrounds, mutually transforming intelligibilities in such a way that the discipline plays a more vital role in the society. Constructionist ideas also invite the scholar to consider the advantages of resuscitating and enriching the compendium of mental discourse. Given a keen concern with the moral and political context, the scholar engages in forms of theoretical poetics that open the culture to new, forgotten or otherwise suppressed intelligibilities and, thus, new alternatives for action. Finally, we have seen how constructionist views can stimulate the development of relational alternatives to the traditional conception of the self-contained individual. In significant respects, these revisionings of the person are intended as resources for societal change. There is no necessary antagonism between constructionism and psychological inquiry. Rather, informed by constructionist metatheory, there is reason to believe that psychology can play a far more vital role within society than heretofore.

Notes

1 For summaries of this work see Gergen (1994a, 1999).

2 For a recent integration of relevant historical literature, see Graumann and Gergen (1996).

3

THE LIMITS OF PURE CRITIQUE

Cynicism . . . is that modernist, unhappy consciousness, on which
enlightenment has labored both successfully and in vain. . . . Well-off
and miserable at the same time . . .

Peter Sloterdijk, *Critique of Cynical Reason*

For the better part of the past twenty years I have been heavily engaged
in critical and reconstructive work in the social sciences. Initial attacks
were lodged against the established practices of behavioural research, along
with associated forms of theory and their justifying base in empiricist
foundationalism. Volleys were variously directed against the traditional
presumptions of cumulative knowledge, value-free theoretical formulations, unbiased observation, knowledge through hypothesis testing,
measurement of psychological processes, and more. Gradually I became
aware of the extent to which this work was both preceded and accompanied
by steadily expanding efforts within philosophy and across the social
sciences, efforts that collectively form what we now see as a genre of *post-
empiricist critique*. The works of Popper, Quine and a host of ordinary
language philosophers wreaked havoc with assumptions of empiricist
foundationalism, and the later works of Kuhn, Feyerabend and other
historians of knowledge, along with a host of sociologists of knowledge,
began to offer alternatives to the traditional understanding of scientific
activity. Over time, these voices were joined by increasing numbers within
the social sciences – humanists, critical theorists, hermeneuticists, constructionists, feminists, phenomenologists, ethogenecists and many others.
Empiricist foundationalism and its associated practices may continue
to be dominant, but for a substantial number of scholars they lie essentially
dead.

Both simultaneous and intertextual with the expansion of post-
empiricist critique have been two other major forms of critical scholarship.
As outlined in the preceding chapter, with the gradual erosion of the
empiricist account, intellectual space was increasingly opened for *ideological
critique* or *unmasking* (see Chapter 2). If theoretical accounts cannot be
rendered authoritative by virtue of empirical data, and if these accounts

enter social life as catalysts or suppressants, then science is opened to a form of evaluation scarcely voiced since the nineteenth century. Specifically, scientific theory can be evaluated in terms of its effects on the culture, the forms of social life which it facilitates and obliterates or, in short, its ideological impact. Such critique was long championed by Marxists and critical theorists, but with the empiricist erosion the way was opened for a vital expansion of ideological critique. At present the range of such critique is ever broadening. Feminist critique has been sharpened to a stiletto-like finish; black, native-American, Asian, Hispanic, and Arabic and gay scholars lend significant new dimensions to existing concerns. Even the erstwhile victims of such critique – typically the right-wing, male-dominated establishment – now responds with its own form of ideological critique: the argument against the tyranny of political correctness.

The weapons of attack within the domains of post-empiricist and ideological critique have been further strengthened by developments in *post-structuralist critique* (see also Chapter 2). Reader-response theory undermines the presumption that texts carry inherent wisdom or profundity; texts contain only so much authority as interpretive communities are willing to grant. Deconstruction theory further demonstrates the internal tensions of the text, the dependence of the said on the unsaid, and the eternal aporia of the apodictic. With deconstruction theory, not only the object of the text disappears as a serious matter, but so does the mind of the author as an originary source. And, coupled with reader response and deconstruction theory, rhetorical analysis further reveals the bag of tricks, ruses and hijinks essential to the intelligibility and persuasive appeal of any text. Under these conditions, all attempts by authorities to establish knowledge, convey wisdom or establish values are placed under suspicion.

We thus stand at present with a mammoth arsenal of critical weapons at our disposal. The power of such technology is unmatched by anything within the scholarly traditions of longstanding. There is virtually no hypothesis, body of evidence, ideological stance, literary canon, value commitment or logical edifice that cannot be dismantled, demolished or derided with the weapons at hand. Only rank prejudice, force of habit or the anguished retaliation of deflated egos can muster a defence against the intellectual explosives within our grasp. Everywhere now in the academic world the capitalist exploiters, male chauvinist pigs, cultural imperialists, neo-colonialists, warmongers, WASP bigots, wimp liberals, scientistic dogmatists, and fundamentalists and essentialists of every stripe are on the run. Nor are these capacities for deflation and decimation limited to the academic establishment. Post-empiricist critique finds ample targets throughout society. Foundational or essentialist presumptions can be located within all domains of high-level decision-making – in government, business, the military, education, and so on. Similarly, the targets of ideological critique are scarcely limited to the academy. Feminists, critical theorists and minority groups find oppression and bigotry at every turn

– in film, art, architecture, clothing preferences and even the design of public toilets. And in the wake of post-structuralist critique, all that passed for trustworthy opinion – in the political sphere, the news media, the courts, the ministry – now teeters on the brink of blather. The revolution is on, heads are rolling everywhere, there is no limit to the potential destruction.

It is at this juncture, however, that my present inquiry begins. For I am not at all sanguine about our present condition and the future which it invites. It is not simply that we who share the arsenal do not always share turf, and these weapons may turn internecine. (Already, there are antagonisms among various post-empiricist enclaves, feminist camps, gay and lesbian groups, and post-structuralist clans.) Rather, my chief concern is with the limits of critique – and most particularly the emerging body of critique – as a genre of scholarship. We find ourselves now in a position not unlike that of the French revolutionaries: echoes of 'Liberty, equality, and solidarity' (a politically correct replacement for 'fraternity') abound. But is the result to be an ingurgitating bloodbath? Will there be no trustworthy or honoured views, only a dismantling that ultimately turns to destroy itself? As Seyla Benhabib (1992) comments: 'Postmodernism, in its infinitely skeptical and subversive attitude toward normative claims, institutional justice and political struggles, is certainly refreshing. Yet, it is also debilitating' (p. 15). It is precisely this latter potential that will concern us here. Sober reflection seems essential on the forms of our interrogations – their intelligibility, coherence and societal effects.

In what follows I shall identify five substantial problems that seem to me inherent in the critical effort.[1] The initial shortcomings seem relevant to all forms of existing critique; the latter two are specifically germane to lines of recently emerging critique. Attention will finally turn to possible alternatives.

The closure of conversation

Critique acquires both its impetus and intelligibility from a preceding advocacy. An assertion (or network of assertions) must be put forward in order to stir and make intelligible the impulse towards negation. In this sense, critique is a symbiotic enterprise, requiring assertion as its parent. Yet, owing to its genesis critique acquires certain characteristics – namely, those possessed by its progenitor. That is, critique is not free to speak with its own voice; rather, the terms of critique are established by the ontology (actual or attributed) of its predecessor. If the assertion is that 'armed intervention is necessary', critique is limited to a linguistic domain in which the binary 'war–not war' serves as the pivotal defining agent. To respond to the advocacy of armed intervention with 'I shall have a cup of tea' or 'I am for the Greens' would not be to engage in critique (indeed, one might view such rejoinders as nonsensical insertions into the interchange). The status of such rejoinders as critique *could* be sustantiated, but only if it could be shown that drinking tea or voting Green represents the negation of armed intervention (for example, as a display of disdain in the case of drinking tea, or with reference to the anti-war stance of the Green in the second).

At the outset, this symbiotic condition means that the critic's voice will operate so as to reify the terms of the binary. In effect, the critique renders support to the ontology implicit in the initial network of assertions, an ontology that might wither or dissolve without the critical impulse. Feminist theorists have been most sensitive to this issue. As many have pointed out, arguments against male dominance simultaneously reify a distinction between men and women; they operate to essentialize gender as a factual difference. Similarly, as various criticisms are couched in the language of racial conflict, the concept of essential differences between races is sustained; to speak against upper-class domination is to engender the reality of class differences. Once reality has been struck in terms of the binary, the contours of the world approach stasis.

This problem is closely coupled with a second, namely that of a dissolving periphery. For as arguments proceed within terms of the binary, other realities, values and concerns are removed from view. It is the terms of the binary that furnish the interlocutors with the basis of their relationship and, indeed, the foundation of their identities within the relationship. In battling against the destruction of the environment, for example, issues of racial equality recede from view. Critiques of racial unfairness are insensitive to gender inequality, and so on. Of course, it is difficult to argue simultaneously about all issues. However, as interchange is polarized around a single continuum, there is a deadly flattening of the world and a silencing of other voices. Each interlocutor, in the face of the other, loses dimension; all human characteristics, relationships, investments and viewpoints unrelated to the binary are suppressed. And the interlocutors themselves become deaf to all those voices – family, friends, the needy, and so on – who do not share the reality which they create and sustain. As David Harvey (1993) puts the case:

> Concentration on class alone is seen to hide, marginalize, disempower, repress and perhaps even oppress all kinds of 'others' precisely because it cannot and does not acknowledge explicitly the existence of heterogeneities and differences based on, for example, race, gender, sexuality, age, ability, culture, locality, ethnicity, religion, community, consumer preferences, group affiliation, and the like. (p. 102)

There are further ramifications of this condition. Once the arena of reifications has been established, the opposing sides come to depend on the image of the other for their very sustenance. Each position remains intelligible and important only so long as the opposition is sustained within the discourse. Should the opposition be removed from view, the favoured position lapses into insignificance. Thus, for example, so long as religious converts can sustain the category of 'the infidel', they retain a distinctive quality and a reason for commitment. For the committed, critique from the outside may even be welcomed because it sustains or strengthens their cause. Here the critic doesn't undermine the target, but enhances the strength of that which is abhorred. Those in political power, for example, may facilitate a certain amount of critique (from let's say, university students) as it can inspire continued commitment to 'the cause' (consider the common slurs on left-wingers, homosexuals, liberals and other 'unAmericans' in universities).

Illustration is furnished by my own early experiences in the Society for Experimental Social Psychology. The association was initially developed to sustain a tough-minded, systematic approach to understanding social interaction. The term 'experimental' was adopted not so much out of a commitment to laboratory experimentation per se, but because experiments were believed to be the most sophisticated means of warranting statements about causal relations. Indeed, many participants in the association employed interview methods, questionnaires, field observation and other research techniques. Semiotically, the term 'experimental' was merely to function as a synonym for 'systematically scientific'. As the association rapidly grew stronger and more elitist, some of us became concerned that the choice of names was unfortunate. For, it seemed, the term 'experimental' was sanctifying the laboratory experiment as the only acceptable methodology. Other forms of research were being discouraged and systematic theoretical and conceptual work was being abandoned altogether. At this point I joined with several colleagues in mounting an attempt to challenge the name of the organization, to remove or replace the term 'experimental'. The succeeding debate led to a heated defence of experimental methodology (not itself under attack at the time), an attack on all other methods as inferior and a renewed commitment to the existing organizational name. Handbooks and textbooks now repeat the defence as a virtual litany. Periodically the second-status journals of the field will feature a contrary view, but the very appearance of such critiques in the peripheral journals serves only to strengthen the intelligibility of 'experimental superiority' within the dominant establishment. In effect, the critical attack primarily served to delineate a binary, to stimulate its defence and to ensure that further criticism remained at the margins of disciplinary consciousness.

Critique as condemnation

In the opening of this chapter I made frequent use of the metaphor of argument as war. The choice was not accidental, for in giving expression to this common norm (see Lakoff and Johnson, 1980) we are better positioned to appreciate the strategic implications of critique. Consider the position of argumentation theorists, van Eemeren and Grootendorst (1983): 'a language user who has advanced a point of view in respect of an expressed opinion must be prepared to *defend* that standpoint and . . . a language user who has cast doubt upon the tenability of that standpoint must be prepared to *attack* it' (p. 1; my emphasis). Given this formalization of a broadly shared conception of argumentation, the posture of one who is targeted for criticism can scarcely be other than defensive. And the dimensions of this defence are profound. In the Western tradition one's words are virtually expressions of personal essence. They are presumed to reflect the inner-most capacities of the individual – the logos – the originary process that sets humans above the brutes (and, traditionally, gives the human kinship with God). To criticize another's views is not, then, a mere linguistic exercise; within the Western tradition it is to invalidate the originary essence of the self. Or, to extend the symbolic laminations, criticism transforms the target's attempt at self-expression to mere foolishness, knavery or idiocy. It is to rob one's words of authority; to threaten one's likeness to God, king, hero and father; and to return one to the status of errant child – now corrected by a knowing parent.

Given this provocative context, how is the target of criticism to respond? Scarcely with zest for open and balanced exploration, with eagerness to see the issues resolved justly and impartially. When one is subjected to forces of annihilation – of one's sense of self and one's dignity – there is little choice but to seek all means of vanquishing the threatening force. Critique thus invites counter-critique, and once the counter-critique is set in motion we enter a scenario with little means of termination.

Even if protagonists are forced into civil interchange, there are principled reasons why critique and rebuttal can scarcely move toward unanimity. In open dialogue one can continue indefinitely to remain secure in his/her beliefs – unaffected by counter-argument – because the very structure of dialogue ensures this possibility. The principal reason for this essential undecidability is derived from a relational view of understanding.[2] As proposed, whether one's words are granted meaning, and the particular meaning they are allowed to possess, is importantly determined by one's audience. One's utterances stand as multiply interpretable texts, subject to appropriation from myriad standpoints. To the extent that this is so, any advocate within an argument fails to control the meaning of his/her case; the words stand open to a variety of interpretations or selective appropriations, and such choices are likely to reflect the adversary's investment. In the same manner, the adversary's utterances are subject to a reciprocal reconstruction. In effect, each interlocutor confronts a situation in which 'I cannot control your interpretation of what I say, but I am positioned so as to grant (or deny) intelligibility to your reply, or to bend your words to my interpretive designs'.

The means for destroying the other's intelligibility are as vast and varied. Sentences may be lifted from context, concepts altered through recontextualization, arguments pressed to absurd extremes, examples transformed through parody, insidious intentions imputed, and so on. The critical movements described above – anti-empiricist, ideological and post-structural – add incrementally to the means of deflating the opposition and reclaiming the high ground for oneself. There are, then, myriad means of ambiguating, complexifying, doggerelizing or transforming any utterance for one's own gain. Resultingly, there is no principled end to argumentation – unless participants are subjected to outside requirements (as in a court of law), or severely restricted by rules of procedure (as in the case of mathematics). Each combatant retains control over the effective contents of the opponent's position.

A brief illustration from Paul Feyerabend's (1978) *Science in a Free Society* is illustrative. In his earlier writings Feyerabend developed a series of vigorous attacks against foundationalist views of science, arguing that virtually all the rules of procedure used to 'advance knowledge' by traditional standards would indeed stifle attempts in this direction. Counter-critique was rapidly forthcoming – much of it highly sophisticated. Ideally one might envision this as a context for an extended dialogue, guided by hopes of enhanced understanding. Consider, in contrast, Feyerabend's reactions to his critics:

> . . . I thought I was confronted with individual incompetence: the learned gentlemen (and the one learned lady who joined the dance) were not too bright and rather badly informed and so they quite naturally made fools of themselves. Since then I have realized that this is a rather superficial way of looking at things. For the mistakes I noticed and criticized do not merely occur in this or that review, they are fairly widespread. And their frequency is not merely an accident of history, a temporary loss of intellect, it shows a pattern. Speaking paradoxically we may say that incompetence, having been standardized, has now become an essential part of professional excellence. We have no longer incompetent professionals, we have professionalized incompetence. (p. 183)

Needless to say, dialogue between Feyerabend and his colleagues came to a virtual standstill.

The atomization of community

This concern with the rhetorical effects of critique is scarcely limited to the relationship between antagonists alone. As advanced in preceding chapters, language serves to sustain communal patterns of conduct. As communities reach ontological and valuational consensus, so do patterns of relationship stabilize. To agree, for example, on the concept of work – its referents and its value – is to lay the groundwork for a mutually acceptable way of life. Thus, to abandon one's assertions in the face of critique is not simply to give way in a contest of logic and evidence. Rather, it is to threaten one's forms of relationship and ways of life. To convince the pacifist that combat is indeed virtuous, would not only be a loss of argument but, more importantly, the demise of the relationships and traditions sustained by the language of protest.

In this light, consider a group of persons among whom communication is open, fluid and unproblematic. Each member of the group is acknowledged and accepted by the others, and efforts are made at common understandings. In effect, the body of available signifiers circulates with relative ease, making it possible for new combinations to develop, and for the language of understanding to evolve over time. Now consider the insertion of critical practice into the community. Critique first serves to generate common consciousness among those placed in question. A category is either created (e.g. 'fundamentalist') or foregrounded ('homosexual') that might otherwise go unnoticed. The targets of critique are thus put on notice that all who share their particular assumptions (and associated practices) are discredited. Not only are their identities imperiled, but also the relationships in which they are embedded. Under these conditions the culture offers little opportunity for other than collective defence. Those under attack reaffirm their relationships, articulate the value of their tradition and locate myriad ways in which their attackers are unjust and misinformed. The banner of defence, along with its *raison d'etre* are all furnished by those who have raised significant question.

As the process of reaffirmation and justification takes place, simultaneously the efforts of the critics are thwarted. Not only do their criticisms go unheeded, but the targets seem to defend themselves with 'cheap ruses' (further masking their faults) and mount unjustified counter-attacks. The culturally sensible response to such loutish reactions to critique is to increase the intensity of the attacks, reaffirm solidarity within the ranks and to proselytize for further strength. Should these efforts prove successful, they will be countered by similar investments among the target group. In effect, the result is a polarizing split within the community as a whole. Mutual acknowledgement and a common quest for understanding are destroyed or, more precisely, reserved for relations within the restricted boundaries of each group. The coordinated actions necessary for generating common meaning deteriorate and, as the language within each camp evolves, communication across boundaries becomes increasingly arduous. The interpretive communities come to share argots within that are unheard, unacknowledged or found absurd within the opposing community. Mutually exclusive realities (incommensurable paradigms) solidify with little means for reconciliation.

Illustration is useful. Some of my earliest critical work took place in the context of what was – in the mid-1970s – called 'the crisis in social psychology'. My attempt at that point (Gergen, 1973) was to undermine the presumption that social psychology was a cumulative science, moving steadily toward the establishment of ahistorical truths, and to replace such an orientation with historically embedded and ideologically sensitive forms of inquiry. In the years immediately following this critique, there was an enormous amount of debate within the field. Major journals carried the dialogue. Yet as my interests became increasingly allied with those of other dissidents, the established journals slowly sealed themselves off from the controversies. Time and relationships have since moved on, and I now find myself deeply immersed within a large and heterogeneous community of anti-foundationalists. We now have our own journals, associations, lines of scholarship and agendas. Traditional social psychologists would understand little of what we talk about – so much jargon, mystification and real-world irrelevance to them. And if they did understand they would be appalled and offended at the picture our literature paints of them. At the same time, they continue business as usual; the crisis is settled. (Ironically, a 1991 book of 'classic readings in social psychology' carries *a critique* of my initial criticism; the original thesis itself is no longer included.) By the same token, were any of *us* to attend *their* meetings or read their articles we would find their efforts archaic, naive and politically shallow. The atomization of communities is virtually complete.

These three problems – the containment of conversation, rhetorical impasse and atomization of community – are all endemic to the process of critique itself, at least as it has functioned within the Western cultural tradition. I wish now, however, to touch on two problems particularly relevant to post-empiricist or post-foundational critique. As critique is mounted from these quarters there are emerging tensions of considerable magnitude.

Critique and the totalizing impulse

Much contemporary critique is designed to undermine any form of totalizing discourse, that is, any set of descriptions, explanations, principles, criteria of acceptability, directives or metatheories that curtail the array of voices allowed speak to any issue or state of affairs. This concern is evidenced, for example, in social constructionist critiques of empiricist metatheory, feminist critiques of androcentric language, Marxist critiques of capitalist economic theory, deconstructionist critiques of marginalization practices and postmodern critiques of modernist foundationalism. Virtually all of these efforts attempt to undermine the dominant discourse and augment the range of voices determining our cultural future.

Yet, in what degree does the critical impulse truly serve the function of democratization? As we have seen, the problems begin with the symbiotic nature of the critical form. Once an assertion is followed by a critical negation, there is a radical truncation in the range of relevant voices. As the grounds of battle are solidified so does any voice registered outside the binary become irrelevant. If we are arguing over abortion rights, there is no room for an advocate of migrant workers rights; psychologists debating over experimentation versus more humanistic alternatives are unprepared for entry of advocates of the spiritual in psychology. Once the binary has been struck, it is not any voice that can be heard, but only those that remain within the reified world of the debate as structured.

Further, because antagonists are traditionally annihilistic in aim – attempting to eradicate the evil or wrong-headedness of the other's position – there are incipient tendencies toward totalitarianism within the critical exchange. As the voice of dissent attempts to demolish those discourses that appear unjust, inhumane, exploitative, and so on, so does it offer itself as a successor. Yet, this successor discourse leaves no space for that which it has set out to destroy. Should the critic prove successful the accomplishment is not thus the broadening of the discursive domain. It is the replacement of one form of totalization with its opposite number. It is an inversion of the binary, with results no less stifling.

By way of illustration, for some time I have been engaged in attacks on the discourses of deficit generated by the mental health professions.[3] I have argued that as the languages of mental disease are disseminated to the public, they are employed by people to understand themselves. By constructing themselves in illness terms, a need is further generated for the very profession that creates the language. And, as the profession is consulted and remunerated, so does it grow and prosper. With its prosperity there is further growth in deficit terminology. In effect, we are witnessing a spiralling growth of terms that enfeeble the population, and the chief focus of critique is the system of mental health diagnosis. In present terms, the binary is thus established between the *production of mental deficit terms* and *non-production* (or, more specifically, the production of alternative, and more promising constructions). The favoured position would, of course, increase the number of available perspectives, in effect broadening the range of available voices. However, the critical form of argumentation operates in such a way that the intelligibility of the new alternative is established in terms of the opposition's demise. There is no space carved out for the mental health professional to continue disseminating the 'bad old language' of deficit, for it is this language that operates against the alternatives. In effect, the symbiotic character of critique operates to silence the voice of the target; the other's totalizing discourse is obliterated in order that the opposition (favoured by me) may take its place.

The problematics of principle

Within the interlocking critiques of recent years we find a deep distrust of existing structures of knowledge, belief systems and ideologies. All that was secure, foundational and established is thrown into question. For post-empiricist constructionists, this suspicion is based on the view that our taken-for-granted understandings are not required by 'the way things are', but are derived from social interchange. Existing beliefs in knowledge, logic, morality and the like have no transcendent foundations, but are culturally and historically situated. From this perspective, all that is held to be so could be otherwise; all existing constructions could be replaced by myriad alternatives. For those engaged in ideological critique, the pervasive distrust stems primarily from a concern with motivational base. Agreeing with the constructionists that our taken-for-granted understandings are not required by the way things are, they explore the ideological or self-serving interests at work in the dominant discourse. Whose interests are being served by existing understandings? Who is dispossessed or marginalized? Poststructuralists add an additional lamination of doubt in their concern with the internal logic of representation itself. Linguistic representation does not function mimetically, but is determined by the conventions of signification itself. Once these semiotic and/or rhetorical devices have been located and dissected, representation ceases to tell us about the world; it essentially displays its own rules at work.

As proposed, these various lines of argument also form a critical arsenal of devastating potential. Each form of critique essentially robs the opponent's assertions of any form of validity or rhetorical force. At best, the opponent's words are reduced to hearsay or personal prejudice; at worst they are deprived of meaning altogether.[4] Yet, at this point the problem of critique begins. For while it has become enormously effective in undermining the opposition, such critique simultaneously casts aspersions on its own production. The grounds of its arguments stand subject to the same forms of deconstructive analysis. To demonstrate the social basis of scientific fact is, by implication, to reduce this demonstration to mere conversation; to attack the class bias underlying a given policy is to transform the attack itself to class bias; and to deconstruct the rhetoric of war is to transform the case for peace to rhetorical flourish.

To demonstrate, consider one of my attempts to undermine research justifying propositions about the relationship of mental processes to the surrounding world. My proposal in this case (Gergen, 1987) was that empirical evidence cannot inform us about the relationships of stimuli (the environment) to mental states (cognition, emotion, etc.), or about the relationship between such states and resulting action. This is so, I asserted, because all intelligible propositions linking mind to world are derived from a forestructure of understandings already available within the culture. Any proposition that is antithetical to this forestructure, or that falls outside its domain, is either absurd or incomprehensible. For example, it would be impossible to demonstrate that all elephants are perceived as rabbits, not because this is untrue, but because the dualism of the Western tradition presumes that the elephants in the material world stimulate elephant-like reflections in the mind. No amount of evidence to the contrary could dislodge the presumption. Yet, while the critical attempt is interesting and intelligible enough, in the end it cannot substantiate itself. For once I have deconstructed 'mind' and 'world' as evidential sites – casting them instead as linguistic integers – so have I also thrown my critique into jeopardy. For where are we to locate the 'forestructure of understandings', the 'culture', 'the propositions', and so on, all of which are essential elements in my argument? If they are not part of the world or of the mind – now fragments of a castaway ontology – to what world do they belong? Why should the use of such terms in my argument count against the position I am assailing? If 'real world' existents are irrelevant to the propositional network under attack, then the rationale for my critique is also placed beyond what we might otherwise index as 'real world concern'.

Critique as a rhetorical form

As I am proposing, the common form of discursive confrontation – with assertion and critique as the pivotal pair – is deeply problematic. Critique feeds from the ontology of the assertion, thus sustaining its intelligibility, reifying the terms of disagreement, removing other entries from the ledger and galvanizing the opposition. Further, critique as a rhetorical move has the effect of demeaning the opposition, generating animosity, atomizing the culture and occluding the way to resolution. Contemporary critique, informed by post-empiricist, critical and poststructuralist thought, carries with it the additional difficulties of favouring the very kinds of total-izing discourses against which it is set and destroying the grounds of its own rationality. Now, this is not to deny the many positive ends served by critique, nor am I attempting in any way to argue for its abandon-ment (another totalizing move). However, it does seem clear that we must raise significant questions regarding the centrality of critique within the scholarly (and cultural) arena. Under what circumstances is critique most effective, for whom and to what ends? Are there other, more promising means of reaching some of the more positive ends to which critique has traditionally been directed? These are important questions and a space must be opened for continuing discussion.

Within this space, it seems to me that a thorough exploration is needed of the rationale for critical deliberation. We need especially to consider the means by which critical argumentation gains its intelligibility. At present, the critical impulse largely acquires its justification from a family of interrelated suppositions, including but not limited to the following: (a) adequate or adaptive behaviour is guided by processes of rationality within the individual mind; (b) in matters of rationality certain states of mind (e.g. logical, objective) are more desirable (or adaptive) than others; (c) the process of critique is essential to reaching a state of optimal rationality; (d) critical thought enables the individual to resist humbug, tyranny and the pressures of the social group; and (e) critical thought at the individual level is a necessary ingredient of a democratic society. Yet, as suggested in preceding chapters, there is not one of these suppositions that can withstand close scrutiny, not one that can viably sustain the critical impulse. Within the contemporary intellectual climate the presumption of individual rationality, capable of autonomously reflecting on the world as it is found wanting on both conceptual and ideological grounds. Were these the only reasons for critical deliberation, we might wish for significant restraint.

At the same time, if we reconsider the aims of the critical venture, abandoning the search for individual enlightenment, additional options may be opened. As I proposed in Chapter 2, there are good reasons for relocating the source of rationality. Rather than viewing rational process as occurring within individual minds, such process can fruitfully be placed within discourse – or, more fundamentally, within the ongoing relations among persons. From this standpoint, there is no universally superior state of rationality, that is, no transcendental optimum in the constitution of human discourse. Further, by adopting this relational standpoint we are invited to reconsider both the utility of critical deliberation and possible means of modifying the process. For if critique is not a means of achieving some form of optimal rationality, what social purposes does it achieve? And if these are desirable purposes from some point of view, is critical deliberation in its current form the best means of attainment? Or, in short, what do we wish to achieve in the social world through critical discourse, and are there superior alternatives to contemporary practices?

Relational means to critical ends

A relational view of language does not itself favour any particular process or goal of deliberation. However, it does invite interlocutors to consider more self-consciously what they wish to achieve through their interchange. Is the aim of argument to sharpen and elaborate opposing positions, yield victory to one side or another, locate areas of compromise, entertain, develop public support, or something else? I have very little doubt that current forms of critique do achieve certain of these goals and, as indicated earlier, I am not at all opting for an abandonment of the critical enterprise. However, by articulating the relational goals, interlocutors may be able to open alternatives to traditional practices of unremitting contention.

To open discussion on such possibilities, let us consider but a single goal, the attempt to maximize participation in cultural decision-making. Many would agree that in general it is a better society when all of its participants are allowed entry into the arenas of decision-making – both grand and local – than when institutions, policies and projects are fixed by only a minority. Such a hope is not only part of our democratic heritage, but one might say that broadscale dialogue is essential to a reasonably harmonious way of life. Now, as commonly reasoned, critical activity is one means of expanding the range of available voices. If assertions are never confronted by counter-assertions, all voices outside the range of assertion are rendered mute. The stage is thus set for tyranny, oppression and conflict. Critical practice, it is reasoned, is essential to broadening the array of participants. Critique enables alternative interests to be made known and thus stands as a cultural resource for achieving democracy.

Yet, given the desideratum of maximizing participation, the critical tradition is significantly flawed. As previously advanced, critique operates on a fundamental axis of opposition: assertion and counter-assertion, with two debilitating results. First, as the binary is established the grounds for entering the dialogue are constrained. It is war vs. anti-war, the political left vs. the right, pro-life vs. pro-choice, and so on. The enormous complexities surrounding any decision, and the enormous array of possible constructions, are thus narrowed to a minimal set. It is not just any voice that may now be heard, but only those voices relevant to the dimension in question. And, as debate continues, the terms of the binary become increasingly objectified and its putative referents increasingly palpable. The possibility for alternative voices – those that speak to the conditions but not 'to the point' – are increasingly subdued. In effect the polarization realized by contemporary forms of critical deliberation move only minimally to expand the democratic spectrum. In this light it may be said that the critical move threatens us with the subversion of the democratic process.

To further this line of argument, the critical move often functions to close down the democratic process altogether. As proposed, critique typically alienates the opposition. Born of the process of assertion and critique are self-sustaining and self-satisfying enclaves of antagonists. In this sense critique serves to insulate groups from the 'good reasons' of the other. Critical voices go either unheeded or are bludgeoned because they are critical. The result is the same in either case: decision-making issues not from common deliberation – with participation by all – but rather through a jockeying for power, inside position or private control of outcomes. The atomization of culture does not mean an increase in the range of voices that may be heard, but more often a constriction. The realities of those in control comprehend only themselves.

Required then is inquiry into alternative means toward democratic dialogue. It is at just this point, however, that the reader will realize we now confront much the same kind of questions faced in Chapter 1. In that context we found realism and constructionism in a mutually destructive orbit. What alternatives, we asked, could be located to the ingurgitating conflict? It is now convenient to ask whether such alternatives could be applicable in the case of critique. Two such possibilities seem especially promising.

Separating self from discourse

As discussed, critique is often ineffective because it takes place within a tradition emphasizing mutual annihilation on the one hand, and arguments as expressions of one's core self on the other. The question, then, is whether key elements of the rhetorical form may be changed without damaging the possibility for exploring contentions, contraries and contexts. For example, in what ways could we remove from the field the emphasis on ego, the sense of authorial ownership of arguments and the threat of destroyed identities? None seems essential to critical reflection, and by separating self from discourse a less polarizing exploration might ensue (see also pages 20–1).

To explore this issue more concretely, my students and I have experimented with a procedure we call 'argumentation from nowhere'. The attempt here is to remove insofar as possible the sense of self, intention or agency from the centre of deliberation, and to emphasize the dependency on discourses already available within the culture more generally. We attempt to remove the grounds either for claiming assertions to be 'one's own' or for viewing counter-assertions as challenges to one's integrity. To assert, in this procedure, is simply to offer one possible card from the culture's repository of meaningful sayings. The attempt is to challenge the participant to explore the array of available arguments within the culture that might accompany any given assertion. For example, if one advocates strong birth control measures in Third World countries, there is an immense range of argumentation that might, by contemporary convention, serve to strengthen such a position (treating, for example, issues of health, economy, education and modernization). At the same time, for each assertion and its accompanying structure of argumentation, there is an enormous range of counter-argument available (concerning, for example, cultural exploitation, historical factors, spiritual issues and the ills of modernity). And each of the accompanying assertions will also harbour a justifying base that can be articulated, leading to a further array of assertions and counter-assertions in an outward-expanding network. Further, each element in the network is also subject to critical analysis, ideological biases, rhetorical construction, and so on. In effect, we could potentially unpack the enormous array of intelligible and interrelated sayings surrounding the issue of birth control in the Third World.

In the 'argumentation from nowhere' programme, we ask a wide variety of persons to contribute computerized entries into a broader (and in principle interminable) network of argumentation. The participant is introduced to a single conflict – for example, the pro-life vs. pro-choice conflict, or the debate over capital punishment. After reading a short description of the countering positions, the participant is asked tocontribute to an emerging computerized document that lays out arguments and critique on both sides of the issue. Participants are asked to set aside their 'own' position on the matter and to generate as many arguments as possible advocating either side. After generating such arguments participants are asked to return once again to their offerings and to generate possible criticisms of what they have proposed. After an accumulation of a small corpus of arguments, counter-arguments and so on, any new participant is given the opportunity to read all that has been entered into the network of arguments. He or she may then add new possibilities, or is free to write rejoinders to any positions already extant. The result is a multiplex array of discourse surrounding the issue at stake – or essentially a map of possible arguments, justifications, citations of evidence and the like on both sides of the issue.

Judging from the entries and reactions of the participants to the procedure, we have found the following: participants are generally capable of generating a multiple array of arguments and criticisms. Although they are more articulate in advancing what they feel to be their 'own' position upon entering the programme, they are also generally capable of generating intelligible arguments for the opposition. Further, they are capable of disclosing weaknesses in the position to which they initially subscribe. While they may defend a given position, they are also generally aware of weaknesses within their assertions. Third, although there is no principled end to what can be said on the issues in question, there is a tendency after a half-dozen participants make entries into the programme for redundancy to occur. Practically speaking, there is a limit to what people (at least within restricted sub-cultures) can sensibly say on such matters.

In reaction to the procedure, participants generally agree that they learn a lot; they feel they see the issue in far more complex terms as a result of the exercise. Of special significance, they indicate that it would be difficult to resolve the issue by simply declaring one side the winner. In effect, the participants seem much more prone to seek compromise solutions, or possible temporary or situated policies. We might say, then, that there is an expansion in sensitivities, sophistication and the range of relevance. To be sure the process muddies the waters, but the failure of clear and simple solutions also becomes more manifest. The process may in this way reduce tendencies toward strong commitment, but as we have seen the heady romance with causes comes at significant cost. Whether 'argumentation from nowhere' can have broader application remains to be seen.

Polyvocal potentials

In the analysis of 'arguments from nowhere', I noted the potential of participants for locating weaknesses in their preferred assertions. This tendency is also reflected in the work of Billig and his colleagues (1988) on the discourse of ideological dilemmas. As their analysis suggests, most people are seldom univocal in their stands on various issues, and often harbour suppositions that would also support their opposition. More broadly we may characterize persons as *polyvocal subjects* (see also Chapter 1). Simultaneously, the implications of this polyvocal condition for critical futures are substantial. First, if persons are capable of articulating many sides of an issue, then it is possible to reconceptualize 'true belief' as a form of social positioning. That is, rather than being defined in terms of a unified core – possessing a single coherent position – we may see the person as fundamentally multiplicitous.[5] Whether an individual claims a particular view to be 'my belief', 'my value' or 'essential' and 'true' is not the result of introspective discernment (e.g. 'I know it is my opinion because I can feel or see that it is'). Rather, the claim to possession is the result of social positioning, where the individual is placed at a given time *vis-à-vis* ongoing interchange. For example, authors may claim their written opinions to be 'theirs', or abandon them as 'once my beliefs, but no longer'. One may heatedly defend a position in an argument, only later to admit, 'That was too extreme; I got carried away'. Or the mother may say to the child, 'I was just saying that because it was for your good'. Having a view, then, derives from a particular form of social process as opposed to an interior origin.

Along these lines, Richard Harvey Brown (1987) extends a line of philosophic work from Socrates to Kierkegaard in developing a case for what he terms 'dialectical irony'. Dialectical irony involves taking both a position and its contrary, not so as to negate oneself but to emancipate oneself from the demands of either position alone. The dialectical ironist 'simultaneously asserts two or more logically contradictory meanings such that, in the silence between the two, the deeper meaning of both may emerge'. This 'deeper meaning', proposes Brown (1987), 'is dialectical. It does not inhere in either the initial literal assertion or its negation; it is rather the tension and completion set off between them that constitutes dialectical ironic awareness' (p. 173). Or, in present terms, one comes to understand the broader dialogic process from which the structure of assertion and counter-assertion emerges.

Moreover, to manifest one's polyvocality is also to demonstrate a degree of similarity to one's putative antagonist. Rather than demonstrating the kind of coherence designed to repudiate all who would differ – thus establishing an unbreachable gap between self and other – the revelation of one's counter-capacities renders one 'part of the other'. A space of vulnerability is created which invites the other in as a collaborator as opposed to an antagonist. In certain respects the present chapter attempts to achieve this end. The chapter is, after all, a critical assessment of critique itself. However, to illustrate my arguments, I have sometimes used myself as the focal point – putting my own foibles and failings on display. By implication I also suggest that the present proposals may be flawed. By my undermining my own case the reader may sense that these are not attempts to 'launch a perfect gunboat', a vehicle that camouflages its weaknesses and resists all opposition. Of course, I simultaneously risk credibility – admitting 'weakness' – but the hope is that in doing so the reader is more likely to join in productive dialogue.

Whether a polyvocal stance can be sustained in normal life is unclear. However, I have participated in a specialized process of such remarkable efficacy that recounting is merited. At the beginning of a three-day conference on construction in education,[6] the organizers arranged a confrontation between radical constructivism and social construction. The former position was to be represented by Ernst von Glazersfeld and the latter by me. For this duel we were each to bring 'seconds' who would act as critics of the opposing position. The subsequent critiques were unsparing, the defences unyielding and as the audience was drawn into the debate polarization rapidly took place. Voices became more agitated, critique turned *ad hominem*, anger and alienation mounted. As the moderator called a halt to the proceedings, the prospect of three days together seemed to echo Sartre's words, 'Hell is other people'. Sensing the impasse of the condition, a group of family therapists, lead by Karl Tomm and Sue Levin, invited the conferees to a rump session. Here Tomm, who had been working therapeutically with multiple selves, asked if he could publicly interview von Glazersfeld and me, but each taking the part of the other. As he reasoned, our exposure to each other should have allowed each of us to absorb aspects of the other – intellectual views, attitudes, emotions – which we now carried with us. Could we allow these to speak? Tomm deftly probed each of us – playing out 'the other within' – ranging over issues of theory, views of the other, doubts, fears, personal relationships, feelings about the conference, and so on.

The results of the procedure were striking. As both we and the audience learned, we could say sensible and sympathetic things from within the other's framework. Each could give voice to the reasonableness of the other. Further, the binary was successfully broken. Rather than a showdown between competing epistemologies, the debate could be understood within the context of a lengthy professional relationship, imbricated friendships, private aspirations and doubts, the demands of public debate, and so on. A new level of discussion ensued. The conference was thereafter marked by its civility of interchange; there was expression without domination, careful listening and sensitive reply. No, this did not mean a resolution of differences. However, it did allow for productive exploration to take place in a context in which victory and defeat were removed from view.

In conclusion

Contemporary critique stands as a manifestation of a long and venerable tradition. As a cultural form it can be viewed as a major advance over the use of physical coercion or arms to achieve the ends of moral ordering. From the teacher's classroom correctives, a judge's condemnation of a steroid use by an athletic team, to a scholar's bromide on the state of cultural life, critique can set in motion social processes that improve, restore and engender reflexive deliberation. However, as a form of life born and bred within particular historical circumstances, we may also call critique into question. Are our responses to human foibles and failings limited to physical removal and critique alone? If the academy is any example, assertion and critique have become virtually the only staples of exchange. Given the limitations on critique explored in the present chapter, the major challenge is to locate and develop alternative forms of reply. Again, this is not to suppress differences nor to subvert the process of emancipation. However, it is to ask whether in the context of increasing globalization – where cultural differences are increasingly manifest – a new range of resources are now required. The present chapter has opened discussion on two possibilities, the one emphasizing the diminution of the ego and the second its expansion into polyvocality. These are but bare beginnings, and broad discussion is needed to explore the potentials. More important is the expansion of possibilities. It is entirely possible that critique is a form of life largely shared within the strata of the highly educated. Perhaps other alternatives have been developed in other contexts of cultural life. Ethnographic inquiry into the range of grass roots alternatives would seem a valuable undertaking at this juncture. In this case the scholar may well benefit from enlightenment in civil practice.

Notes

1 I shall employ the term 'critique' in this chapter as a form of discourse designed to display the weaknesses of a given position with the aim of removing it from contention or replacing it with an alternative. This is to separate critique from the process of *correction* and *coaching*, both of which demonstrate shortcomings or domains of potential improvement for purposes of strengthening a given position.

2 For a more detailed account, see Gergen (1994a) Chapter 11.

3 See, for example, Gergen (1994a), Chapter 6.

4 The avowal aim of critique within this body of work is often emancipatory. Or, as Brian Fay (1987) puts it, we participate in 'the humanistic variant' of a tradition of critique with roots in Platonic philosophy. Such critique should be 'capable of interpreting in a cognitively respectable manner the social world in which we live in such a way that this world's oppressiveness is apparent, and in such a way that it empowers its listeners to change their lives' (p. 23). Although such a goal is surely salutary, the question raised in the present chapter is whether critique is the best means for securing such ends.

5 For a more extended account of multiple selves, see Gergen (1991).

6 Proceedings from the conference are contained in Steffe and Gale (1996).

4

WHO SPEAKS AND WHO RESPONDS
IN THE HUMAN SCIENCES?

A constructionist consciousness is inherently reflexive, sensitive to the ways in which one's own actions contribute to the cultural presumptions of the real and the good. And so it is that in the scholarly world that we have become increasingly concerned with the forms of reality generated within our privileged sanctuary and the ways of life to which our work contributes. As evidenced in the preceding chapter, there is an enormous body of self-reflexive scholarship devoted to the ideological implications of theories, research agendas and methods of inquiry in the sciences. Within this domain there is also substantial concern with forms of scientific representation, and particularly forms of writing.[1] While much of this work is concerned with writing as reality creating, my aim in this chapter is different. As we write within the human sciences so are we sustaining and re-creating certain forms of life as opposed to others. My concern here is with the authorial voice in human science writing. How do the available traditions of writing define the author, how do they situate the audience and what are the implications for our conceptions and practices of science and societal life?

In the wake of widespread critique of the essentialized self, it is increasingly difficult to speak of authorship as originating within the minds and hearts of individual scholars. It is perilous indeed to attribute the theoretical insight, the rational elaboration, the acute observation or the ideological impulse to some person in particular. Nor can we easily speak of 'the impact of ideas' on readers, as if there were virginal minds awaiting passively for the 'seminal inputs' of the more knowing or experienced. Rather, we are drawn to understanding 'voice' within the scholarly spheres as owing to communal traditions, to negotiated understandings among interlocutors as to what counts as insightful, rational, objective or moral discourse. Communal traditions of representation largely determine the rhetorical power of our writing. When framed in this way, it is useful to address the question of 'who speaks' in the human sciences in terms of power relations. What are the institutionalized positions to which status or significance is accorded, and what are the characteristic forms of discourse associated with (expected from, appropriate for) those who occupy these positions?

To frame the issue in this way also leads us to inquire into appropriate postures of reply to those who are given voice. Given that we accord significance to those occupying certain positions and speaking in a manner appropriate to these positions, what are the conventions of reply? How is the reader interpellated or called into being by the form of writing? For example, we accord political candidates a right to voice, and when they speak in a manner appropriate to candidacy, listeners are positioned within the democratic tradition as evaluators or judges. Deliberation on the positive and negative aspects of the candidate's views are appropriate. Under ideal conditions, interrogation and dialogue might appropriately follow. In contrast, while newscasters are also accorded voice in contemporary society, the acceptable modes of address are quite different from those of the politician, and the typical mode of response is not that of opinion evaluation but information seeking. It would not be customary (good reasons not withstanding) to debate with the newscaster the wisdom or ideological grounds of his/her report.

Historically speaking, the human sciences are of relatively recent origin, acquiring intelligibility as self-conscious disciplines largely within the last century. There is little means of establishing a wholly novel voice within culture, that is, a position of authority with associated speech forms that stands in complete disjunction with cultural tradition. A completely novel argot would function much like a Wittgensteinian 'private language'; no one would comprehend its significance or appreciate its illocutionary force. In this sense, in asking 'who speaks' in the human sciences we must attend to their pre-history to appreciate the ways in which positions of traditional authority and their rhetorics have been appropriated and transformed. In effect, to give an account of authoritative voice in contemporary human science, we must listen with an ear to the distant historical traces that are carried. In asking the question in this way we are also drawn into considering modes of reply. How do these traditions position their audiences and with what effects for human science inquiry?

In what follows the attempt is to identify several traditions from which contemporary scholars derive their privilege of intelligibility. Further, I shall consider the manner in which these forms of discourse position the reader. We shall be concerned, then, with what we inherit from the Western tradition as forms of authoritative voice and their contrasting invitations to their audiences. Four modes of traditional voice will be considered: the mystical, the prophetic, the mythic and the civil. To place a reflexive edge on the analysis, I shall then take up recent developments in the rhetorics of the human sciences. The very intellectual movements spawning interest in the literary and rhetorical means by which texts achieve their authority have also given rise to new forms of voice and associated rhetorics, along with repositionings of the reader. We shall be particularly concerned with the potential gains and losses afforded by two of these alternatives: the autobiographical and the fictional.

A preliminary caveat is required. Any attempt to characterize discursive forms in the human sciences confronts a vast and ever-shifting terrain. There are no binding sanctions over discursive forms, and with erosion, appropriation and recreation in motion, it is difficult to locate pure rhetorical forms. Even within the same work, or even the same passage, an author may invoke a range of tropes extracted from disparate traditions and inviting different responses. The present analysis proceeds, then, by elaborating a range of ideal types, offering them as a 'way of listening' that may help us to critically evaluate our rhetorical legacy and its contemporary alternatives.

Telling traditions

Given a broad range of discursive practices, what dominant themes, traditions or images do they evoke? And drawing from the Western tradition of authority more generally, how and with what effects do these dominant postures position the reader? Let us consider, then, four primary registers.[2]

The mystical tradition: priests and apostles

Although typically allied with the secular world as opposed to the sacred, we can locate within many corners of the human sciences remnants of a tradition originating in early mysticism and carried forward in both the Jewish and Christian religions (with the *Cabbala* playing a central role in the former case and Neoplatonism in the latter). In the mystical tradition, the right to convey to the public the profundities of the supernatural world has generally been assigned to those occupying high positions within religious hierarchies. Those occupying such 'priestly' roles have been accorded enormous respect over the centuries, and there is much to be gained within the human sciences from importing mystical discourse into the scholarly domain.

In my view the chief components of mystical writing within the human sciences include a high reliance on metaphor (and avoidance of the literal), the linguistic construction of realities beyond observation and a strong evaluative terminology. The use of metaphor and the suppression of the literal enables the rhetor to lift the realities of the text out of the realm of common sense logics and assumptions; through metaphor things are other than what they seem. Curiosity and wonderment are invited. With the text removing the reader from quotidian reality, the way is prepared for the textual creation of a second-order world. This is a world beyond the senses and beyond reason and, most importantly, it is a world to which the priest alone is privy. Often the sense of the unknown is achieved through subfuscous tropes, linguistic manoeuvres that disrupt the ordinary, that create puzzlement and furnish the general sense of a world that is beyond the realm of common understanding. Finally, a reliance on an evaluative language brings this world into the realm of the palpable, not directly transparent and not subject to rational analysis. Rather, through an appeal to the register of emotions, one can literally *feel* the presence of the unknown. Further, evaluative language serves to establish the significance of the discourse. Frequently it warns of punishment to those who are impervious to the new reality and offers significant reward to those who accept. In effect, the rhetoric of mysticism in the human sciences carries evocations of dread and joy.

Mystical discourses have been integral to the human sciences since their inception. Freud's debt to the Jewish mystical tradition is well documented (Bakan, 1990).[3] Partly owing to his psychoanalytic training, and partly to his father's clerical profession, Carl Jung's writings may also be singled out for their manifestations of the mystical. Consider a fragment from Jung (1945):

> In reality . . . the primordial phenomenon of the spirit takes possession of the person, and while appearing to be the willing object of human intentions, it binds his freedom, just as the physical world does, with a thousand chains and becomes an obsessive *idée-force*. (p. 91)

In effect, we have the creation of a new reality, a 'primordial phenomenon of the spirit', and without recognition of its power, one's freedom is bound 'with a thousand chains'. The transparent mysticism in this work reappears frequently in psychiatric writings. Consider R. D. Laing, writing in 1967:

> True sanity . . . the emergence of the 'inner' archetypal mediators of divine power, and through this death a rebirth, and the eventual re-establishment of a new kind of ego-functioning, the ego now being the servant of the divine, no longer its betrayer. (p. 100)

Jacques Lacan's works are interesting in their extension of the psychoanalytic reliance on the mystical. They draw significantly from the tradition, but face the challenge of a culture to whom much of the psychoanalytic reality has now moved into the realm of the literal. Through novel and highly complex circumlocutions Lacan breathes new life into the possibilities of the unfathomable. Consider the sense of the supernatural forged by the following:

> Seizing the original and absolute position of . . . ' In the beginning was the Word' . . . is to go straight beyond the phenomenology of the alter ego in Imaginary alienation, to the problem of the mediation of an Other who is not second when the One is not yet. (1953: p. 203)

Here Lacan writes obscurely but with a confidence that exudes first-hand knowledge of otherwise unfathomable mysteries. He makes direct connection with the biblical tradition, and lets the reader know that we confront here emotionally significant issues of alienation and incompletion.

It is useful at this juncture to distinguish between the discourse of the priest as opposed to the apostle. The priest speaks *ex cathedra*, knowingly and confidently conveying the sense of clairvoyant connection to the mysterious realities themselves. In contrast, the apostle is not so much an official bearer of the mysteries as a personal emissary – one who humbly and with a sense of awe, bears personal witness of the 'mysterious one'. The apostle will speak more 'for him/herself' as a mortal being than as a direct bearer of the mysteries. In addition to many of the tropes of mystical writing, the important feature of apostolic writing is its frequent reference to 'the holy one', that is, the individual who *is* the bearer of mystical powers or knowledge. It is the words of this one who are clarified, defended and praised by the apostle. A fragment of John Shotter's (1993b) writing provides an illustration of apostolic writing:

> But how can we investigate the nature of something that lacks specificity . . . This is where Wittgenstein's notion of 'perspicuous representations' play their part . . . All the metaphors used by Wittgenstein . . . bring to our attention aspects of language, and of our knowledge of language, that were previously rationally-invisible to us . . . (pp. 58–9)

Although Shotter's work displays many marks of the mystical, it is not in this instance suffused with moral judgment. More purposefully judgmental is the emerging genre of cultural studies writing, a genre that frequently makes use of apotheosis (with such figures as Althusser, Benjamin and Ray Williams frequently occupying the Pantheon), and employs their divine powers in the service of condemning various habits of contemporary society. Consider Hebdige's (1987) use of (Saint) Genet:

> So Genet brings us full circle . . . back to an image of graffiti, to a group of blacks, immured in language, kicking against the white-washed walls of two types of prison – the real and the symbolic . . . he brings us back also the meaning of style in subculture and to the messages which lie behind disfigurement . . . Like Barthes, he has secret insights, he is involved in undercover work. (pp. 136–7)

Let us turn to the issue of interpellation: how by virtue of our traditions is the reader positioned by the various forms of mystical discourse? At the outset, such discourses establish a hierarchy between the writer and the audience. The writer is one who possesses words of profound significance; the audience, in contrast, is presumed ignorant or unaware. The mystical rhetor never addresses an equally enlightened colleague. The form of address is that of revelation; a reader is thus required who 'has yet to see'. However, while the audience is treated as unknowing, it is not thereby devalued. Rather, the hierarchy is benign: the revelation is humane, intended to bring the supplicant into a state of grace, emancipation or renewal. In effect, the text invites the reader into a redemptive posture; by forsaking past realities and their attendant commitments the reader may be redeemed. At the same time, for much of this writing a third party is invoked, one who is neither the writer nor the reader. The third party occupies the lowest position in the hierarchy for it is he or she who has chosen not to listen, who remains in ignorance or sin (e.g. inauthentic, unemancipated, one-dimensional, falsely conscious). It should finally be noted that writing in the mystical tradition is typically impersonal and monologic. The rhetor does inhabit the text as a flesh and blood individual, replete with common foibles, but as a channel for the divine. At the same time, the reader is not included in the text, except possibly in the form of an imagined interlocutor invented by the writer (a la Freud) as a foil.

The words of the prophet

The prophetic tradition is closely linked to the mystic in that the earliest prophets served, in early Greek culture, as 'mouthpieces' for the gods. The particular importance of the prophet, however, derives from the capacity of the oracular utterance to foretell the future – to warn and advise on the yet to be. In later Israelite society, the prophets occupied a distinct religious class, separated in important ways from the priestly. And in Christianity, while apocalyptic writings (e.g. the Book of Revelations) served (and continue to serve) an important religious function, they are separated from the inspirational role played by the books of the apostles. Owing to its close association with the mystical tradition, the prophetic voice shares many of its rhetorical modalities. The strong emphasis on metaphor adds to the capacity of the prophet to create a visual picture of a future not yet available to the senses. In prophetic writing there is also a strong emphasis placed on moral evaluation. However, whereas the mystical voice offers redemption by virtue of 'believing' ('seeing the light'), the apocalyptic voice tends to gain moral sway through warning. Catastrophe is at hand unless people change their ways.

In the human science struggle to achieve cultural authority, the prophetic forms have been valuable adjuncts. One might single out the Hegelian-inspired work of Marx as providing the touchstone for much apocalyptic writing in the human sciences. The prophetic voice in the service of moral ends is most clearly evident in *The manifesto of the Communist Party* (with Engels):

> The bourgeoisie . . . is unfit to rule because it is incompetent to assure an existence to its slave within his slavery, because it cannot help letting him sink into such a state that it has to feed him, instead of being fed by him. Society can no longer live under this bourgeoisie, in other words, its existence is no longer compatible with society.

The moral weight of warning wrought by the invocation of coming catastrophe also reverberates throughout the works of many critical school writers, most notably Horkheimer (1974) and Marcuse (especially *One Dimensional Man*). More recently, we find the prophetic vein effectively mined by authors who, while not themselves Marxists, share in their critique of contemporary social conditions. Christopher Lasch's volumes, *The Culture of Narcissism* and *The True and Only Heaven*, both warned against the deterioration of cultural life and used jeremiad to incite social change. Similarly, the work of Bellah and his colleagues, *Habits of the heart*, finds intimacy and community under siege, and in the face of coming catastrophe asks for a return to earlier but now obscured moral traditions.

More interesting in their rhetorical modalities are recent prophetic offerings from the French context. They are fascinating, for one, because they make abundant use of the mystical rhetorics with which the prophetic tradition is intimately intertwined. Such rhetorics have been more easily absorbed into the Continental cultural traditions than the Anglo-American. Further, while these works contain a strong moral message, they allow little in the way of redemptive potential. Rather, one senses a coming doom from which there is little escape. Consider, for example, a fragment from the mystically saturated work of Deleuze and Guattari (1983): 'The schizophrenic deliberately seeks out the very limits of capitalism; he is its inherent tendency brought to fulfillment, its surplus product, its proletariat, and its exterminating angel' (p. 35).

Jean Baudrillard presents an interesting variation on the apocalyptic theme. After an early commitment to neo-Marxist ideas, Baudrillard turned his attentions to the mass circulation of signifiers within the culture, a move that essentially undermined the structural foundations of Marxist theory. However, in spite of his defection, Baudrillard nevertheless continued to draw from the prophetic tradition. To illustrate: 'Behind this exacerbated mise-en-scène of communication, the mass media, the pressure of information pursues an irresistible destructuration of the social' (1994, p. 81).

In its positioning of the reader, the prophetic genre is similar to the mystical. Again, a hierarchy is established with the high ground, both ontologically and morally, claimed by the rhetor. The reader is again treated as unenlightened and, with few exceptions, a redemptive option is presented to remove the threat of the future. However, in the prophetic genre, we seldom find the extended hierarchy, with the reader privileged over the invoked hordes of the unrepenting. Rather, the apocalyptic message is addressed to all; one gains no special credit for attending. Finally, prophetic writing is also impersonal and monologic.

The mythic tradition

A third voice in the human sciences may also be singled out for its roots in early religious practice. Originating somewhere around the ninth century

BC, stories about divine beings came to occupy an important place in cultural life. Myths essentially narrated a sacred history, relating events in a primordial time to give intelligibility to the origin of things present. Myths played an important role in emerging religions because they typically demonstrated ways in which supernatural powers broke into the realm of the natural, and explained how significant patterns in the visible world resulted from divine action. Where the prophetic voice linked a natural present with a divinely revealed future, the mythic voice placed the present within the history of a divinely ordered past. And, like the prophetic voice, mythic narration frequently carried with it moral messages, condemning certain actions while condoning other. Over the centuries, the mythic tradition has been absorbed into many forms of writing, including the Gospels in Christianity, along with folk tales, fairy tales, allegories and fables in the secular realm. It is a tradition that also flourishes in contemporary human science.

In addition to many of the rhetorical markings of the mystical and prophetic traditions, mythic writing places a strong reliance on common rules of storytelling or narrative. Within the Western narrative tradition emphasis is placed on establishing story beginnings, sequences of inter-related actions or events (*fabula*) and the sense of a conclusion. Further, there is typically the establishment of a morally invested end-point, something towards which the events or actions are directed (a *telos*) and from which derives the capacity of the story to produce drama (the sense of a 'high point' or climax). Put in these terms, we can see that a substantial range of scholarship in the human sciences draws sustenance from the mythic tradition. Accounts of unknowable but inferred origins are (or have been) particularly popular in anthropology, archeology, history, psychology and sociology. Illuminating here is Landau's (1991) analysis of prominent theories of human evolution in terms of their conformity to narrative convention and the way in which competing theories depend on available options in narrative forestructure. Gergen and Gergen (1986) have also contrasted Freudian and Piagetian theories of human development in terms of their narrative properties, and most particularly the ways in which the dramatic impact of these theories is derived from narrative convention. In their approximation to mythic writing, Weber's *The Protestant ethic and the spirit of capitalism*, Elias's *The civilizing process*, Ong's *Orality and literacy*, Luhmann's *Love as passion* and Foucault's *The History of sexuality* would all lend themselves to similar analyses.

In its filliation with the mystical tradition, mythic rhetoric establishes a hierarchical relationship with the reader. The rhetor again provides impersonal, monologic pronouncements, intended to illuminate and inform an unknowing audience. While the narrative lends intelligibility to the known through the metaphoric construction of the unknown, the narratives are frequently freighted with moral implication. The point is well recognized by critics of Whiggish history, accounts of the past that valorize or rationalize existing practices and conventions.

More subtly, we find in Piaget's (1954) account of the epigenetic development of cognition strong value placed on the ultimate achievement of human development, namely abstract reason. In contrast, Freud's theory of psychosexual development portrays the emerging adult as necessarily 'neurotic', bearing the burden of multiple laminations of repression. The human trajectory, in this sense, is a downward spiral, with psychoanalytic intervention required to place reason on the throne.

The civil voice

While contributing significantly to the rhetorical power of the human sciences, the preceding traditions are marginal to the dominant form of social science writing. Within the vast cadres of 'the behavioural sciences' there is little left of the moral and emotional expressivity of the preceding traditions, the metaphors of the mystical are largely replaced by literal language and obscurity is abandoned in favour of 'straight talk'. Divine beings now reappear in secular form as 'seminal' thinkers; the drama of prophecy is shorn in favour of experimental prediction and actuarial prediction. Not only does the prevailing 'scientific style' strive for dispassionate and mundane clarity, but it manifests an unfailing concern for evidence and serves as a model of careful restraint.

Although much has been written about the rhetoric of the dominant discourse in the human sciences, far less attention has been paid to its social and political origins. Perhaps the most extensive account of this kind is contained in Steven Shapin's *A social history of truth*, a work richly elaborating the emergence of the scientific style in the 'early modern' culture of seventeenth-century England. As Shapin proposes, the English 'gentle class' – demarked by wealth, ancestry and education – came to serve as the dominant models for discursive interchange within the emerging practices of natural sciences. As the elite turned their attentions to natural philosophy and natural history, and the experimental work of Robert Boyle and others was becoming increasingly salient, the civil manner of speaking became the argot of science. Among the primary characteristics of civil discourse were a respect for the other (as a class equal, deserving of honour), the avoidance of hostility or direct antagonism (which would disrupt class congeniality), the avoidance of excessive persuasion (respecting the other's capacity for good judgment), impersonality of reporting (respecting the other's personal experiences) and modesty (emphasizing the equal standing of all gentlemen). Finally, authorial credibility was importantly linked to assumption that all gentlemen reported truthfully on their individual experiences. Thus, strong reliance was placed on evidence from first-hand observation.

There is surely much more to be said about the transformations in style and significance of scientific discourse since the seventeenth century. However, for present purposes Shapin's account provides a convenient means not only of indexing a predominant form of discourse, but of comprehending the origins of its rhetorical potency. Exemplars of the civil tradition are everywhere at hand, and the present offering serves in many respects as a local instantiation. Remaining at question, however, is the issue of author–reader relationship. To be sure the civil tradition is more fully respecting of the reader than the preceding genres. Rather than plunging the reader into a position of helpless ignorance, one finds the reader enjoined as a potential commentator. The reader is thrust back upon his/her own experiences and reason as resources for rendering judgment. Further, civil discourse proceeds without diminishing the reader in terms of moral worth. The reader's integrity is never in question.

Yet, it is a mistake to conclude that civil discourse ensures equality among participants in the profession. In numerous and subtle ways civil discourse renders some more equal that others. As groups very civilly create scientific realities, those who do not share the language are either found 'wrong headed' or symbolically exterminated by never being recognized at all. As we also explored in Chapter 3, the form of civil argumentation is essentially that of war, with each side bent on eliminating the opposition. Thus, while the dominant discourse in the human sciences does invite participation in the fellowship, it is a fellowship in which the fight for survival is ever apparent.

After the discursive turn

These voices from the distant past are lathered throughout the contemporary texts of the human sciences, and serve to position our subject matters along with those who acquiesce to their illocutionary promptings. However, in recent years we have also witnessed the entry of a new range of rhetorics into the scholarly arena, forms of voice and reader–author positionings that bear significant attention. In large measure these new forms of writing gain impetus from the extensive and intensive critique lodged against the presumption of scientific discourse as truth bearing. As variously reasoned, there is no justification for a view of language as a picture or a map of reality in the raw, or the companionate presumption that scientific discourse is demanded or driven by nature. Rather, it is argued, we inherit in the sciences various traditions of writing and speaking, discursive genres that function as necessary forestructures of comprehension and communication. Accounts of self and society, then, are substantially shaped by textual traditions, rhetorical demands and conventional forms of relationship between author and reader. It is this shift in intellectual posture, of course, that gives birth to the present account.

Most important for the present analysis, this discursive turn in the human sciences has two profound effects on the practice of inscription. First, the traditional privilege of authority accorded to the writer is undermined. In the context of the discursive critique, it becomes increasingly difficult to accede to the author's claims to be bearing truths from mysterious worlds, prognosticating the future, telling reputable origin stories or sharing providential information. Rather, the reader informed by these texts is prompted to resist the positions into which such writing has traditionally thrust him/her, positions of repentance, awe or respect. Or, more exactly, the reader approaches the text with a dual consciousness: on the one hand prepared by tradition to join a good-faith bond with the author, and simultaneously knowing that the pleasure of belief is bought at the price of substantial suppression.

Coupled with such challenges to the traditional rhetorics and their illocutionary force, contributions to the discursive turn also invite the human scientist into a creative stance towards representation. Can means be located, one asks, for stepping outside the comfortable but constraining traditions, developing new forms of writing and reshaping the relationship between author and reader? Specifically, as scholars have become increasingly sensitized to the politics of hermeneutics, and concerned with the potentials for totalitarianism, suppression and injustice subtly secreted into the stices of writing, experiments in inscription have begun to flourish. It should be recognized that these emerging forms are not, nor can they be, genuinely new. All achievements of intelligibility must draw from some pre-existing tradition. Thus, we find the emerging forms of voice 'new' by virtue of the fact that they draw on different traditions from those prevailing heretofore. Let us consider two significant flourishings.

The autobiographer

Although the term 'autobiography' did not emerge until the late eighteenth century, I will use the term broadly here to encompass a genre of writing in which the author serves as the chief focus of concern – both as a unique individual and possibly as a lens through which to understand the world more generally. We may thus include here not only autobiographical works as such, but personal diaries, memoirs and travel journals. Such writing acquires its authority in several ways. It first enables the reader to gain access to a curious 'elsewhere', into a period in history, a culture or a particular personality – often of broad significance. Further, there is often an educative function. For example, St Augustine's *Confessions* informs one of the travails of achieving spiritual purity; the autobiographies of Benjamin Franklin and William Carlos Williams provide insights into the creative process; Donald Trump tells the reader how to achieve economic success. Finally, autobiography borrows from both mythic and fictive traditions, providing both narrative understanding and entertainment.

With respect to rhetorical markings, autobiographical writing in the social sciences generally avoids the mysterious worlds of mystical writing. The autobiographer typically attempts to present the fullness of life as experienced. Similar to the mystical and the prophetic, autobiographical writing is replete with expressions of value. However, such expressions are not typically in the service of chastising the reader for his/her deficiencies, but used for justifying actions taken. The reader is left, then, to draw object lessons from these accounts. Autobiography, while sometimes used for purposes of sustaining civil society, is more frequently employed by those who are in some way unusual – either non- or anti-normative. The autobiographer will often 'reveal the dirt' that the civil reporter would wish to suppress. Perhaps the most significant characteristic of the genre is born of its attempt to share subjectivity, to enable the reader to stand in for the writer. This often means a high reliance on affectively charged language (e.g. values, passions), heavy reliance on quotidian discourse (the reality shared by all) and a substantial reliance on metaphor (enabling the reader to sense the qualities of a unique experience).

In my view it is the autobiographical voice that informs major movements in scholarship since the discursive turn. The genre was already present, influencing early scholarship in anthropology and clinical psychology. However, we now find a significant flowering of the autobiographical genre, in qualitative research, narrative inquiry, ethnography, case reports, feminist research, and more. Such of this writing is double-voiced. First there is the presence of the author's subjectivity ('my experience as researcher'). Here the scholar resists appearing as someone other than a personal self (e.g. priest, prognosticator, civil fellow) and attempts to make his/her own interior available to the reader. In the second, there is an acknowledgement of the subjectivity of the other, and an attempt to render it transparent through his/her own open expression. To illustrate, in an analysis of 'nonunitary subjectivity in narrative representation', Leslie Bloom (1996) begins her ethnography by situating her own experience as the lens through which the world will be refracted: 'When I met Olivia in 1991 . . . ' (p. 179). With her subjectivity installed, she then acts as a conduit through which the voice of Olivia is heard.

> I had just gotten rid of one of the biggest sexual perverts . . . at the organization. He was a senior executive. And I went after him. And I got him fired . . . ' (p.180)

Similarly, Amia Lieblich (1993) introduces a discussion of immigration and the self, with:

> When I experience loss of familiar orientation, such as being unable to find my way (lost!) on the freeway . . . I shudder for the immense loss of my young Russian new-immigrant students. (p. 93)

Soon, however, the immediate sense of empathy we feel for Lieblich is extended to Natasha, her subject of concern. In Natasha's words:

> You know, you are the first adult outside my family with whom I had the opportunity to talk at length since my arrival . . . (p. 105)

Further developments in what is called 'autoethnography' (Ellis, 1995; Ellis and Bochner, 1996), enable authors to use their own lives as lenses through which the reader may gain a broader understanding of various life situations.

Writing in the autobiographical mode invites the reader into a posture quite unlike those previously considered. Whereas the mystical, prophetic, mythic and civil forms tend to place a distance between author and reader, autobiographical rhetoric has the reverse effect: the reader is invited to identify or be at one with the writer. Because the author relies on tropes within the common vernacular, and particularly those reserved for more intimate or open circumstances, the reader can more easily resonate with the writing, that is, locate a host of personal experiences to which the writing would speak. The reader is invited to feel the account as 'one's own'. When the author features the narrative account of another, there is a triple fusing: the narrator, the author and the reader are ideally bound (and bonded) within a common subjectivity.

The fictionalist

Let us consider a final form of enunciation, a genre entering common consciousness primarily within recent centuries. Myths, folk tales, fables and epic poems long served to convey truth, insight and direction in Western culture. However, as civil discourse, the language of dispassionate objectivity, became increasingly prevalent, and claims for its significance increasingly vocal, a delineation between fiction and factual writing became increasingly focal. The former discourse was to be taken seriously, matters of life and death depend on its depictions; the latter was more typically viewed as a contribution to cultural wisdom or simply a diverting entertainment. In the past century the term fiction has become increasingly identified with prose, and particularly the novel; however, with the recent explosion in experimental (postmodern) writing, the term fiction tends to be reserved for writing that does not employ systematically gathered facts to warrant its case.

It is within fictional writing that human scientists wishing to break from traditional modes of inscription find resources of enormous richness. Fictional genres are deeply respected for their contribution to cultural life – providing wisdom, insight and inspiration. The scholar may thus draw from these traditions to arouse, provoke, entertain, challenge and intrigue. There is no limit to the possibilities. Further, the genre of fiction inherently operates as a counter to the dominant discourse of 'fact', while simultaneously functioning in the human sciences to blur or destroy the fact/fiction binary altogether. To be sure it is difficult to characterize the 'fictional genre' in terms of rhetorical specifics. Rather, for the human scientist who is at once restless to break with common traditions, and who is informed by the fictional tradition, virtually all forms of writing become available for use (including pre-modern and modern traditions).

Furthermore, there are no general agreements as to appropriate criteria of evaluation. In terms of rhetorical form, virtually 'anything goes' – with one exception: because the fictionally oriented scientist is not bound to any specific rhetorical convention, such writing runs the risk of unintelligibility. If a reader cannot identify what the writing is intended to do, and how he/she is being positioned by the work, then it may be found opaque or eschewed as nonsense. It is imperative, then, for the scholar to presume a readership immersed in the intellectual context giving rise to such experimentation. If the assumption cannot be made, prefatory, 'straight-talk' elaborations may be essential to render the work 'rational'.

Although the range of experimental writing in the human sciences continues to expand, for present purposes I wish to focus on a single rhetorical form. In my view, the most significant contribution afforded by the genre is its expansion of vocal registers. That is, in a variety of contrasting ways, authors have enriched the number of realities, rationalities or values embraced within a single work. All of the genres considered heretofore depend on and reinstantiate the assumption of singular authorship. They create the sense of the author as a unified subject, of one mind, one consciousness, a coherent rationality of moral integrity. To be other than unified is to invite epithets of incoherence, self-contradiction or moral muddlement. However, the fictional impulse provides broad licence for the dispersion of authorship.

One of the earliest and most provocative illustrations is Michael Mulkay's 1985 book, *The word and the world: explorations in the form of sociological analysis*. The book is extraordinary for its range of polyphonic experimentation. In the introductory chapter, the voice of a querulous interlocutor is interspersed throughout the text. The expository Mulkay speaks of 'extending the range of analytical discourse to include forms not previously considered appropriate' (p. 10). The interlocutor replies: '*That sounds very attractive in principle, but it ignores the important distinction between fact and faction . . .*' (p. 10). Mulkay goes on to explain that, even within science, 'what is fact for one (scientist) is no more than fiction for the other' (p. 11). The interlocutor rebuts: '*Aren't we in danger of confusing two different meanings of "fiction?"*' Later chapters include an exchange of correspondence between Marks and Spencer, letters from these individuals to Mulkay himself, a one-act play, a multi-participant discussion in which several of the 'fictitious' participants are models of living and identified scientists, and a discussion among a group of inebriated participants at the Nobel ceremonies.

While intellectually resonating with Mulkay's work, Stephen Tyler's 1987 book, *The unspeakable*, opens a new range of formatics. For example, in one attempt to dislodge the scientific view of language as carrying specific meaning (and therefore transparently revealing truth), Tyler playfully deconstructs a phrase from semiotics ('movement along the syntagmatic axis . . .') by showing that when the meanings of each word are fully traced the phrase actually means 'the second world war pitted the anally fixated Germans against the orally fixated British'. In a mirthic burst, Tyler then rapidly heaps one discursive tradition on another to animate the argument: 'The simultaneity of paradigmatic implication interrupts the urgent forward flow of signifiers in the singualrity of time. Don't follow forking paths! Don't fork! Get thee behind me Borges! Time marches on!' (1987: p. 6).

However, the rhetorical richness of the piece is perhaps best illustrated by the lyric mode with which Tyler completes the chapter: 'Beneath the glimmering boreal light, mirrored polar ice groans and heaves, the flame flickers feebly on the altar hearth, in the heart, into the moldy breathing darkness of the antipodal night' (p. 59).

A final illustration of the polyvocality of fictional experimentation is provided by Stephen Pfohl's 1992 work, *Death at the parasite cafe*. The volume begins with five different '(w)riting prefaces': from the editor, the translator, the author, the graphic artist and the copy (w)riter, each representing a different position of authorship, but all bearing the marks of an overarching subjectivity. The remaining chapters are collages of richly variegated forms of writing, including the mystical: 'This is a story of . . . one (who is (k)not One) to pass throughout the HORRORS of being orphaned. Without transcendence or the sublime assurance of genius. Without heroics or the call to war . . . ' (p. 264); the prophetic: 'This is the Parasite Cafe, a dark if brilliantly enlightened space of postmodernity where a transnational host of corporate inFORMational operatives feed upon the digitally coded flesh of others' (p. 8); the autobiographical: 'I'd like to inFORM you that my recollections of that field research in Florida represent the "origins" of the words you are reading' (p. 54); the civil: 'To take seriously the situated character of all knowledge is not to deny the objectivity of social scientific truths but to demand of objectivity that it reflexively locate the (always only) provisional adequacy of its own partial positionings with the world it studies' (p. 79); and the generic fictional: 'It's incredible to be here. I never thought I'd be writing these words in prison and with such fear' (p 59). All the genres are interlarded with photographs, headlines and visitations by various 'factional' characters such as Black Madonna Durkheim, Rada Rada, Marty Martin and Jack O. Lantern.

With respect to reader positioning, it is useful to compare fictional endeavours with the autobiographical. In both cases there is an attempt to break the traditional hierarchical relationship between author and audience. Both avoid authoritative, well-defended monologues. However, the fictionalist undermines his/her own authority as well through the inclusion of multiple and often competing voices. Closely related, both the autobiographer and the fictionalist shift the emphasis toward a dialogic as opposed to monologic relationship with the audience. The autobiographer typically establishes an interdependent relationship with the reader ('As autobiographer I am open and available to you, to your feelings and opinions.), while the fictionalist may rely on a dialogic relationship among differing textual traditions (the polyphonic novel). Both the autobiographer and the fictionalist are also permitted to break with the civil tradition in their display of passion and commitment.

Finally, we must consider a way in which the fictional voice is unique within the present family considered. Here it is useful to array the various genres along a continuum of author/reader distance. The mystical, prophetic and mythic voices clearly demark the author from the reader. The author in these cases is an independent being, a knower who in/forms the reader. The civil voice draws the reader closer, in speaking to a common (albeit competitive) 'brotherhood' of well-intentioned and rational truth-seekers. The autobiographer brings the reader even closer to the author. His/her experience (soul) is rendered transparent and accessible. With fictional writing, however, we discover a new domain of *ironic distance*. On the one hand the genre invites a high degree of author/reader intimacy. The author does not adopt a god's eye-view, coherent, impersonal and contained. Rather, he/she enables the reader access to the full complexity of being – the passionate, the playful, the sophisticated, the brutish, and so on. Further, drawing on the tradition of fiction as entertainment, the genre invites the reader to enjoy the experience, to indulge in the pleasures of the text. Yet, it is this very context of entertainment that gives rise to the ironic distance. For every evidence of textual crafting – of 'writerliness' – is simultaneously evidence of an authorial presence that is removed from the text, one is not authentically present but a 'wizard behind the curtain'. The earmarks of the fictional suggest a created world that is not to be taken seriously after all, one which is crafted by an authentic author in the service of enthralling an audience.

Inscription in question

With historical sensitivities sharpened, we find playing through contemporary human sciences the voices of mystics, prophets, makers of myth, civil fellows, autobiographers and fictionalists. The aim of this analysis is not, however, deconstructive. The substantial literature on the rhetoric of the human sciences has already generated broad consciousness of the constructed character of truth telling. Nor is a recognition of our modes of rhetoric and the traditions from which they draw fully emancipatory. To be aware of the role of tradition, literary convention and rhetorical rules does not permit escape. Even the recognition is reliant on the same resources it may serve to discredit. In this sense, the present analysis is fully dependent on the same rhetorical forms that it attempts to illuminate (most especially the civil and the mythical). Rather, I see the most fruitful reflection generated first from issues of comparative value and second from the challenge of expanding modes of expression. Several comments will be useful in seeding these dialogues.

With respect to comparative merit, there are at least three major (and interrelated) criteria to consider: purpose, audience and politics. It should be clear from the above analysis that the human sciences are scarcely unified in conception of purpose. Whereas goals of prediction and control are paramount in certain circles, others are variously committed to generating insight, emancipating the reader, moral moulding, providing conversational resources and constructing cultural futures. To the extent that we recognize these multiple goals as legitimate, we must also welcome the broad variation in traditions of voice. Mystical writing may be of little value in predicting drug use or suicide, while civil discourse is morally torpid; and so on. In effect, we may value the full panoply of available rhetorics and attend to their relative strengths as we range over possible scholarly and scientific goals.

Concerning audience, we find a strong tendency for scholarly enclaves to coalesce around particular genres of writing, with a concomitant disparagement of the alternatives (e.g. for variously being 'mystifying,' 'banal', 'impractical', 'mawkish', 'merely entertaining', etc.). In general, scholars are unprepared to enter author/reader relationships outside their specialties. For example, to encounter a mystical writing from a background in civil discourse is tortuous and unrewarding; at the same time the autobiographer will often find civil discourse agonizingly flat and technical. The problem is exacerbated in terms of the capacity of the human sciences to reach audiences outside the academy. Although the scientific genres borrow heavily from common cultural traditions, as they continue to circulate within the academy and scholars continue to search for more sophisticated forms of enunciation (more mystifying, arousing, precise, inventive, and so on), their intelligibility wanes within the public sphere. We find, then, that in selecting only one of the existing genres the scholar vastly reduces the potential audience for his/her work. We shall return to this issue shortly.

Regarding political implications, I have placed particular emphasis on the ways in which these various modes of voice favour or fashion forms of relationship. In effect, in selecting a genre one simultaneously invites a particular form of life; genres themselves function as mechanisms of social production. In this sense it is important to place not only the content of various works but the forms of writing themselves under evaluative scrutiny. In the manner of positioning self and other, to what forms of society does the scholar wish to contribute? The ramifications of such queries are many, from matters of educational policy and peda-gogical practice, to issues of familial and societal organization. However, to the extent that one favours cultural democratization, the dialogic generation of truth and morality, and reducing the experienced distances among people, severe limitations inhere within our more traditional forms of writing.

Yet, we may finally ask 'why writing?' Can we not create a new register of relations with our culture by pressing beyond written expression? There are enormous possibilities awaiting those conjoining scholarship with performance – drama, dance, music, art, multi-media and the like (see, for example, Blumenfeld-Jones, 1995; Case, Brett, and Foster, 1995; Gergen, 1995b). While visual artists have long used their medium to speak of the human condition, we now find human scientists turning to art as a means of communication (see, for example, Gergen and Walter, 1998). Similarly, human scientists are increasingly turning their attention to potentials of film and video as forms of professional expression. From the early films by Fred Wiseman to the rich offerings of the Media Education Foundation the border between academic inquiry and entertainment is increasingly threatened. Most importantly, the shift toward performance, poetry, art and visual modalities threaten the scholar/non-scholar binary. And while scholarly authority is undermined, the sciences are richly laminated in expressive capacity. Further, these expressive genres reduce the hierarchy between performer and audience. In the case of film and video, in particular, it might be said that rhetorical success depends importantly on the degree to which the work resonates with the orientation of the audience. The audience does not anticipate 'working in order to understand', but being pleasured through the 'author's' understanding of them. Finally, the emerging range of genres opens an unparalleled possibility for human science scholars to reach audiences outside the academy itself. Whereas the success of the existing genres is largely dependent on a sophisticated coterie of initiates, the move to art, theatre, poetry, film and the like is more populist. Particularly in the case of film and video, the audience is vast and thoroughly prepared.

In conclusion

As we find, there is no single or univocal form of voice in the social sciences, but rather a rich array of varied traditions. Further, within the past several decades there has been robust experimentation in our forms of representation. Whether traditional or iconoclastic, both author and audience are constructed entities and certain forms of relationship privileged over others. In this sense the politics of representation extends far beyond a concern with the ways in which social scientists treat those whom they portray. Rather, political concern extends to the relationship between author and audience created by the genre of writing. While I have been critical of certain forms of address, I have not attempted to argue for the overall superiority of one of these genres over another. Each creates a different form of culture, but as should be clear from preceding chapters, there is good reason to avoid a transcendent hierarchy of the good. Rather, in my view it is important to make a place for all such traditions, as each will nourish a certain sector of society, serving as a valuable resource under certain circumstances. This is not to argue for blindly sustaining the status quo. Rather, it is my hope that the present offering will serve to invigorate the kind of dialogue enabling us to make more propitious choices for future society.

Notes

1 See, for example, Bazerman (1988), Clifford and Marcus (1986) and Simons (1989, 1990).

2 There are alternative means of arraying the rhetorical forms within the human sciences, including, for example, root metaphors (Pepper, 1942) and narrative forms (van Maanen, 1988). The hope of the present alternative is to enhance sensitivity to the historical nexus from which the 'right to voice' in contemporary writing derives.

3 See also Kirschner's (1996) analysis of the manifestations in contemporary developmental theory of Neoplatonist mystical writings. More direct attempts to introduce spiritualist elements into scientific writing are described by Garroutte (1992).

5

HISTORY AND PSYCHOLOGY: CONFLICT AND COMMUNION

Psychologists and historians have not always been congenial companions. For many historians psychology has been a suspicious enterprise, an uneven fledgling in the intellectual world, disingenuously arrogating itself to the status of a natural science. Further, psychology's implicit agenda is hegemonic. In the present case, if psychological science furnishes foundational knowledge regarding human behaviour, and historical study is largely devoted to understanding just such conduct across time, then history stands to be absorbed by the science – ancillary and subsidiary. Psychology's attitude toward history has been equally distant. As a child of cultural modernism, psychological science has treated historical inquiry with little more than tolerant civility. Psychology has been an enterprise struggling to develop general laws through scientific (and largely experimental) methods. Because of its commitment to progress through empirical methods, preceding inquiries into the the mind or scholarship about earlier mentalities was necessarily impaired. In an important sense the past was a shroud to be cast away. Psychologists might scan accounts of earlier times in search of interesting hypotheses or anecdotes, but the results would most likely confirm the widely shared suspicion that contemporary research – controlled and systematic – was far superior in its conclusions. From the psychologist's standpoint, historians are backward looking, where the proper emphasis should be placed on building knowledge for the future.

Slowly, however, these disciplinary antipathies have begun to subside. With the emergence of new cultural topoi – globalization, ecology, information explosion, multi-culturalism and postmodernity among them – we encounter increased sensitivity to the artificial and often obfuscating thrall of disciplinarity. Division and specialization are increasingly replaced by curiosity, dialogue and an optimistic sense of new and fascinating futures. It is with the shape of this future that this chapter is concerned. A marriage of history and psychology can take many forms, and reflexive concern over their differing potentials and shortcomings is essential. It is not only a matter of intellectual and scholarly promise, but longstanding traditions hang in the balance – to be strengthened or dissolved accordingly. And these traditions are further linked to broader societal practices of moral and political consequence. In choosing our mode of inquiry, so do we fashion a cultural future.

With these concerns in mind, I wish to consider three contrasting orientations to this blending of psychology and history. The first orientation may be viewed as *interactionist*: with psychological states giving rise to historical change, and historical conditions influence psychological states. The second is a *radical historicist* orientation, in which historical conditions create what we take to be mental states. The third orientation focuses on the *historical production of psychological discourse*. Each approach is lodged in a different logic, with each logic potentially obliterating the alternatives. My hope in this case is that through comparative exploration we may move beyond this condition of pantagonism. Indeed, informed by a constructionist sensibility, my hope is that we may find openings to a more congenial and enriching future.   These remarks are not intended as conclusive – the end of a conversation – so much as invitations to collective reflection the building of a viable futures.

Empiricist grounds for psycho-historical interaction

Of pivotal concern in the present analysis is the set of assumptions traditionally grounding central inquiry in both the psychological and historical domains. While inviting certain forms of communion between history and psychology, these assumptions are also problematic and delimiting in significant respects. They are well elaborated within twentieth-century philosophy of science (as emerging within 1920s positivism and extending through logical empiricism to the Popperian extenuations in critical rationalism), and deeply embedded as an implicit forestructure within the everyday activities of scholars and scientists themselves. Briefly, to recapitulate four of the central working assumptions within psychology and history, we find commitments to the following:

An independent subject-matter. Until recent years, historians and psychologists have assumed the existence of their subject matters independent of the particular passions and predilections of the inquiring agent. This obdurate subject-matter – given in nature – is there to be recorded, measured, described, and analysed. Experience of this subject-matter may serve as an inductive basis for the generation of knowledge or understanding. Contrasting accounts of human behaviour – past and present – may be compared against the range of existents to determine their relative validity.

An essentialist view of mind. Historians have largely joined psychologists in presuming that, among the important subject-matters to be explored, are specifically mental processes, their antecedents and manifestations. Because human action is based on a psychological sub-stratum (including, for example, emotion, thought, intention and motivation), an illumination of psychological functioning is essential for historical knowledge (lest history become a mere chronicle of events). And, or course, the mind is the pivotal focus of psychological science.

Inquiry as objective and cumulative. Psychologists have expended great effort to insure the objective assessment of their subject matter. Instrumentation, computer control, experimental design and test validation studies are only a few of the safeguards to objectivity. Although few historians would claim the world of the past to be transparent, most would agree that through the examination of manuscripts, letters, diaries and other artefacts one's accounts of the past can shed increasing light on actual occurrences. Objective understanding may not be fully achievable, but the goal can be approximated in ever-advancing degree. Further, in both disciplines objectivity serves as the foundation for cumulative knowledge. With increasing study of a given phenomenon – whether psychological depression or the Great Depression – scholars can achieve more fully detailed understanding.

Value neutrality. The pervasive tendency in historical and psychological inquiry has been a claim to ideological non-partisanship. To be sure, scholars and scientists may harbour strong personal values, but ideally these should not influence the assaying of evidence or the resulting account of the subject-matter. The quest for objectivity in both cases is simultaneously linked to a belief in objectivity as liberation from ideology.

In large measure, these shared assumptions are responsible for the emergence of the major orientations relating mind to history. It is useful for the present analysis to draw these enterprises into focus, and to examine several problematic implications. With these issues in place, we can turn to further developments that offer alternative weavings of the historical and the psychological.

Assumptions in action: psycho-historical interaction

At the outset, if we presume the existence of psychological process (entities, mechanisms, dispositions, etc.), along with an objectified historical context (that is, a context that exists independently of mental representation), then we are disposed to analyses that causally link mental predicates with historically specific events or actions. Two major forms of inquiry are favoured: the first illuminating *psychological origins* of historically located actions (psychology as cause), and the second focused on the *psychological outcomes* of specific historical conditions (psychology as effect). While interactions between psychological and historical conditions are rare but noteworthy, most research tends to favour one of these polar types or the other. In the case of psychological origins, perhaps the premiere efforts have been those of psychohistorians (see, for example, Brown, 1959; DeMause, 1982; Loewenberg, 1983), in which the scholar typically presumes the existence of various psychodynamic processes, and the focus of the analysis is on the ways in which these processes manifest themselves in various historical events. Such analyses may consider the psychodynamic conditions of people at a given era of history (for example, Fromm, 1941), or the individual psychology of significant historical figures (for example, Erikson, 1975). While Martindale's work (especially, 1975, 1990) on psychological motives giving rise to aesthetic appreciation and interests, places primary stress on the mind as origin of history, his work is especially interesting in demonstrating that the effects of these states create a context that loops back to alter the psychological state. Thus, for Martindale there are predictable historical trajectories derived from psychohistorical inter-actions.

Increasingly prevalent, however, is research in which mental states and expressions are positioned as effects of particular historical conditions. This work does not propose that psychological processes are products of these conditions; rather, the analyst presumes the existence of funda-mental psychological processes (e.g. cognitive, emotional, motivational), and views the historical context as shaping their content, character or expression. In effect, we might say, there is a *historical texturing* of the psychological. Work of this sort has sprung from many sources. There has been a longstanding concern, for example, with the ways in which processes of child development are situated within particular historical milieus (Aries, 1962; Kessen, 1990; van den Berg, 1961). Wide-ranging works such as those of Elias (1978) on the civilizing process, Ong (1982) on forms of cognition favoured by oral as opposed to print cultures, and Elder (1974) on the psychological effects of the 'Great Depression' also stand as impor-tant contributions to this form of inquiry. Researchers such as Simonton (1984, 1990) have even attempted to generate means of quantifying historical variables so as to predict historically specific levels of creativity, genius or leadership. Perhaps the most extensive and concerted work within this domain has been that of the Stearns, including their history of anger in the American context (Stearns and Stearns, 1986), the evolution of jealousy in recent history (Stearns, 1989) and the fate of Victorian passions in twentieth-century life (Stearns, 1994). Further exemplars of inquiry in these various domains are contained in the volume *Historical social psychology* (Gergen and Gergen, 1984).

The limits of tradition

As we find, each of the traditional assumptions outlined earlier are robustly manifest in several lines of psycho/historical inquiry. Each presumes the independent existence of its subject-matter, the psyche as a 'natural kind' available to objective appraisal and research as cumulative and non-ideological. Significant enrichment has resulted from pursuing these assumptions, including the development of the social/behavioural sciences as significant disciplines on the cultural landscape; an emerging sense of unity in questions of knowledge, its importance and how it is to be pursued and taught; and an enormous body of inquiry serving to stimulate scholarly deliberation. Yet, while there is much to be said for these endeavours, it is also important to realize their limitations. That we should applaud the traditional efforts is not in question; whether a single paradigm should suffice is yet another matter.

Three particular issues demand attention in the present context. At the outset, it is important to realize that the assumptions giving rise to this form of inquiry are themselves derived from a historically situated intelligibility. The assumptions as articulated give the impression of 'first principles', – foundations that transcend historical and cultural context. Yet, the historically sensitive analyst will draw attention to the conditions under which these assumptions emerged and the part they may have played within the political, economic and social conditions of the time (see, for example, Shapin, 1996). The assumptions, then, derive their legitimacy not from transcendent verities but from specific conditions of society. And, if this is so, then there is no binding necessity for maintaining them to the exclusion of others. Or, more positively, because they are optional they may be opened to broad-ranging scrutiny and the consideration of alternatives.[1]

Such scrutiny begins in earnest when it is realized that these grounding assumptions furnish no means of critical self-reflection. Once set in motion, there is neither a means of questioning their premises nor of intelligibly raising questions falling outside the ontology they circumscribe. Once it is agreed that knowledge is accumulated through empirical assessment of the world's givens, it is difficult to challenge this assumption. To question it on grounds that did not assume the ontology (e.g. on spiritual grounds) would be irrelevant to the venture (e.g. 'mere mysticism'). To put empiricism to empirical test would be equally problematic. It would be conceptual mischief to suppose that empirical methods could prove themselves untrue.

Yet the problem is not limited to an incapacity for self-reflexivity. As we find, once the paradigm is in motion all questions falling outside the bounded domain of empirical knowledge are placed in jeopardy. In particular, critics have long been concerned with the inability of the traditional orientation to speak to questions of human value. Because the language of value cannot be unequivocally linked to events in the material world, issues of value have been largely removed from discussion. Further, the pursuit of knowledge is concerned with establishing what is (or was) the case, it is said, and not with promulgating a canon of 'oughts'. Objective inquiry is not in the business of ideological propaganda. Yet, as critics persist, in one's choice of descriptive terminology, explanatory base, method of exploration and rationalizing metaphysics, the scientist/scholar is also acting into the world and inevitably shaping its future for good or ill. In spite of erstwhile claims to value neutrality, then, traditional pursuits are inevitably ideological. Means must be found, it is argued, to restore a sense of moral and political responsibility to such endeavours.

There is a final issue, less profound in implication but nonetheless significant. This concerns the tensions inhering in the dominant traditions of history and psychology, and the ways in which they are resolved within various forms of interdisciplinary work. Of particular concern, psychological study has generally, though not exclusively, been a generalizing discipline. That is, the chief attempt is to establish knowledge of human functioning that transcends both time and culture. In contrast, most (but not all) historical analysis has tended to be particularizing, concerned with the unique configuration of circumstances existing at different periods of time. In terms of our preceding discussion, these differences in propensity are not without political significance. For the generalizing disciplines a conception of human nature as relatively fixed (of genetic origin) tends to prevail. For many psychologists, there is a resulting preference for explaining various social ills (e.g. aggression, poverty, drug use) in terms of individual, inherent tendencies, with an associated preference for strong state controls and political conservatism (one cannot change human nature, but only control its excesses). For the particularizing scholar, the tendency is to view human nature as more mutable and multi-potentiated. Societal problems are more likely to be understood in terms of the particular configuration of circumstances (e.g. economic, attitudes and values, quality of governance), with solutions favouring collaboration and creativity over control and punishment.

In this context many of the psycho/historical efforts just described, in their assumption of human action as an effect or expression of a fixed psychological substratum, will tend to privilege the universal over the particular. For example, the existence of the emotions, is never doubted in such research; only its expressions and effects are historically constituted. Such expressions may be controlled, channelled or suppressed, but the psychological fundament remains fixed. Thus, psychological process remains a prevailing force in the generation of historical events and the history of psychological processes can only be written in terms of variations on the fundamental theme. These contentions are amplified when we consider a second orientation.

The historical constitution of the psyche

In important respects, the second line of psycho/historical inquiry represents a more extreme version of the texturing approach just discussed. However, rather than the historical context serving to give content or conditions of expression to an otherwise fixed domain of psychological functioning, here we find that the historical is the origin of the mental. That is, mental processes – both the ontology of the mind and the specific manifestations – are byproducts of antecedent historical conditions. These conditions may be material: for Marxist historians psychological conditions of self-alienation and false consciousness are the specific outcome of conditions of labour. The reconfiguration of labour would essentially eradicate these particular states of mind. For the most part, however, scholars have looked to the social conditions as the primary formative agents of psychological process.

This approach has been most inviting for a range of psychological states that are either marginal or controversial to society more generally. Thus we are not at all discomforted by accounts of the social history of romantic love (for example, Hunt, 1959; Kern, 1992). Possibly because many feel uncertain about their own experiences of such a state, and possibly because romantic love threatens the Enlightenment ideal of the rational mind, there is a certain relief attendant upon historization. However, the intellectual and ideological stakes are raised considerably when such analysis turns to psychological concepts more pivotal to our Western institutions. Consider, for example, the radical implications of Lev Vygotsky's (1978) proposal that, 'There is nothing in mind that is not first of all in society' (p. 142). In effect, for Vygotsky the processes of thinking and memory are not there in nature, prior to culture, but owe their very existence to cultural antecedents. Also exemplary of this view is Badinter's (1980) analysis of the sense of the mother's instinctive love for her child, its genesis traced to particular political and intellectual conditions of the eighteenth and nineteenth centuries. My own work (Gergen, 1991) has traced the erosion in the concept of an essential, unified self to current technological conditions. Harré and Finlay-Jones's (1986) explorations of *accidie* and *melancholy* in the early European context are also apposite. Although cross-cultural in its focus, Lutz's work on the social constitution of emotions such as *fago* and *song* in the Ifaluk people of the south-west Pacific is highly compelling. Additional contributions to Harré's (1986) edited collection, *The social construction of emotions*, add important dimension to this historicizing of the mind.

For many, the implications of such work for traditional empirical psychology are little short of devastating. At the outset, such inquiry challenges the essentialism so endemic to psychological science and so necessary to its claims to be studying 'universal man'. Not only is the search for transhistorical and transcultural generalizations thrown into question, but the very assumption of the science as cumulative is jeopardized. Today's empirical results, on this account, are not indicators of universal truths, but of historically contingent customs (see Gergen, 1994c). Or, in terms of our previous concerns, this form of analysis reverses the privilege of the psychological over the historical. Here psychology becomes a tributary of historical analysis.

Yet, the implications do not stop here. Ultimately the analyst confronts the historical contingency of the very conceptions of knowledge giving rise to historical study itself. For example, if mentalities are socially constituted, what are we to make of the concept of objectivity as a state of mind and the assumption of an unbiased relationship between a private subjectivity and the objects of study? The very idea of a mind as separate from the world, existing within the body, and reflecting the contours of an external world becomes open to historical reflection (see, for example, Rorty, 1979). If subjectivity is socially constituted, then isn't all scientific description and explanation coloured by (if not derivative of) the community conventions of the time? Self-reflexive dialogue becomes essential.

Further, a view of the mind as historically constituted begins to generate a moral and political sensitivity. In particular, if the mental is socially constituted, then forms of psychological being are essentially optional. And if optional, we may inquire into the desirability of existing modes of being and the potentials inherent in potential alternatives. To illustrate, Averill (1985) argues for anger as a form of culturally situated performance. Anger in Western culture, for example, is not duplicated elsewhere. Under these circumstances, we in contemporary Western culture can raise questions about the desirability of our current construction of anger. For example, Tavris (1982) has argued for a transformation in our cultural construction of anger. We must abandon the traditional view of anger as a natural act, biologically determined and triggered by particular circumstances. Such a view, proposes Tavris, rationalizes acts of family violence, physical retaliation, jealous violence, and the like. To construct anger as a cultural performance is to sensitize people to their responsibility for their actions and the possibilities that they could act otherwise. More recently, Averill and Nunley (1992) extend these arguments to propose that people should create the emotional forms essential for fulfilling lives.

Finally, we find in this orientation the seeds for a dramatic recasting of the role of historian in matters of psychology. As suggested in the preceding analysis, once mentalities are essentialized they will tend to circumscribe all historical analysis. However, if the mental world is historically constituted, then historical understanding is essential to any further analysis of mind. The work of the historian becomes a necessary prolegomenon for understanding in psychological science. To launch research into any psychological 'phenomenon' without a grasp of the textual history giving rise to the very presumption of a phenomenon would be cavalier to say the least. To carry out research without a sense of the socio-cultural forestructure that sets limits to the project's generality would be myopic.

Psychological discourses in historical context

The most recent turn in scholarship grows from the array of interrelated movements variously indexed as poststructural, post-empiricist, postfoundational, post-Enlightenment and postmodern. As outlined in previous chapters, these movements tend to converge in their concerns on the construction of reality through language and within community. Further, as it is commonly argued, because such constructions create and sustain particular forms of conduct they simultaneously operate as forces of control or power within society. Most pointedly, those standing at the margins of such communities may become subject to what for them are oppressive if not annihilative consequences of construction.[2]

These have been stirring if not dramatic dialogues, and their implications far-reaching. Of particular relevance to the present chapter, they have stimulated an alternative form of scholarship, devoted in this case to the historical and cultural circumstances giving rise to particular vocabularies of mental life and the part played by these vocabularies in the ordering of social conduct. The argument here is not that mental events are socially constituted, as in the previous case. For most of these scholars the existence of mental life itself is undecidable. That is, whether or not there is 'mental life' and how (if it exists) it is constituted are not questions generally felt to be answerable outside the confines of a particular interpretive community. The major concern, then, is with the discourses of mental life, people's actions made apparent or possible through such discourses, and the functioning of these discourses (and associated actions) within society over time.

Emotions as discourse: an illustration

To appreciate the logic of this work it is useful to illustrate with the discourse of the emotions. Attempts to define the emotions and elucidate their character have ornamented the Western landscape for over two thousand years. Two characteristics of this continuing colloquy are particularly noteworthy: first, the presumption of palpability and, second, the interminability of debate. In the former case, until the twentieth century there had been little doubting the existence of the emotions. In the second book of the *Rhetoric*, Aristotle distinguished among fifteen emotional states; Aquinas' *Summa theologiae* enumerated six 'affective' and five 'spirited' emotions; Descartes distinguished among six primary passions of the soul; the eighteenth-century moralist David Hartley located ten 'general passions of human nature'; and the major contributions by recent theorists, Tomkins (1962) and Izard (1977), describe some ten distinctive emotional states. In effect, Western cultural history is one in which there is unflinching agreement regarding the palpable presence of emotional states.

At the same time, these deep ontological commitments are also matched by a virtual cacophony of competing views on the character of the emotions – their distinguishing characteristics, origins, manifestations and significance in human affairs. For Aristotle the emotions constituted 'motions of the soul'; for Aquinas the emotions were experienced by the soul, but were the products of sensory appetites; Descartes isolated specific 'passions of the soul', these owing to movements of the 'animal spirits' agitating the brain. For Thomas Hobbes (1651), the passions were constitutive of human nature itself and furnished the activating 'spirit' for the intellect, the will and moral character. In his *Treatise on human nature* (1739), David Hume divided the passions into those directly derived from human instinct (e.g. the desire to punish our enemies) and those which derive from a 'double relation' of sensory impressions and ideas. A century later, both Spencer's *Principles of psychology* and Darwin's *The expression of the emotions in man and animals* attempted to place the emotions on more seemingly certain biological grounds.

This interminability of debate is most effectively illustrated by considering the 'objects of study' themselves, that which is identified as an emotion. For example, Aristotle identified *placability, confidence, benevolence, churlishness, resentment, emulation, longing* and *enthusiasm* as emotional states no less transparent than *anger* or *joy*. Yet, in their twentieth-century exegeses, neither Tomkins (1962) nor Izard (1977) recognize these states as constituents of the emotional domain. Aquinas believed *love, desire, hope* and *courage* were all central emotions, and while Aristotle agreed in the case of *love*, all such states go virtually unrecognized in the recent theories of Tomkins and Izard. Hobbes identified *covetousness, luxury, curiosity, ambition, good naturedness, superstition* and *will* as emotional states, none of which qualifies as such in contemporary psychology. Tomkins and Izard agree that *surprise* is an emotion, a belief that would indeed surprise most of their predecessors. However, where Izard believes *sadness* and *guilt* are major emotions, they fail to qualify in Tomkins analysis; simultaneously, Tomkins sees *distress* as a central emotion, where Izard does not.

There is a certain irony inhering in these two features of emotional debate – palpability and interminability. If the emotions are simply there as transparent features of human existence, why should univocality be so difficult to achieve? Broad agreement exists within scientific communities concerning, for example, chemical tables, genetic constitution and the movements of the planets; and where disagreements have developed procedures have also been located for pressing the nomenclature toward greater uniformity. Why, then, is scientific convergence so elusive in the case of emotions? At least one significant reason for the continuous contention derives from a presumptive fallacy, namely Whitehead's fallacy of misplaced concreteness. Possibly we labour in a tradition in which we mistakenly treat the putative objects of our mental vocabulary as palpable, whereas it is the names themselves that possess more indubitable properties. Because there are words such as love, anger and guilt, we presume that there must be specific states to which they refer. And if there is disagreement, we presume that continued study of the object will set the matter straight. After two thousand years of debate, one is ineluctably led to suppose that there are no such objects to which such terms refer.

This latter possibility has become far more compelling within recent years, and particularly with the development of ordinary language philosophy. Wittgenstein's *Philosophical investigations* was the major stimulus in this case, both questioning the referential base for mental predicates and offering an alternative way of accounting for such discourse. As Wittgenstein (1953) asks:

I give notice that I am afraid. – Do I recall my thoughts of the past half hour in order to do that, or do I let a thought of the dentist quickly cross my mind in order to see how it affects me; or can I be uncertain of whether it is really fear of the dentists, and not some other physical feeling of discomfort? (p. 32e)

The impossibility of answering such a question in terms of mental referents for the emotion terms demands an alternative means of understanding mental terms. This understanding is largely to be found in Wittgenstein's arguments for use-derived meaning. On this view, mental predicates acquire their meaning through various language games embedded within cultural forms of life. Mental language is rendered significant not by virtue of its capacity to reveal, mark or describe mental states, but from its function in social interchange.

Historicizing psychological discourse: instances and implications

Arguments of the preceding kind inform a genre of historical work concerned not only with emotion but the full range of discourses on the nature of psychological functioning. The focus of inquiry is variously on the genesis and sustenance of psychological discourse, its modes of functioning within society and the values and groups that it sustains (and suppresses). Illustrative are Suzanne Kirschner's (1996) exploration of the way in which contemporary conceptions of psychological development echo the narratives of neo-Platonist theological texts; David Leary's (1990) edited collection on the place of metaphor in the history of psychological theorizing; Gigerenzer's (1996) analysis of the influence of statistical methodology on psychology's conception of cognitive functioning; Hacking's (1995), *Rewriting the soul*, a historical inquiry into the conceptions of multiple personality and the politics of memory; Spacks's (1995) exploration of the emergence of boredom in the eighteenth century; and Herman's (1992) inquiry into the political roots of the discourse of psychic trauma. A broad sampling of historical work on psychological discourse is also contained in *Historical dimensions of psychological discourse* (Graumann and Gergen, 1996).

Such work begins to form a significant alternative to the stance of value neutrality pervading both the preceding psycho/historical enterprises. That is, rather than simply reflecting on the nature of the past, these inquiries often use historical work in the service of moral/ethical critique. This kind of value-based analysis is specifically invited by the assumption that what we take to be mental functioning is neither given as an essence nor fixed within individuals as cultural disposition; rather, concepts of mind are woven into the fabric of discursive understandings. Thus, if the scholar can alter such forms of understanding – as in the case of the historization of psychological discourse – then we enter a clearing in which choice is possible. To understand that the psychologist's conceptions of emotion, for example, are not maps of human nature but the outcomes of cultural tradition enables us to reflect on the relative value of these conceptions in comparison with other possibilities. The discourse is not fixed but is rendered optional. Particularly illustrative of the critical posture are Rose's (1985, 1990) Foucauldian explorations of the role of the discourse and methods of professional psychology in the political 'disciplining' of the society; Lutz's (1988) critique of the androcentric biases fostered by the discourse of emotions in contemporary Western culture; and Sampson's (1988) analysis of the individualist ideology sustained by cognitivist conceptions of mental life.

The implications of this growing corpus of work for more traditional historical and psychological work seem, at the outset, little short of annihilative. From the discursive perspective, it is difficult to locate a subject-matter that is independent of the discursive/theoretical projects of the investigating agents. The very idea of an 'independent subject-matter' – whether the mind or history itself – lapses into incoherence. And with this turn, of course, so do essentialist conceptions of mental events or processes deteriorate. If anything, these inquiries demonstrate the tenuous (if not tautological) relationship between our language of the mind and its putative referents. Further, the aspiration for an objective science/history begins to wither. Yes, the sense of objectivity may be achieved within a particular community of interlocutors. However, the scientist/scholar loses the warrant for claiming truth beyond community, some privileged relationship between words and world. Similarly, knowledge may accumulate but only by virtue of the standards shared within an interpretive community.

Yet, in the end, the annihilative implications of these arguments cannot be sustained. As proposed in Chapter 2, should the discursive critic make claims to the truth of his/her proposals, then the very grounds from which they issue are removed. More positively, this is to say that discursive inquiry does succeed in avoiding the pitfalls of gainsaying its own rationale. Whereas traditional inquiry has no means of questioning its own premises (e.g. presumptions of objectivity, value neutrality), the discursive scholar is invited into a posture of self-reflection. The discursive critique of the traditions must itself be viewed as a discursive move, a means of carrying on intellectual life within the scholarly community and relating this community to the broader society. The arguments essentially serve as an invitation to forms of conversation and relationship that may offer new alternatives for inquiry and new roles for the scholar.

History and psychology: towards polyphonic prosperity

We have surveyed three significant departures in the marriage of historical and psychological scholarship: the first draws on traditional essentialist assumptions regarding both history and psychology; the second emphasizes the historical constitution of the psychological domain, and the third transforms both history and psychology to discourse. How should we now regard these ventures in terms of future investments? Should the traditional endeavours, still very robust, simply continue unabated? Do the emerging alternatives now make it impossible to return to traditional work? Is there some form of amalgam that we should seek? These are complex questions and discussion should remain open. However, we may draw several conclusions from the preceding discussion that may serve as useful entries into the dialogue.

At the outset, I find myself compelled by the various arguments seeding the discursive turn in social analysis. To be sure the chief outcomes of historical and psychological scholarship are bodies of discourse – books, articles, lectures and the like. The extent to which these bodies of discourse are referentially linked to events outside language must always remain in question; word–object relations are forever in motion ('infinite semiosis') and words themselves are easily objectified even when there are no ostensible referents. Further, when we attempt to describe the world to which discourse could be linked, we again enter the corridors of discourse.

With this said, however, we do not locate within the discursive orientation any foundational arguments against the preceding lines of investigation. Unlike the empirically based traditions, there is no presumption that research may proceed in an unbiased way to reveal what is (or was) the case.

Thus, there is no means of discrediting a particular form of inquiry because it fails to participate within the empirical/essentialist paradigm. Rather than ruling out forms of inquiry, the discursively sensitive scholar should ideally welcome a range of possible endeavours, each of which would speak for a given community, its traditions and values. The aim should not be to obliterate traditions of language but to enrich them. At the same time, we are sensitized by the logic of discursive inquiry to the potential effects of our study on intellectual, political and societal life more generally. Thus, while not discrediting any particular form of study out of hand, there is a strong invitation to explore the societal implications of all our inquiries, whether oriented around psychological process, historical analysis or discursive process. To publish work without preliminary attention to the moral and political implications within one's cultural/ historical context would, from the discursive standpoint, be arrogant if not inhumane.

In conclusion

What seems favoured in the end is a dialogic marriage among equals. With no ultimate grounds of dismissal on any side, it may be possible to appreciate the interdependencies of these various forms of inquiry, along with complementarities and potential affinities. With respect to interdependency, for example, with all its critique of objectively accurate analysis, discursive inquiry must indeed rely on the rhetoric of objectivity to render its analyses intelligible. Concerning complementarity, analyses favouring both the social constitution and discursive construction of the mind do tend to privilege social change over stability (liberal and trans-formative agendas over conservative). However, it is very unlikely that any analyst would favour a complete overhauling of all societal investments; absolute change would be the equivalent of absolute chaos. Transformation is only possible against the backdrop of a deep stability. And, finally, there are opportunities for coalescence. For example, there is a high degree of overlap between the social constitutionalist and the discursive construc-tionist efforts. With the former shifting the emphasis from psychological states to culturally situated performances, and the latter embedding discourse within embodied actions, powerful forms of historical analysis would be consolidated.

Notes

1 See Levy (1989) and Modell (1989) for discussions of some of these limitations.

2 For a detailed analysis of the position of historical analysis within these debates, see Novick (1989).

PART II

SOCIAL CONSTRUCTION AND SOCIETAL PRACTICE

6

THERAPY AS SOCIAL CONSTRUCTION

With Lisa Warhus

As we pass into a new century we are witnessing a gradual but ever intensifying convergence in conceptions of the therapeutic process. At the heart of this convergence lies the human activity of generating meaning. First and foremost we find the therapeutic relationship one in which human meaning is not only focal but pivotal to the process of therapeutic change. Significant preparation for the contemporary movement has come from many sources, including humanistic/phenomenological/hermeneutic psychology, cognitive constructivism (Kelly, 1955; Neimeyer and Mahoney, 1995) and recent object relations theory (Ashbach and Schermer, 1987; Mitchell, 1993). The work of the Palo Alto group (Watzlawick, Beavin and Jackson, 1967) centred on interdependent meanings within families, and Milan systemic therapists carried this orientation forward into a range of new and challenging practices.

As these early dialogues on meaning have unfolded and interacted the therapeutic community has become increasingly open to the vortex of critical and constructionist interchange within the broader intellectual community.[1] The result has been a persistent though uneven shift towards a common conception of meaning – away from its traditional locus within individual minds to its creation within relationships – from mental to social construction. For some the shift is subtle and adjustments are minor; however, in its more radical form this transformation does nothing less than subvert all existing foundations of therapeutic thought and practice. To be sure, this movement has provoked a substantial degree of antagonism

(cf. Held, 1996; Lannamann, 1998; Mancuso, 1996; Sass, 1992b). More pro-
ductively, however, a range of significant questions has emerged: what, if
any, are the significant threads uniting these diverse movements; are there
important differences; how does a constructionist shift disrupt and/or
enrich existing therapeutic traditions; should we anticipate or hope for a
singular mode of treatment; how are these orientations to be reconciled
with traditional investments in diagnosis and mental health policies; what
is being lost in this transformation and what is gained?

It is this context of ferment and self-reflection that gives rise to the
present undertaking. In what follows we shall attempt first to extricate a
number of pivotal assumptions playing through the emerging dialogues
on relational meaning, to sharpen them through comparison with the extant
traditions and to treat some of the central problems which they raise. This
will illuminate and clarify a family of interlocking assumptions to which
participants in the dialogues subscribe in varying degrees. The attempt is
not to articulate a new foundation for therapy, nor a canonical formulation
of 'postmodern therapy'; both aspirations would be antithetical to social
constructionist dialogues. Rather, the hope is that such a discussion can
contribute to generative conversation, a maturing of sensibilities and
the emergence of new practices. This latter aim will become focal at the
chapter's end.

Social construction and therapeutic posture

For this analysis it is convenient to consider first a set of four transitions
that characterize the emerging conception of therapy as a process of
relational construction. While these transitions have a variety of practical
implications, they are not centred so much on specific techniques as they
enkindle the therapist's sensitivities, invite deliberation on options and
provoke reflection on ongoing process.

From foundations to flexibility

Traditional orientations toward therapy have derived from what are
commonly viewed as *rational foundations of knowledge*. These foundations
are typically lodged within what is narrowly defined as an empiricist
conception of knowledge,[2] but more broadly within the Zeitgeist of cultural
modernism.[3] As outlined in the preceding chapter the major crucible for
testing knowledge claims has been systematic observation. With continued
and rigorous study we should approach a true and objective understanding
of both normal and aberrant action. Further, continued research should
reveal which of a variety of therapeutic practices is most effective for
treating various forms of abnormality. There may be many candidates
for truth about persons, dysfunctions and cure, but empirical research
should, on the traditional account, ultimately enable us to winnow the
many to a few – and ultimately to perhaps one.

For the social constructionist theories of human action are not built up or derived from observation, but rather grow from a community of engaged interlocutors. It is the conventions of intelligibility shared within one's professional enclave that will determine how we interpret the observational world. Thus, a psychodynamic therapist will find evidence for repressed desires, while a cognitive therapist will locate problems in the individual's mode of information processing and a family systems therapist will be drawn to the realities of family communication patterns. Because theories serve to construct the world in their terms, there is no means of empirically testing between them. Each 'test' would inevitably construct the field of relevant facts in its terms. Outcome research is subject to the same problem; a positive outcome from one standpoint (e.g. symptom reduction, expressions of anger) will signify a regression or problem exacerbation for others.

Based on this line of reasoning constructionism invites an abandonment of the search for foundations – a single view of human functioning its foibles and cures. As we have seen in previous chapters, this is also to place constructionism itself into question as a final philosophy (see Doan, 1998). We are encouraged instead to relinquish the longstanding competition among schools of therapy, along with the related conceptions of fixed diagnostics, 'best practices' of therapy and outcome comparison. More positively, if we view the various therapeutic schools as communities of meaning, then each school possesses transformational potential for some population. Each offers an opening to a form of life. Lynn Hoffman (1990) captures much the same idea in proposing that theories 'represent sets of lenses that enforce an awareness that what you thought looked one way, immutably and forever, can be seen in another way . . . At the cost of giving up moral and scientific absolutes, your social constructionist gets an enlarged sense of choice' (p. 4). Similarly, Cecchin, Lane and Ray (1992) write: 'Having too much faith in any position, any story, we run the risk of creating an inflexible, impoverished therapeutic reality, (which is why) we pose the question, how can we train ourselves to be disloyal to any story when or if it becomes no longer useful' (p. 14).

In terms of therapeutic practice, the therapist is thus invited to prosper from the entire domain of therapeutic intelligibilities and to employ whatever may be serviceable in the immediate context. In this sense, there is no 'social constructionist method' of therapy. To formalize any method – to canonize its principles – is to freeze cultural meaning. It is to presume that effective processes of forging meaning in the present will remain so across time, circumstance and context of interpretation.[4] This is also to say that the common critique of the therapeutic community – that the multiple and ever-shifting fields of theory and practice reveal a state of confusion and a lack of real knowledge – is ill founded. This very richness of intelligibility and the capacity of the therapeutic community continuously to refashion understanding represent its very strengths.

Yet, the implications of this position are more radical than an advocacy of eclecticism. Within the foundationalist tradition the professional account of people's problems was privileged over that of the common culture. Whereas the quotidian understandings of the culture were said to be fraught with bias, misunderstanding and superstition, the discourse of the profession furnished more comprehensive and accurate understanding. For the constructionist the criterion of 'more accurate or objective understanding' is removed; all forms of understanding are culturally embedded constructions. Effective therapy may – and typically will – require the use of many speech genres, including those of the culture at large. This is to say that for purposes of therapeutic practice, the door is opened to the full range of cultural genres. To be sure, this may include all existing forms of therapeutic discourse – from psychoanalytic, behaviour modification, cognitive, primal scream, and more. At the same time, we must be prepared to radically expand the arena of usable meanings. For example, there is strong support here for those wishing to include spiritual discourse within the therapeutic process (see, for example, Butler, Gardner and Bird, 1998; Griffith and Griffith, 1992; Richards and Bergin, 1997). For much of the population such discourse speaks in a powerful way; to neglect its significance is therapeutically myopic. However, the complete therapist should not shun the discourses of romance, New Age, Marxism, Zen Buddhism, and more. The skilled therapist in a constructionist mode might be as much at home speaking the language of the street, the locker room, or the nightclub as mastering the nuances of Lacanian analytics. Each new intelligibility enriches the range and flexibility of the interactive moment.

We should not conclude, however, that professional theories are without special merit or that concern with therapeutic outcomes should be abandoned. Professionally developed theories may be especially significant in their capacity to offer alternatives not easily located within the common culture. Therapeutic theories represent some of the century's most important innovations in making human action intelligible. In this sense the culturally deviant theory of the professional may possess unique generative power. In deviating from common sense it may significantly challenge the status quo, shake the cage doors of conventionality and offer genuinely new possibilities for action. Further, professional languages enable therapists to engage in communal deliberations – to speak meaningfully with each other and thus to coordinate their efforts more effectively. Such discourse enables the therapeutic community to reflect critically on the common intelligibilities of the culture – which reflection cannot be done from within these intelligibilities themselves (e.g. one cannot reflect critically on spiritual discourse from the standpoint of a committed spiritualist).

Similarly, the abandonment of foundations does not mean the end of inquiry into outcomes (see also Amundson, 1996). Every outcome – from reducing alcohol consumption, domestic violence or depression to that of creating a sense of personal growth or consciousness of archetypes – reflects a tradition, a way of life or an enclave of value. The point, then, is not to abandon traditional investments. Rather the more profitable path is to (1) expand on the range of value considerations taken into account in any outcome (e.g. broaden consideration on what may count as a positive outcome), and (2) set in motion dialogues in which competing and conflicting values or outcomes may be preferred.[5] By taking into account multiple criteria of 'wellness' we not only expand the domain of what it means to be adequate, but generate a more differentiated picture of what counts as 'the good', when and for whom.

From essentialism to consciousness of construction

As suggested, the modernist therapeutic tradition trucks in truth. Thus, therapy is typically oriented toward locating 'the real problem', the 'causes of the difficulty', 'the forces at work', 'the determining structures', and the like, and assessing the effects of contrasting therapeutic practices on outcomes. For the constructionist there are no problems, causes, forces, structures and so on that do not derive their status as such from communally based interpretations. This is not to propose that 'nothing exists' or that 'we can never know reality' – common misunderstandings of constructionism – but rather that when we attempt to articulate what exists, to place it into language, we enter the world of socially generated meanings. It may be more helpful, then, to say that constructionism operates against the tendency to *essentialize* the language, that is, to treat the words as if they were pictures, maps or replicas of essences that exist independent of we who interpret our existence in this way. In this sense, constructionism serves as a continuous reminder of Gregory Bateson's dictum, 'the map is not the territory'.

Of course, the proclivity of therapists to point out ways in which clients' accounts of self and world fail to match the territory have been a professional mainstay since Freud's revelation of repression. However, until recently most schools of therapy have presumed both the existence of the territory and the function of words as mapping agents. It is only under these assumptions that such terms as 'delusion,' 'distortion' 'misperception' and 'misattribution' are intelligible. Constructionism, in contrast, invites us to see such terms in a horizontal rather than a vertical plane, that is, as indicators of an alternative way of constructing the world as opposed to the necessary or superior way. To accuse others of being deluded is primarily to say that they do not share your interpretive conventions. Early movement toward the horizontal plane can be found in the Milan school practice of circular questioning. Circular questions are not aimed at revealing 'what is the case', but rather attempt to generate information that can make a difference in the shared understanding of family members (Selvini-Palazzoli et al., 1980). A circular question such as 'Father, which of your two children do you think your wife is closest to, Vicki or Joe?' does not function to illuminate the truth about family structure, but rather to bring forth possible ideas that might challenge the problematic logic shared by the family. A similar move toward consciousness of constructionism is evident in brief therapy, and particularly the work of de Shazer (1994). As Berg and de Shazer (1993) propose, 'Meanings arrived at in a therapeutic conversation are developed through a process more like negotiation than the development of understanding or an uncovering of what is "really" going on' (p. 7).

This emphasis on constructed realities must be accompanied by an important caveat. Constructionism does recognize the significance of *truth in context*. Within any community of interlocutors there will be tendencies to essentialize the commonly shared modes of discourse, and this essentialization is of inestimable importance in sustaining the community's traditions. We may name this infant Diana and that one David, and while the names are arbitrary the essentializing moves (e.g. 'Diana is my daughter', 'David is at school') are necessary to maintain the local orders of family, school, friendship, and so on. Similarly, while the language of biology is not required by 'what exists', agreement on the way in which the language of genes and chromosomes is used within the profession is essential for what we call 'in vitro fertilization' and 'DNA testing'.

This is also to say that consciousness of construction does not necessarily invite therapists into a posture of deconstructing client realities. Effective therapy does not require ontological crisis and, indeed, is more likely to leave most of the client's understandings intact. As Harlene Anderson (1997) puts it: 'My role as a therapist is to participate with a client in a first-person linguistic account of his or her relevant life events and experiences' (p. 114). Similarly, Tom Andersen (1991) writes: 'If people are exposed to the usual they tend to stay the same. If they meet something un-usual, this un-usual might induce a change. If the new they meet is very (too) unusual, they close up' (p. 19). Consciousness of construction is most valuable as a posture that invites the suspension of reality at any moment the taken-for-granted or essentialized reality proves painful or problematic. If a client's 'problem' seems intractable then deconstruction of meaning may be an essential precursor to reconstruction.

From expertise to collaboration

As proposed, there is no singular set of practices that follow from a constructionist metatheory. For example, there is nothing about constructionism that would necessarily opt against 'taking an authoritative stand' in a therapeutic relationship; strong opinions may sometimes be useful. However, if we play out the implications of constructionist metatheory new doors are opened to practice. In particular, constructionist theory invites the therapist to consider alternatives to the traditional position of authority, and particularly to adopt a collaborative orientation to the client. The shift in style is no small undertaking. As Hoffman (1993) writes: 'the change from a hierarchical to a collaborative style . . . is a radical step.

It calls into question the top-down structuring of this quasi-medical field called mental health and flies in the face of centuries of traditional western practice . . . To challenge these elements is to challenge the whole citadel' (p. 4). As Andersen (1995) describes his therapeutic work, it has moved toward 'heterarchy'. 'Hierarchy governs from the top and down, and heterarchy governs through the other . . . More common words for a heterarchical relationship might be "democratic relationship," an "even relationship," or a relationship with equally important contributors' (p. 18).

More controversially, in their 'collaborative language systems' approach, Anderson and Goolishian (1992; Goolishian and Anderson, 1987) propose a collaborative partnership with the client in which the therapist enters with a stance of 'not knowing'. Not-knowing refers to

> an attitude and belief that a therapist does not have access to privileged information, can never fully understand another person, always needs to be in a state of being informed by the other, and always needs to learn more about what has been said or may not have been said . . . Interpretation is always a dialogue between therapist and client and not the result of predetermined theoretical narratives essential to a therapist's meaning, expertise, experience or therapy model. (Anderson, 1997: 134)

This is not to say that the therapist does not bring uniquely valuable skills to the relationship. It is to say, however, that such skills are not derived from a mastery of understanding. They are primarily skills in *knowing how* as opposed to *knowing that* – of moving fluidly in relationship, of collaborating in the mutual generation of new futures.

For many constructionist therapists an animus has developed toward traditional, strategic options. More generally, strategic interventions are seen to be monologic (as opposed to dialogic), dictated by the therapist's private standpoint. For the collaborative specialist, such strategic action not only seems manipulative, but generates a sense of inauthentic participation in the therapeutic relationship (e.g. the therapist's reality is concealed off-stage). In our view, these reactions are not entirely warranted. Again, nothing is necessarily ruled out by constructionism and surely no one would wish to abandon the process we take to be 'rational deliberation'. Thus, rather than abandoning the strategic orientation, we might opt for dialogues of difference, that is, discussions of how and why strategic intervention can be advantageous and under what conditions it is problematic. We might move, then, to an orientation of *situated strategy*.

From value neutrality to value relevance

From the modernist/empiricist standpoint therapy is not a forum for political, ideological or ethical advocacy. The good therapist, like the good medical doctor, should engage in sensitive observation and careful thought, unbiased by his/her particular value investments. Critiques of value neutrality have long been extant. The works of Szasz (1970), Laing (1967) and participants in the critical psychiatry movement have made us acutely conscious of the ways in which well-intentioned therapists can contribute to forces of oppression. Congenial with Foucault's (1979) critique of the 'disciplining' effects of therapeutic practices, more recent analysts have focused on the ways in which various therapies and diagnostic categories contribute to sexism, racism, heterosexism, individualism, class oppression and other divisive biases.[6] From a constructionist standpoint even a posture of non-engagement or 'neutrality' is viewed as ethical and political in its consequences (MacKinnon and Miller, 1987; Taggart, 1985). Whether mindful or not, whether for good or ill, therapeutic work is necessarily a form of social/political activism. Any action within a society is simultaneously creating its future for good or ill by some standard.

Many therapists, cognizant of the relationship between therapeutic constructions and societal values, now explore the implications of ethically and politically committed therapy. Rather than posturing as unbiased and non-partisan, value realization constitutes a therapeutic *raison d'être*. We have, then, the development of therapies that are specifically committed, for example, to challenging the dominant order (e.g. White and Epston, 1990) and pursuing feminist, gay, socialist and other political ends. Feminist therapists, for example, frequently focus on female oppression as a fundamental therapeutic theme, or deconstruct gender categories to provide clients an expanded set of options (Ussher, 1992). With the expanding power of identity politics there is every reason to anticipate an increase in such investments.

While such movements are invited by constructionist dialogues, there is also good reason for critical reflection. For we confront here the possibility of an anguished fragmentation – the development of multiple therapeutic enclaves each claiming a moral high ground, each isolated and righteously indignant. We approach a bellicose state in the therapeutic world of all-against-all. From our standpoint this condition would stand in stark contrast to the constructionist emphasis on plural realities. A Hobbesian condition of generalized animosity would lend itself not to an expansion of viewpoints but ultimately the eradication of all but one. Most important, then, is the constructionist premise that there are no foundations – no final justifications – for any ethical or political claim. Thus, constructionism also invites the politically engaged therapist into a posture of self-reflexivity and a curiosity about those who differ. This does not mean avoiding value positions; as in the above, we can scarcely step out of culture and we should scarcely wish to abandon attempts to create the good society. However, constructionism does remove the ultimate authority of such investments – just the kind of commitments that, in our view, are most frequently used to silence or obliterate those whose voices differ from one's own (see also Parre and Sawatzky, 1999). And it does invite therapists into mutually transformative dialogue with clients who do not share their views on such matters as abortion, divorce, physical abuse, and the like.

Finally, in its emphasis on the ultimate interdependence of all meaning, constructionist arguments suggest a new and different role for therapists. Supplementing the options of either avoiding political issues or ardently pursuing social change, therapists may fruitfully explore the possibilities of bringing disparate groups into coordination, rendering alienated languages more permeable, enabling people to speak in multiple voices and ultimately reducing the potential for mutual eradication. As we shall explore more fully in Chapter 10, value commitment is replaced by practices of co-creation.[7]

Social construction and therapeutic practice

As we propose, constructionist dialogues favour four major movements in therapeutic posture – movements toward flexibility, consciousness of construction, collaboration and value relevant practice. However, such dialogues also invite a new range of practices. Here we trace the emerging forms of practice, along with constructionist re-theorizing of traditional practices. Five central dimensions of change will be treated.

From mind to discourse

Traditional therapy is focally concerned with individual mental states. From the psychoanalytic emphasis on psychodynamics and Rogerian concerns with self-regard to contemporary cognitive and constructivist therapy, it is the central task of the therapist to explore, understand and ultimately bring about transformation in individual minds. Even group psychotherapy has retained a strong investment in psychodynamic principles. It is within what began as systems-oriented family therapy that we find the most concerted shift outward – from mind to language. To be sure, vestiges of psychological essentialism have remained – embedded, for example, in second-order cybernetic orientations – but the significant move has been toward understanding the process of communication. Yet, within the emerging dialogues on social construction it has become evident that even these moves are insufficient. For in the main they have issued from a modernist/empiricist orientation in which the communication structures or dynamics are typically essentialized, objectified and treated from a position of 'knowing that'.[8] Further, because meaning among persons is largely achieved through conversation, then it is to discursive processes that primary attention shifts. Or as Sluzki (1992) has put it, therapy may be understood as a process of 'discourse transformation'. If meaning is chiefly generated within linguistic processes, then it is to these processes that attention is drawn (see Kogan & Brown, 1998).

This shift to discourse is perhaps the most widely apparent aspect of therapy in a constructionist frame and has given rise to a broad range of therapeutic innovations. The vast share is congenial with the groundswell of social science interest in narrative or essentially the storied construction of self and world (Bruner, 1986; Polkinghorne, 1988; Sarbin, 1986). For many therapists Donald Spence's *Narrative truth and historical truth* represented a critical turning point. Here was a scholar/therapist of long experience who argued that historical truth was seldom reflected in the patient's accounts of his/her early life. In contrast, Spence began to explore the positive uses of the narrative truths developed in therapy. Perhaps the most prominent expression of this shift to discourse is found in what McLeod (1997) calls the 'postmodern narrative movement'. As developed by therapists such as White and Epston (1990), and enriched and expanded in numerous ways over the years (see, for example, Freeman, Epston and Lobovits, 1997; Freedman and Combs, 1996;Larner, 1996; McLeod, 1997; Neimeyer, 1999; Parry and Doan, 1994; Zimmerman and Dickerson, 1996), the prevailing concern is with the ways in which language constructs self and world, and the implications of these constructions for client well-being. More radical than Spence – who assumed that historical truth was achievable in principle – the radical implication of such work is that life events do not determine one's narratives but, rather, linguistic conventions largely determine what counts as a life event and how it is to be evaluated. It is much the same concern with the constructive force of language that has sparked the therapeutic use of metaphor (Combs and Freedman, 1990; Schnitman, 1996; Snyder, 1996), the combination of narrative and metaphor (Goncalves, 1995) and the development of client writing practices as therapeutic tools (Bacigalupe, 1996; Lange, 1996; Penn and Frankfurt, 1994).

Yet, while much has been gained from this watershed, dangers and limitations are also at hand. First, even with an abiding construction-ist consciousness, there is a pervasive tendency to objectify discourse, that is to treat narrative discourse as simply 'there in nature'. For the constructionist to speak of narratives is to create a conversational object – only 'one way of putting things' – and not ideal under all circumstances. Practically speaking, there may be instances in which it is more fruitful to treat a life history, for example, as a manifestation of psychodynamic processes or a reflection of actual fact. In effect, it is important to sustain the reflexive posture in which even constructionism itself is treated as one perspective among many. In this sense, constructionist practices do not deny the existence of mental events (e.g. experience, emotion). How-ever, the therapeutic emphasis shifts away from mental exploration and plumbing the depths of emotional life to the consequences of speaking in these terms.

Further, there exists a strong tendency to treat discourse as a personal possession, with meaning originating in individual consciousness. Indeed, a mainstay of the Western tradition is the belief that words are manifes-tations of meanings created within the individual mind. However, this emphasis on personal meaning obscures the constructionist emphasis on language as relational and pragmatic, generated not within but between persons in their relationships.[9] Or, for the constructionist, one can never have meaning isolated from relationship. This emphasis on the personal is often coupled with a third problem, which is that of treating a change in discourse as tantamount to cure. As often reasoned, if one learns to narrate life in a different way, or shift from a culturally dominant to an individualized story of self, then improvement has been achieved. Such assumptions not only borrow from the individualist heritage (e.g. 'Changes in mind yield changes in action') but favour as well a view of meaning as an originary force in one's life. If narratives and metaphors are forms of discourse, as constructionist writings suggest, then they do not so much determine one's actions as they are resources used by people in generating meaning together (Gergen and Kaye, 1992; Newman and Holzman, 1999). If stories are social performances, we must raise questions concerning the value of a single life-narrative (which diminishes one's capacity for relationship) and the capacity of therapeutically generated narratives to survive in the social world more generally. We shall return to this issue shortly.

Finally, many of the emerging therapies are limited in their narrow definition of discourse – principally to spoken or written language. Given our traditions this is a comfortable starting point, enriched as well by an expansive literature on semiotics, literary theory, rhetoric and linguistics. At the same time such a preoccupation is reductionistic. First it reduces discourse to the utterances (or writing) of the single individual. Yet, if meaning is the byproduct of relationship, then such a focus is blind to the relational process from which any particular utterance derives its meaning. In effect, words mean nothing in themselves, and it is only by attending to the flow of interchange that we can appreciate the origins, sustenance and decay of meaning. Further, the emphasis on words strips discourse of all else about the person (and situation) that is essential to generate intelligibility. One speaks not only with words, but with facial expressions, gestures, posture, dress and so on. Ultimately it is important to add what we might commonly call corporal and material dimensions to the discursive domain.[10] Again, this is not to objectify the more expanded view of discourse any more than the restricted vision. Rather, with each new lamination in the concept of discourse so do we add to the range of possible practices.

From self to relationship

The traditional emphasis on mental states is closely allied with a focus on individual treatment and cure. Relationships, on this account, are built up from associations among otherwise private individuals. Effectively, relationships are secondary or artificial contrivances, constructed from the raw materials of independent selves. Movements in group and family therapy have offered a range of alternative practices built around such concepts as group dynamics, family structure and psychological interdependence. However, in many (but not all) of these cases relational activity is treated as a derivative of fundamentally private, psychological process. With the constructionist shift from mind to discourse the focus moves significantly towards the primacy of relationship. In effect, language is fundamentally a relational phenomenon. Much like a handshake or a tango, it cannot be performed alone. On this account, meaning is not located within the mind of individual actors, but is a continuously emerging achievement of relational process (Gergen, 1994a, Chapter 11). It is in this context that we appreciate more fully the earlier described emphasis on co-construction. It is within the matrix of therapist–client exchange that meaning evolves.

Yet, while most therapeutic practices included in this analysis share this premise, the emphasis on relationship (as opposed to individual minds) expands in many directions. It is useful here to think of concentric circles of relationship, starting first with the therapist–client and expanding then to the client's relationship with immediate family, intimates, friends and the like. Within this outer circle, some therapies press backward in time to consider earlier relationships. As Mary Gergen (2000) proposes, we carry with us a cadre of 'social ghosts'. To tap into these often significant relationships, Penn and Frankfurt (1994) sometimes ask clients to write letters to a lost loved one. Further expanding the circle, still other therapies take into account the broader community – the workplace, church and the like. In Sweden, Egelund (1997) and his colleagues include in their 'town therapy' parents, teachers, social workers and others whose opinions bear on the case. Broadening the circle even further, some therapies are vitally concerned with the relationship of the individual to the broad social context – to institutions of power, cultural traditions of suppression, and the like. The 'social therapy' of Newman and Holzman, for example, attempts to link individual problems with the broad social conditions of society – race relations, employment opportunities and community action. In the same vein, Freeman, Epston and Lobovits (1997) write: 'Since problem-saturated stories are nested in social, cultural, economic and gender assumptions about roles and behaviour, we inquire about these factors and strive to be aware of how they are affecting different family members' (p. 51). With each move outward in the circle new moves in practice may emerge.

While challenging and innovative, therapeutic moves in the relational direction do require continuing attention. There is, for one, the constant danger of reviving social determinist metaphors, in which the self becomes the victim of others' influences – family, the work place, the economic structure and the like. Social constructionism is not a social determinism; the emphasis is on meaning through coordination. Here we are in accord with Kathy Weingarten's (1998) view that 'I am subject to the same world-making and unmaking processes as everyone else, I can never locate myself as an objective outsider, but must always know myself as a participant' (p. 5). With this shift in emphasis we are also invited to reconceptualize the 'I' as always already a constituent of relationship (see Chapter 2). This is not to objectify the domain of the relational in such a way that individual exploration is abandoned (see also Parre and Sawatzky, 1999). Again, constructionism is not about the destruction of traditions. Rather, we are invited to situate the exploration of the self, to consider the pragmatic consequences of relational as opposed to individualist understandings.

From singularity to polyvocality

Traditional therapies were enchanted by metaphors of the singular and unified. First there was the commitment to the singularity of objective truth and the aspiration for a unified discipline. Further, there was the traditional ideal of a self whose mental world is coherent, integrated and unified. It is thus that we often speak pejoratively of psychological tensions, mental splitting, multiple personality disorder and schizoid personalities. With the emergence of constructionist consciousness, these traditional romances with unity are placed in question. The argument for multiple constructions of the real – each legitimate within a particular interpretive community – renders the concept of the 'single, coherent truth' both parochial and potentially oppressive. Further, with people embedded in multiple relationships – each constructing one's identity and the world in a different way – the ideal of a unified self seems increasingly unappealing if not counter-adaptive (Gergen, 1991). To thrive under these conditions may require something akin to a protean personality (Lifton, 1993). It is within this intellectual and cultural context that a new range of therapeutic practices has been nurtured.

At the outset such therapies often press toward multiplicity of client realities. As Weingarten (1998) writes: 'a postmodern narrative therapist is generally uninterested in conversation that tries to ferret out the causes of problems. Instead, she is extremely interested in conversations that generate many possible ways to move forward once a problem has arisen' (p. 14). Or as Riikonen and Smith (1997) put it, 'It would be a mistake to think that inspiring worlds can only be built in one way' (p. 90). Here the work of Tom Andersen (1991, 1995) and his colleagues on the reflecting team provided an important breakthrough. When multiple observers of a family therapy session share their views with family members, and the family is invited to comment on these interpretations, they are set free to consider all options – including those they may themselves develop as alternatives. There is no attempt here to determine the 'true nature of the problem', but rather to open multiple paths to alternative futures.

In addition to practices of interpretive enrichment, other therapists have specifically focused on self-multiplicity. Most pointedly, for example, Karl Tomm (1999) has developed a process of 'internalized other interviewing', during which he interviews the voice of another person within the client. For example, if overcome with anger at another person, the client might be asked to enter as deeply as he/she is able into the other's experience and speak from the 'I' position of the other. In a more general frame, Penn and Frankfurt (1994) find that many of their clients enter therapy with 'constricting monologues': as therapists they encourage the development of 'narrative multiplicity'. They first introduce the possibility of alternative voices – for example, positive, optimistic or confident – into the conversations with clients. Then, the client is encouraged to write – for example, letters to persons living or dead, dialogues, notes between sessions, journal entries, poetry – in a manner that evokes the new voices. Penn (1998) has also experimented with introducing new, imaginary voices into client narratives. Similarly, Riikonen and Smith (1997) are concerned with the ways in which culturally dominant discourses constrict individual action. Classic are cases of physical or sexual abuse, where victims too quickly embrace conventional views in which they are defined as unworthy or deserving the abuse. The therapist asks such questions as: 'Where do you think these oppressive descriptions come from? Which other types of descriptions/voices in you have been silenced? Have you been able to listen to other ideas? What might it mean if you were able to listen more to those different ideas?' (p. 123). As Hermans and Kempen (1993) further detail, the new voices set in motion internal dialogues that have significant potential for change.

While this exploration of multiple selves represents a movement of far-reaching consequence, we also confront significant questions. To encourage multiple realities is to violate common conventions, and for many represents a condemnable relativism. If there are multiple interpretations, then what is truly valuable and what is ultimately worth doing? Some clients – longing for 'the answer' to their problems – may find themselves lost in a vertigo of options. If no option is more reasonable than another, then how is choice possible? It seems clear that like other constructionist practices, pressing toward multiplicity must be situated; care must be given to when and where it is useful (or not). In the case of multiple selves we locate further challenges. Many highly valued institutions are based on a conception of singular selves; to foster the reality of polyvocality may place such traditions in jeopardy. For example, traditional forms of intimacy are lodged in the capacity to trust – to know the other as he/she truly is. Yet, the polyvocal other may seem thinly committed; too often he or she may appear glib, superficial, a mere player of games. Similarly, the capacity to hold one responsible depends on a conception of 'the one' (or singular agent) who acts. If every action is only one reflection of a large cast of inner characters, then who is to be blamed or credited for their actions? These are only representative of issues now on the horizon.

From problems to prospects

Traditional therapy is based on a medical model of disease and cure in which patients (clients) confront problems – typically indexed as pathologies, adjustment difficulties, dysfunctional relationships, etc. – and the task of the therapist is to treat the problem in such a way that it is alleviated or removed ('cured'). It is the assumption of 'the problem' that underwrites the process of diagnosis and indeed, fuels the development of diagnostic criteria (e.g. the DSMIV). From a constructionist standpoint, however, this entire array of interlocking presumptions and practices engages in the realist fallacy of presuming that 'problems' (diseases) exist independent of our forms of interpretation. For the constructionist the term 'problem' is an optional interpretation. There are no 'problems' in the world that require such discourse. Again, this is not to abandon problem terminology in its conventional usages but, rather, to give us pause to consider the consequences. For, as many reason, to define the world in terms of problems often essentializes a reality in a way that is intractable. When therapists set out to explore the client's problems, so do they generate a conversational reality that increases in magnitude and palpability. Options become fewer and anguish is sustained rather than alleviated. There are special shortcomings attendant upon using diagnostic terminologies. In their locating the source of difficulty within the client (or the family), the therapist positions the individual (or family) in a dependent and disparaged role, simultaneously creating him/herself as expert. Cure depends on the therapists' skills and not the clients'.[11]

With these arguments in hand, therapists have developed a range of practices that attempt to avoid the reification of problems and shift attention to a discourse of positive prospects. As Riikonen and Smith (1997) put it: 'We have been accustomed to talk about analyzing problems as a prerequisite of solving, dissolving or deconstructing them. It seems in most cases more useful to talk about actions, experiences and thoughts which can help to make things better' (p. 25). In narrative therapy there is also exploration of the significance of positive events in relating one's history (Suddaby and Landau, 1998). Most visible in this respect is the work of solution-focused therapies (for example, Berg and de Shazer, 1993, de Shazer, 1994; O'Hanlon and Weiner-Davis, 1988). Here problem talk is almost entirely abandoned in favour of exploring resources and goals for the future. The 'miracle question' is essentially an invitation to a new domain of dialogue in which the creation of future realities takes precedence over the objectification of past problems.

Again, however, it is important to remain sensitive to possible shortcomings in prospect-oriented practices. As emphasized in Harlene Anderson's (1997) work, honouring the client reality is essential to a productive relationship. Or as William O'Hanlon (1993) proposes, 'if clients don't have a sense that you have heard, acknowledged, and valued them, they will either spend time trying to convince you of the legitimacy of their pain and suffering or they will leave therapy with you' (p. 7). Thus, by rapidly moving towards deconstruction or dissolution of 'the problem', the therapist may run the risk of undermining rapport. Further, while it is possible to relativize a client's account of the problem, his/her definition may be importantly tied to relations outside therapy. Regardless of the reconstructive possibilities, for most people 'physical abuse' or 'incest' remain problems within the broader culture. To suppress such accounts runs the risk of alienating the client from his/her relational surrounds. This point is also related to the earlier discussion of moral engagement. Problems are always such by virtue of a particular tradition of value; to undermine a report of 'my problem' is also to place in question the related tradition. None of this is to argue against prospect-oriented practices; rather it is to encourage reflection on the use of such practices within the broader matrix of meaning-making.

From insight to action

Traditional therapies, focusing on individual psychological deficit, have also viewed the individual psyche as the site of therapeutic change. Whether, for example, in terms of transference, catharsis, self-understanding, self-acceptance, re-construal or cognitive change, most therapeutic practices have been built around the assumption that successful therapy depends primarily on a change in the mind of the individual. Further, it is typically supposed, this change can be accomplished within the therapeutic relationship. The concept of the 'therapeutic breakthrough' epitomizes this point of view; once change is accomplished in the therapeutic chamber there is hope that the transformation will remain after departure. We may use the phrase *individual insight* to index this class of practices.

Yet, as we shift the emphasis from individual minds to discursive relations among individuals, we find the traditional array of practices delimited if not shortsighted. From the constructionist standpoint, the process of generating meaning is continuous and its form and content likely to shift from one relationship to the next. The individual harbours multiple discursive capacities, and there is no strong reason to anticipate that the meanings generated within the therapeutic relationship will be carried over into outside relationships. The dramatic insight shared between therapist and client is essentially *their* achievement, a conversational moment that derives its significance from the preceding interchange and cannot easily be lifted out and placed within another conversation remote in time and place.

When we locate the source of meaning within dialogic process, we are essentially viewing the meaning-making process as social activity. Meaning, then, is not originated within the mind and stored there for future use, but rather is created in action and regenerated (or not) within subsequent processes of coordination. In de Shazer's (1994) terms: 'Rather than looking behind and beneath the language that clients and therapists use, I think the language they use is all we have to go on . . . Contrary to the common sense view, change is seen to happen within language: What we talk about and how we talk about it makes a difference . . . ' (p. 10). In this context the primary questions to be asked of therapeutic co-construction are (1) whether a particular form of discourse is actionable outside the therapeutic relationship, and (2) whether the pragmatic consequences of this discourse are desirable. To illustrate, in a Jungian practice one might acquire an entirely specialized vocabulary archetypes. While this vocabulary will enable a rich relationship to develop within the therapeutic setting, it can seldom be placed in practice elsewhere. The vocabulary can accomplish little in the way of conversational work. In the case of pragmatic effects, primal scream therapy may enable one to dramatically express rage and anguish. Yet, while these expressions can produce significant effects in the marketplace of social life, the consequences are not likely to be helpful to the client.

These twin criteria – actionability and pragmatic outcome – have been slow to surface in constructionist therapies. In some degree this relative unconcern is based on the view that therapeutic conversation (along with internal dialogue) yields results in the external world of relationships. Yet, this assumption is largely a promissory note. Much needed are practices specifically dedicated to forging this link. To illustrate the possibilities, White and Epston (1990) have generated a variety of authenticating practices for giving life to newly emerging narratives. They may conduct celebrations, give prizes with significant people in attendance or generate 'news releases' in which the individual's arrival at a new status is announced to various significant others. White recruits what he terms 'The Club of Your Life', which might include anyone, living or dead, actual or imaginary. Epston and his colleagues (Madigan and Epston, 1995) help clients with eating disorders to develop politically oriented support groups. Social therapists (Newman and Holzman, 1999) enable their clients to engage in political activism as a means of increasing their control over events impinging on their lives. The emphasis on practical action also helps us to appreciate the special qualities of both group and family therapy practices. Here the client's discourse enters directly into the public arena and its pragmatic consequences made more manifest. Further we find new purchase on role-playing therapies. If properly directed, the client gains skills in forms of social expression. In our view, the most important challenge for the therapeutic community is to enlarge these resources for pragmatic consequence.

Reflection and the creative challenge

The shift toward a constructionist sensibility invites both conceptual and practical transformation in psychotherapy. Not only is the general posture of the therapist displaced significantly from its modernist base, but a range of new practices and attendant challenges has emerged. Yet, our purpose in this analysis goes further than articulating the contours of change. We also find here grounds for constructive critique and the creation of new departures. The heuristic value of the analysis can be set in motion by first linking the above dimensions of change with illustrative therapists and/or practices. For example, we propose that each of the individuals or practices in the right-hand column below can effectively illustrate the conceptual dimension to the left:

Flexibility in standpoint	Lynn Hoffman
Consciousness of construction	Milan School
Collaborative orientation	Collaborative Language Systems
Value relevant stance	Feminist therapy
Discursive emphasis	Narrative therapy
Relationship emphasis	'Town' therapy
Polyvocal emphasis	Reflecting process
Prospect emphasis	Brief/Solution focused
Action emphasis	Social therapy

When arrayed in this way the question emerges as to whether a theorist or practice congenial with one conceptual dimension is also coherent with the others. While a given practice may be highly effective in realizing one focal aspect of the constructionist turn, in principle it could be irrelevant or even antithetical to other constructionist directions. Not all therapies that emphasize polyvocality, for example, are politically or ideologically engaged, not all practices focusing on positive prospects also emphasize relational process, and so on. Thus, the analytic categories outlined here can serve as criteria for reflection: given a particular therapeutic practice, in what ways does it reflect (or not) these various dimensions? More importantly, when it does not achieve one of these ends, can we locate potentials for further enrichment of the practice? In effect, deliberation on the ways in which a given practice does and does not take into account the dimensions of change, invites a creative posture in which new practices may be envisioned.

To illustrate, consider first the now classic form of narrative therapy outlined by White and Epston (1990). In a constructionist world such a practice would receive reasonably high marks for its consciousness of construction, collaborative stance, value consciousness and its emphases on relationship, prospects and action. Yet, the practice does appear to be inflexible in these respects; there is little room within the practice for more traditional standpoints or practices, even if their pragmatic utility might in certain conditions be superior. Further, there is a strong tendency within this practice to emphasize singularity in story. The attempt is primarily to help the client escape the grasp of a dismal and dominating discourse and to generate a more useful narrative. Little emphasis is placed either on the multiplicity of stories the client may bring with him/her into therapy or the possibility of moving within a fluid space of multiple narratives. The productive challenge, then, would be to inquire into ways that the orientation might (1) be rendered more flexible, making use of multiple traditions, and (2) introduce multiple voices and visions into the dialogue.

In a similar manner, we might explore new evolutions of solution-focused therapy encouraged by a consideration of political and ideological implications. We might also explore new potentials in reflecting team practices when action consequences are placed in focus. Ideologically based therapies might also gain considerably by moving from problem centred discourse ('societal blame') to prospective possibilities. As we found, dramatic changes in conception and practice of therapy have emerged within the past two decades. However, important challenges are now confronted and the possibilities for new and innovative practices form vistas for an exciting future.

Notes

1 The sense of a converging movement has been captured in a variety of edited volumes over recent years, including McNamee and Gergen's (1992) *Therapy as social construction*, Friedman's (1993) *The new language of change: constructive collaboration in psychotherapy*, Gilligan and Price's (1993) *Therapeutic conversations*, Hoyt's volumes on *Constructive therapies* (1994, 1998) and Rosen and Kuehlwein's (1996) *Constructing realities*.

2 Both psychoanalytic and constructivist advocates might object to this assertion. However, while psychoanalytic theory posits psychodynamic processes that violate empiricist assumptions, the orientation of the analyst – including Freud himself – is towards gaining objective knowledge about these processes. Similarly, while Kelly's (1955) vision of the individual seems to violate empiricist assumptions, the theory essentially sets out to vindicate the image of 'scientific man'.

3 For more on the place of empiricism within Western modernism, see Hollinger (1994), Rosenau (1992) and Gergen (1991).

4 See Goldner (1998) for an excellent use of multiple theoretical/practical standpoints, including constructionist.

5 For an exemplary case of a dialogic orientation to diagnosis and outcomes, see Seikkula, Aaltonen and Alakare (1995).

6 See, for example, Cushman (1990), Parker et al. (1995), Kutchins and Kirk (1997), Mustin (1994) and Gergen (1994a).

7 For further discussion of ways and means of accomplishing such integrative ends, see Becker, Chasin, Herzog and Roth (1995), McNamee and Gergen (1999) and Pearce and Littlejohn (1997).

8 Illustrative, for example, is the movement toward diagnosing relationships (see Kaslow, 1996).

9 For an excellent illustration of the relational genesis of meaning in therapy, see O'Neill (1998).

10 James and Melissa Griffith's (1994) *The body speaks* represents a groundbreaking attempt to unite narrativity and corporality.

11 For an extended bibliography on the problematics of mental and relational diagnoses, see http://www.swarthmore.edu/SocSci/kgergen1/Psychodiagnostics/index.html

7

SOCIAL CONSTRUCTION AND PEDAGOGICAL PRACTICE

With Stanton Wortham

Practices of education are typically linked to an assumptive network, that is, a shared discourse about the nature of human beings, their capacities and their relationship with the world and each other. In the case of education, perhaps the pivotal concept is that of knowledge itself. How, then, do we define or conceptualize knowledge such that educational practices are necessary, and certain practices become favoured over others? Clearly disparate concepts of knowledge will lend themselves to differing views of the educational process. If we believed, along with certain romanticists, that 'the heart has its reason', we might replace books and lectures with intense emotional and spiritual encounters. Should we believe, along with the Ilongot of Northern Luzon, that knowledge is to be gained in the throes of anger or in the hunting of heads, then formal training in schools might be replaced by battle experience. Beliefs about knowledge, then, inform, justify and sustain our practices of education.

Given this concern with grounding assumptions, we wish first to sketch two major conceptions of knowledge dear to the Western tradition, conceptions that continue today to inform the vast share of the educational practices in which we participate. As we shall then propose, these closely related systems of belief are deeply problematic, both in terms of their epistemological and ideological commitments. We shall then outline an alternative to these views, namely one issuing from a social constructionist standpoint. While not attempting to destroy the traditional views, social constructionism offers a significant alternative. In doing so it also opens the door to new ranges of practice.

Knowledge: exogenic and endogenic traditions

Although there are many ways of dissecting our historical traditions, it is helpful here to single out two longstanding orientations to knowledge: *exogenic* (or world centred) on the one hand, and *endogenic* (or mind centred) on the other. The exogenic tradition in education can be traced to empiricist philosophies of knowledge (from Locke to logical positivism), while the endogenic tradition largely owes its intelligibility to the rationalist tradition (from Descartes and Kant through Fodor and the AI movement). Both orientations embrace a mind/world dualism in which the existence of an external world (typically a material reality) is set against the existence of a psychological world (cognitive, subjective, symbolic). From the exogenic standpoint, however, knowledge is achieved when the inner states of the individual reflect or accurately represent (or serve as a mirror of) the existing states of the external world. Exogenic thinkers often place a strong emphasis on keen observation in the acquisition of knowledge, and tend to view emotion and personal values as potential hazards to the neutral or 'evenly hovering attention' required for accurate recording of the world as it is. Further, the exogenecist is also likely to stress the importance of knowledge in the individual's ability to adapt to or succeed within a complex environment. We must possess an 'internal map' of nature, as it is held, if we are successfully to find our way in the world. For the exogenecists, then, the world is a primary given, and the mind operates best when reflecting it accurately.

The endogenic tradition is similar to the exogenic in its dualist foundations and its emphasis on value neutrality. Yet, whereas the endogenic tradition treats careful observation of the world as the key to acquiring knowledge, the endogenecist places the chief emphasis on the powers of individual reason. Where the exogenic educator is likely to focus on the arrangement of environmental inputs necessary to build up an accurate representation, the endogenic educator lays chief emphasis on the human being's intrinsic capacities for insight, logic or conceptual development. In this sense the exogenic theorist is likely to view the external or material world as a given and conjecture about how nature becomes accurately represented in the mind, while the endogenic thinker is likely to view the mental world as self-evident and raise questions concerning the way in which the mind operates so as to function adequately in nature. In debates on the influence of nurture versus nature (environmentalism versus nativism) the exogenecist will favour the effects of nature on the individual; infinite and continuous moulding of the individual mind may be possible. In contrast, the endogenecist will call attention to the inherent or natural capacities and development of the individual mind. Limits to learning may be traced to developmental stages of the cognitive system.

As suggested, each of these orientations to knowledge also serves to justify or rationalize certain forms of educational practice. By and large the exogenic orientation is subject matter or curriculum centred. From the exogenic perspective the student is largely viewed as a *tabula rasa* upon which the educational process should inscribe the essential features of the world. More concretely, the perspective favours an emphasis on the student's direct observation or the experiential enrichment of experience – the collection of samples or specimens, participant observation, laboratory experiments, field trips, and so on. Exposure to books and lectures is also favoured by the exogenic perspective, as it is through these means that the individual can acquire vast amounts of information not otherwise available to direct observation. The exogenic view is favourable to examination procedures in which the primary emphasis is placed on assessing levels of individual knowledge. Devices such as multiple-choice questions, standardized tests and statistical normalization may all reveal in what degree 'the slate has been filled'.

In contrast, the endogenic perspective is child or student centred. Endogenic curricula place the major emphasis on the rational capacities of the individual. It is not so much the amount of information in one's mind that is important as the way one deliberates about it. Thus a strong emphasis may be placed on mathematics, philosophy and foreign languages, all subjects that are said to enhance one's capacities for thought. Class discussion is favoured over lectures, as it is through active engagement that cognitive skills are most fully potentiated. Essay exams and term papers are favoured over standardized tests, as rational analysis is not only better trained through these means but evaluation should ideally be tuned to quality rather than quantity. To be sure, there have been attempts to unite the two traditions. Piaget's (1954) theorizing is exemplary, as he posits two opposing processes of cognitive development, cognitive *accommodation* to real world objects (homage to the exogenic tradition) and cognitive *assimilation* of the world to cognitive structures (sustaining the endogenic tradition). We shall have more to say about such integrations in a later discussion of social constructivism.

The demise of knowledge as individual possession

Although present day educational policy and pedagogy is rendered rational largely through these longstanding conceptions of knowledge, it appears that the traditions are rapidly becoming unravelled. In part, this unravelling is invited by the fact that the traditions have always existed on shaky ground. From within these two perspectives, philosophers have never been able to solve the fundamental question of epistemology – how the mind acquires knowledge of a world external to it. Indeed, the fuel for each perspective is largely derived from the flaws inhering in its opposing number. As many now see it, the problem of knowledge is inherently insoluble (Rorty, 1979). If we commence with a distinction between what is *outside* and *inside* the mind of the individual, we create an inherently intractable problem in determining how the former is accurately registered in the latter. Such conclusions have also rendered both exogenic and endogenic conceptions of knowledge vulnerable to the more recent fusillade of critiques variously labelled post-empiricist, post-foundational, post-Englightenment, poststructural and postmodern (see Chapters 1–3). Within these camps, both exogenic and endogenic conceptions of knowledge have lost virtually all currency.

Yet there is one argument emerging from these more recent dialogues that does require further attention. Both exogenic and endogenic traditions locate knowledge within the minds of single individuals. It is the individual who observes and thinks, and who is challenged to acquire knowledge. It is only by virtue of the individual's possession of knowledge, it is held, that he or she can survive or thrive in a complex world. The shaky grounds for such beliefs are but one reason for hesitation. Perhaps more importantly we must inquire into the effects on cultural life to suppose that this is so? If we declare knowledge to be essential to survival, and to reside in the heads of separate individuals, what forms of cultural practice are invited; what groups are privileged; what traditions or potentials are suppressed or obliterated?

Framed in this way there is reason for resistance. Essentially such a conception of knowledge allies itself with an ideology of *self-contained individualism* (see Chapter 2). To view knowledge as the possession of single minds is consistent with other propositions holding individuals to be the possessors of their own motives, emotions or fundamental essences. Within this tradition, people are invited to see themselves as the centre of their actions – as lone choosers, searchers, finders – confronted with the challenges of survival and success. As critics argue, such beliefs not only favour a narcissistic or 'me-first' disposition toward life, but cast others (along with the physical environment) into a secondary or instrumental role. Persons and environments are viewed primarily in terms of what they can do for oneself. Further, because of the sense of fundamental isolation ('me alone') bred by this orientation, human relationships are viewed as artificial contrivances, virtually set against the natural state of independence. Most importantly, as the peoples of the globe become increasingly interdependent, and as they gain the capabilities for mutual annihilation (either through arms or pollution), the ideology of self-contained individualism poses a threat to human well-being. Under these conditions it is no longer useful to think of me vs. you, us vs. them. We are not then speaking of abstract and arcane philosophy, but of a system of beliefs that in certain respects may be inimical to global well-being (see also Gergen, 1999).

The social construction of knowledge

As these problems with the traditional views of knowledge have become evident, there has been increasing interest in possible successor projects. It is also precisely at this point that social constructionist dialogues acquire their contemporary significance. Much post-foundational critique has centred on restoring to culture that which had been declared natural, that is, replacing the assumption of truth verified by nature with truth as created in community. In terms of the above arguments, this is to view knowledge as a byproduct not of individual minds but of communal relationships. Or, to reiterate a prevailing theme in this book, *all meaningful propositions about the real and the good have their origins in relationships*. This is to bring into sharp focus the site of knowledge generation: the ongoing process of coordinating action among persons. It is to foreground the moment-to-moment interchange between and among interlocutors, and locate meaning within the patterns of interdependency. Following Wittgenstein (1953), there is no private language (a moment prior to relationship in which the individual formulates meaning); rather, language (and other actions) gain their intelligibility in their social use, as they are coordinated with the actions of others. Individuals in isolation do not thereby cease to be intelligible; however, this is to trace the intelligibility of their private actions to a preceding immersion in relationship. Individuals may carry out actions traditionally indexed as 'thought' or 'feeling'; however, these actions may properly be viewed as forms of relationship carried out on the site of the individual.

In preparation for our later discussion of educational practice, more must be said about the significance of relationship. One useful way of putting things is to say that an actor never comes into meaning save through the supplementary actions of another. Whatever is said or written has no intrinsic meaning; it carries no univocal message in itself. Nor is the meaning of a series of words or actions determined solely by the recipient (listener or reader). Rather, an individual's actions (both linguistic and otherwise) operate as indicators of possible relational sequences; they invite certain lines of action as opposed to others. In responding with one or another line of action, the recipient bestows on the initial action one potential form of meaning as opposed to many other possibilities. Thus, the comment, 'Chuck, I think you will find this interesting', invites or makes possible the reaction, 'OK, I'll take a look', which reaction grants the comment meaning as an invitation to share information. However, the equally plausible reaction, 'Yeah (eyes rolling), I bet' positions the utterance in a different way, generating a sense of its meaning as manipulation.

On this account lectures and books have no meaning until students grant them this privilege. Further, neither lectures nor books can determine the meaning which will be assigned to them. They open a variety of alternatives from which different students are likely to select differentially. Through feedback and evaluation, the teacher may narrow the range of alternatives – moving students toward 'approved' sequences. However, feedback and evaluation stand in the same position as lectures and books – subject to a multiplicity of supplements over which they have no determinative control. With these orienting suppositions in place, we are positioned to explore several significant corollaries.

Indeterminacy

Intelligibility is never complete. Any established meaning stands open to infinite re-signification. There is no single point at which the process of generating intelligibility is consummated. There is no fixing of the word, as it were, such that we can ensure what it is a lecture or text will mean – even if the student masters the appropriate supplements within the local scenarios of the school. As time and conversations proceed, the 'true and the beautiful' of today's class can be revisioned as 'trite' or 'ideologically suspect', and today's subject of scorn can turn fascinating. To be sure, we often treat intelligibility as a *fait accompli*. 'That is the correct answer', 'I understand you perfectly' and 'His writing is so clear' are ways of signalling the full achievement of meaning. Yet, these are only frozen moments in a continuing conversation, which realizations may at any time be rescinded ('I thought you had the correct answer until I read further'), and which themselves stand open to further signification by the speaker or others ('You say you understand me but I doubt it').

Polyvocality

As interlocutors enter new relationships and attempt to create intelligibility together, they will rely on preceding practices of making sense. And, because they have typically been party to multiple relationships, scattered over time and circumstance, so will they import into the present a substantial vocabulary of words and action. In effect, we enter each relationship as polyvocal – carrying with us numerous voices appropriated from the past. Any given sentence may thus represent a pastiche of past utterances, cobbled into coherence and set afloat in an uncharted sea without fixed destination. At the same time, by dint of tradition or circumscribed history of interchange, meaning making in any given relationship will tend to reduce the range of usable resources. In French language courses, one's dependency on English will slowly vanish; courses in psychology will invite students to relinquish the common discourses of free will, spirit, and moral responsibility.

Contextualization

The relational generation of meaning employs much more than the words and actions of the interlocutors. Their coordinations will frequently employ objects of various kinds and will always take place within specific material conditions. Thus, the discourse of baseball will not only be interdependent with patterns of action, but with objects such as bats, gloves and balls. And these patterns of coordination will be facilitated and delimited by a playing field. Or, with Wittgenstein (1953), our language games take place within *forms of life*. In this sense, each form of life may contribute to the resources imported by the individual into any new relationship. One doesn't enter merely as polyvocal, but as poly-potentiated in terms of capacities for insinuating objects or calling forth contexts with which to construct meaning in any given relationship. The richer the range of such capacities for coordination, the more flexible and effective persons may be as they enter the ceaseless challenge of the new and novel. More metaphorically, life may approximate a series of jazz concerts in which a continuous array of new partners and venues requires improvisation without end.

Pragmatics

The relational view developed here not only contrasts with the traditional view of language as an outer expression of an inward state, but also with the broadly shared assumption that language can serve as an accurate 'picture' or 'map' of the world (that it can 'tell the truth'). Rather, language chiefly functions as a constitutive feature of relationship. In the same way that lovers may require a vocabulary of emotion in order to create a scenario of romantic love, so does a laboratory team in neuroendocrinology require such terms as hypothalamus and amino acids to coordinate themselves around experimental procedures. In neither case, in love nor neuroendocrinology, does the language picture or map a world outside itself; rather, the language functions as an essential element of doing love or laboratory research (much like smiles and embraces in the former case and assays and journals in the latter). From this perspective we are also able to glimpse the importance of evaluating educational practices in terms of pragmatic implications. In what degree are various discourses of the academy embedded within or relevant to broader patterns of cultural action; what are the pragmatic potentials of the forms of life to which students are exposed in our schools? Before turning to specific issues of practice, however, it will be helpful to examine differences among competing characterizations of construction.

Varieties of construction

Constructionist ideas have taken many forms over time and been used in quite different ways. For example, in their classic work Berger and Luckmann (1966) use social constructionism to represent a particular form of social phenomenology, linked to a structural conception of society. While their concern with the social basis of knowledge remains robust in the present account of constructionism, the assumptive base has been radically altered. Neither phenomenology nor social structural views remain. Similarly, the term constructivism has been used by a number of different theorists, and the term figures in George Kelly's (1955) constructivism in ways that are not fully consistent with those of von Glasersfeld (1988) or Piaget (1954). Because views of construction have played an important role in more recent deliberations on pedagogy, it will prove useful to explore the differences between social constructionism as outlined above and two alternative orientations: *radical constructivism* and *social constructivism*.

The radical constructivism of von Glasersfeld is strongly influenced by Piagetian theory and has much in common with cognitive orientations to education in general. However, unlike cognitivists (who ironically remain wedded to an empiricist view of science), constructivists share with social constructionism strong misgivings with exogenic epistemology and its strong emphasis on knowledge as an accurate reflection of the world. Each questions the view of knowledge as something 'built up' within the mind through astute observation. And thus, each questions the authority traditionally accorded to those who claim truth beyond anyone's standpoint. However, beyond these affinities are also differences of substantial significance. For, as should be clear from the foregoing, radical constructivism does subscribe to a mind/world dualism and places its stake in cognitive (endogenic) process. In von Glasersfeld's (1988) terms, 'Knowledge is not passively received either through the senses or by way of communication, but is actively built up by the cognising subject' (p. 83). Knowledge is not thus a reflection of the world as it is. Rather, as Richards and von Glasersfeld (1979) put it:

> We redefine 'knowledge' as pertaining to invariances in the living organism's experience rather than to entities, structures and events in an independently existing world. Correspondingly, we redefine 'perception'. It is not the reception or duplication of information that is coming in from outside, but rather the construction of invariances by means of which the organism can assimilate and organize its experience. (p. 40)

This account of knowledge is so fully interiorized that it begins to offer the constructivist a means of escaping the charge of dualism. That is, by staking the entire epistemology on an account of the interior, the 'exterior' can be erased from concern and the theory can be viewed as monistic. Yet, to escape a Scylla of dualism in this way confronts the theory with an equally perilous Charybdis, that of a self-defeating solipsism. For if each of us is simply locked into our own experience, constructing the world as we may, then all that we take to be 'the world', all that we believe to be 'other persons' are simply the products of our own design. I simply make up the idea that there is a world, and that there are others in it who possess minds. There is no account, then, of how we manage to get on in the world or, indeed, whether there is even a world which challenges our adaptive capacities.

This is an unfortunate cul de sac for an epistemologist, and von Glasersfeld scarcely wishes to remain there. Thus, to avoid the problem of solipsism, a pragmatic dimension is added to the theory. As von Glasersfeld (1988) writes, 'The function of cognition is adaptive and serves the subject's organization of the experiential world' (p. 83). Or again, 'Radical constructivism is unashamedly *instrumentalist* . . . The concept of adaptation intended here is the basic biological concept in the theory of evolution. It refers to the *fit* with the environment . . . ' (p. 87). Yet, to sustain this position requires two admissions. First, that there is a real world that is separate from one's experiences of it – thus reasserting the dualist assumption. Second, an endogenic account of knowledge is insufficient; it must be supplemented by an exogenic concern with the real world to which the individual adapts. Yet, the latter admission propels the theory once again into the spiral of problems outlined above. How, for example, can one determine what actions are adaptive except through the private experience of construing? Can one be mistaken in his/her assessments of what is adaptive? How could this be determined? On what grounds could the radical constructivist defend his/her position?

These problems are exacerbated when the constructivist attempts to account for communication. As von Glasersfeld (1988) posits, 'the meaning of signals, signs, symbols and language cannot be anything but subjective' (p. 88). Yet, how could one go about determining in the first place that others' possessed subjectivities, that their actions were indeed attempting to communicate these subjectivities, that certain actions communicated subjectivities while others did not, or the linkages between the other's specific actions and a specific array of subjective states? In effect, the individual would be left roaming his/her own private and subjective world, hoping that just somehow, communication was occurring. The dim possibilities for anything approaching genuine communication are recognized by von Glasersfeld. As he surmises, ' . . . at best we may come to the conclusion that our interpretation of their words and sentences seems compatible with the model of their thinking and acting that we have built up in the course of our interactions with them' (p. 90). As a 'best', one might wish for more. For further critical discussion of constructivist orientations to knowledge and education see Phillips (1997) Shotter (1995), Olssen (1996), and Osborne (1996).

In many respects, social constructionism finds a much closer ally in works that can be termed *social constructivist*. By social constructivism we mean to delineate a body of work in which both cognitive processes and the social milieu are pivotal. Vygotskian formulations and other action theories are exemplary (Holzman, 1997; Kozulin, 1998). Social constructivism would also be represented in the educational work of cultural psychologists (Colte, 1998; Seeger et al., 1998; Wertsch and Toma, 1995), and is exemplified in much of the recent writing of Jerome Bruner (1996). Social constructionism is quite congenial with such inquiries in the importance placed on the social sphere. In a certain sense, both look at human knowledge or rationality as a byproduct of the socius. In both cases, the relationship precedes the individual. And, while the specific role of the teacher is different, both view the relationship between teacher and student as pivotal to the educational process.

In spite of these convergencies, however, for constructionists the social constructivist orientation still remains tied to a dualist epistemology and all the philosophical problems that it inherits. The epistemological riddles remain about how external and internal reality are connected. It is in this same vein that the social constructivist will often make mental as opposed to social process a major point of inquiry. A social constructivist would thus find uninteresting, if not obfuscating, a theoretical statement such as 'The chained complex (in the child's movement toward the mastery of concepts) is constructed in accordance with the principle of a *dynamic, temporal unification of isolated elements in a unified chain, and a transfer of meaning through the elements of that chain.*' (Vygotsky, 1978, p. 139). In contrast, social constructionist writings will focus on discourse, dialogue, coordination, conjoint meaning making, discursive positioning, and the like (Bruffee, 1993; Walkerdine, 1997; Wortham, 1994).

Finally, there is a strong tendency for the social constructivist to remain tied to empiricist tenets of value neutrality. Empirical demonstrations are typically used to ground central concepts, but without the kind of political and ethical reflexivity that the constructionalist would favour. For the social constructionist, the pragmatic implications of both theoretical interpretation and methodological implementation are critical considerations. Nevertheless, in their concern with the relational character of the learning process, constructionists and social constructivists are quite allied.

Educational policy and pedagogical practice

We have glimpsed several problems inherent in traditional conceptions of knowledge and have scanned the rudiments of a social constructionist alternative. The challenge now remains of exploring the implications for educational policies and practices. Before doing so two caveats are required. First, there is no attempt in what follows to abandon traditions of longstanding. As stressed in previous chapters, constructionism makes no claims to being a first philosophy, a foundation upon which a new world may be erected. There is no attempt to replace all traditions in the name of truth, ethical principle, political vision or any other universal criterion. Rather, the hope is to augment and expand on existing resources in the service of planetary well-being. This point is closely related to another: there are no policies or pedagogies that cannot be understood through the lens of social constructionism. All traditional practices – for good or ill and with varied efficacy – serve to construct worlds of the real and the good. In effect, all make a certain contribution to the sea of intelligibility. The central question is whether the implications of a specifically constructionist consciousness can open promising new avenues of departure. In this vein we shall also find that many existing innovations are congenial to a constructionist intelligibility. However, as their affinities are articulated we also locate new horizons of possibility. Let us explore five domains of particular relevance.

From hierarchy to heterarchy

Consistent with traditional views of knowledge as cumulative (exogenic) and universal (endogenic), educational institutions are built around what Friere (1985) calls a 'nutritionist' model. The model is essentially hierarchical, with the ultimate authority residing in the communities of knowledge-production. Typically these are experts in the field, like scientists and scholars. Thus, experts discover or reveal the truth that students will ultimately be taught – or 'fed', in Friere's terms. Next within the hierarchy are educational experts such as curriculum designers, who package the knowledge into educational units. Following these are administrators and bureaucrats who select among these units. Teachers enter at the end, as instruments to dispense the educational nutrients to the students. Students are expected merely to consume the knowledge.

Despite widespread criticism of this model, it continues to describe educational practice disturbingly well. Apple (1982) and others have documented the hierarchical processes through which educational content is produced and passed on to teachers. Mehan (1979) and others have shown how students remain generally passive and are expected merely to absorb the knowledge presented. In several significant ways, social constructionists add dimension to such critique. At the outset, constructionists see all claims to knowledge as embedded within particular communities of meaning making. As a result, various bodies of knowledge will inevitably favour particular visions of the good, for example continuous improvement in conditions (perfectibility), materialism over spiritualism, 'reason' over 'emotion', individualism over collectivism. In this sense a hierarchy of knowledge functions in a totalitarian way. Or in Foucault's terms (1979a, 1980), the dissemination of knowledge expands relations of power in which the user ultimately serves as pawn.

On a more subtle level, the constructionist finds the hierarchical model wanting in its tendency to suppress the contextual and pragmatic conditions that give authoritative language its significance. From the constructionist standpoint, 'knowledgeable propositions' gain their meaning within particular contexts of usage and function as a means of coordinating action within these contexts. Knowledge of chemistry, for example, serves to unite a community, to define and grant value to particular projects and identities and to help in generating outcomes of importance to this community. Yet, in the hierarchical model, the knowledgeable propositions are stripped away from this context. Educators extract bodies of discourse (and a limited number of instantiations) from the professional disciplines and pass these extractions on to those beneath them in the hierarchy. The pragmatic function of these discourses within the communities themselves is lost. The discourses lose their significance and students are often left with a promissory note that *somehow* their studies are useful and important. One may, then, learn the chemical tables and perform abstracted laboratory experiments. But the vitality of the language, its practical significance and its life-giving potentials in a relevant community of action are obscure. The epithet of 'irrelevance' gains increasing credibility.

Further, because the authoritative discourses are treated as sacrosanct – the products of 'our best minds' – they tend to travel the hierarchy in insular fashion. That is, they do not move from communities of administrators, to teachers, to students as invitations to 'take away'. The recipients may clarify, order and package, but the authoritative discourses remain, too frequently, intact. Students enter the realm, approximate its ways and then exit. The result is that the authoritative discourses are not easily appropriated for use in exterior realms of life. One cannot easily employ the argots of physics, economics, experimental psychology or algebra in cultural life more generally because their meanings are so fully tied to a specific domain of academic usage. In this sense, the professional discourses operate paramorphically, not so much altering existing forms of conduct in the world, as co-existing in relative isolation.

In addition to problems of power and decontextualization, constructionists point to the problematics of monologic vs. dialogic processes of meaning making. The recipient of a monologue – as in the case of authoritative knowledge – is denied a voice of his/her own. The endpoint to be achieved by monologic education is a student who has fully absorbed that which has been presented – or, in effect, becomes a simulacra of the authority. Whatever talents, insights or specialized education the individual possesses finds little entry into the conversation. And with the denial of voice comes an obliteration of identity and an invitation to lethargy. It is in this vein that Wise (1979) has described how academics and governments impose curricula and methods on schools that largely silence the teacher. Apple (1993) elaborated this analysis in discussing how the standardized curricula imposed on teachers deskill them. Because teachers are treated as technicians, and asked merely to implement prefabricated plans, they lose their capacity to reflect on the larger educational issues and to develop their own solutions. As Aronowitz and Giroux (1991) report, 'many of the [contemporary] educational reforms appear to reduce teachers to the status of low-level employees . . . whose main function is to implement reforms decided by experts in the upper levels of state and educational bureaucracies' (p. 33).

Others similarly argue that the hierarchical model 'deskills' the student. Jackson (1968) has described how the hierarchical relationships in schools discourage creativity and innovation among students. Wood (1988) and others have extended this analysis, arguing that students are shaped 'to take their place unthinkingly in a world that operates beyond their control with no respect for their needs' (p. 174). Once we attend to the relational aspects of knowledge production, we can also see that deskilling does not happen equally to all social groups. Rather, because professional knowledge is largely spawned within a particular segment of the society more generally (predominantly white, English-speaking, upper-middle-class male) its discourses are more meaningful (cohesion building) within this context than others. Students confronting these discourses from other sectors of society may find them remote and irrelevant. It is in this vein that we can appreciate the critiques of Apple (1982), Friere (1985), Walkerdine (1998) and others who describe how certain historically underprivileged groups – because of their ethnicity, gender and class – disproportionately suffer under the traditional educational system.

Given the inherent problems of authority-based knowledge, what alternatives are suggested by the constructionist? The present analysis first calls for a de-sacralizing of professional knowledge. Rather than presuming that the traditional knowledge makers provide 'the best' or 'last' word, let us realize that all claims to knowledge grow from culturally and historically situated traditions. This is not to deny their value, but to realize that such values are also contingent. For example, knowledge of painting typically presumes the value of self-expression or aesthetics; knowledge of medicine presumes the value of curing what we deem to be illness. All such values are circumscribed and negotiable. Thus, rather than monologues to be mastered, we might think of the disciplines as offering resources that may or may not be valuable depending on a particular condition of life. By situating knowledge in this way we invite a shift from monologue to dialogue – from hierarchy to heterarchy. Others are invited into deliberation about the subject-matter, its value and relevance.

John Dewey (1916) once made strong arguments for viewing education as a germinating grounds for democracy. However, these views were put forward at a time when it was generally believed that knowledge was objective and politically neutral. From a constructionist perspective, all knowledge is perspectival and value saturated. Thus, to enter a domain of knowledge is to step into a particular form of life. Such entry is not in itself a step toward democracy; it is to acquire one voice at the possible expense of others. In this sense the present arguments lend strong support to current movements toward plurivocality in education, attempts to empower those who have traditionally been excluded from knowledge production. Beyer and Apple (1988), for instance, have argued that 'meaningful curriculum reform must occur within those institutions, and by those people, most intimately connected to the lives of students: teachers, administrators, students, and community members' (p. 6). Instead of seeing teachers merely as technicians trained to dispense authoritative knowledge, many wish to enhance the role of 'teachers as curriculum makers'. For example, 'action research' projects train teachers to explore their own intuitions about educational processes (see, for example, Hollingsworth and Sockett, 1994). Rather than accepting experts' accounts of teaching and learning, teachers trained in action research gather their own data and address educational questions themselves. In many cases this results in more context-specific utilization of knowledge.

Yet, the process of curriculum making should also include students, parents and the community. Concerning students, Wood's (1988) proposal regarding educational curricula is relevant: 'In its content we (should) provide students with the tools to live a democratic life and the visions of what is possible in our shared social context. In terms of form, the curriculum should engage students in actual decision making in a shared community of equality and justice' (p. 184). Decision-making at the the Sudbury Valley School is illustrative: here a weekly school meeting, composed of all students and staff, deliberates on the day to day practices and policies of the school (Greenberg and Sadofsky, 1992). In another educational initiative, Claire Eiselen has established a supplementary curriculum for gifted students:

> Small groups begin each year with their teacher in an empty classroom. There are as yet no books, no papers, no curriculum. Nothing will enter the room except by way of a student's bringing it. The meaning of things comes from the people bearing and using them. The value of ideas comes in the same way. Ideas and imaginings emerge with the youth and some of these begin to coalesce into projects. Life together begins to need some guidelines. Small groups begin to construct these; larger groups can critique them. Meanwhile projects and ideas begin to proliferate and out of these a larger cultural whole slowly emerges. By the end of the year the room is packed with student-designed items that speak movingly of the human experience while emerging from their constructed culture within our own human community. The classroom looks like many issues of the UNESCO *Courier* enacted in one place. (Mary Fox, 1993, personal communication)

In conclusion, we may follow Lather's (1991) admonition that we abandon claims to universal knowledge fit for a general curriculum and move toward context-specific intelligibilities that include the concerns of all parties involved in the particular educational situation.

Beyond disciplines of knowledge

It is traditional to view the terms of our language as gaining their meaning by their links to specific, real-world referents. We have such words as 'lion', 'rabbit' and 'elephant' because we wish to distinguish between three different species of animals. However, for the constructionist, this picture of language is abandoned in favour of a use-based conception in which the meaning of words is traced to the active relationships in which they play a part. Thus, the meaning of the term 'aggressive' is not derived from a specific datum in the world, but from the linguistic contexts in which it is used by people to do things with each other (e.g. index action, assign blame, prepare a speech). Its meaning will thus change importantly depending on whether one is working with others to deploy troops, develop a business strategy or combat cancer cells. In the same way 'lion' may mean quite different things depending on whether one is speaking about jungles, the stars or a theatre performance. It is largely this polysymous character of words, their capacity to be used in multiple contexts of relationship, that both injects the language with flexibility and allows for the subtle nuancing of action in any given setting.

Over the last century there has been a concerted attempt to delineate fields of knowledge – chemistry, physics, history, and the like. Curricula of study are typically arranged so that students are exposed at least minimally to a variety of the separate fields and ultimately acquire in-depth understanding of at least one of them. However, from the constructionist standpoint, delineations in knowledge are useful primarily for those within a particular domain of study. They enable communities of knowledge-makers to generate achievements in the terms of their traditions. While education in these traditions has much to be said for it, educational processes circumscribed by disciplinarity are deeply problematic.

At the outset most issues of central significance to the culture are either tangential or entirely irrelevant to the existing disciplines of study. Disciplinary agendas are seldom set by national or local agendas; they tend to remain internal – honoured by the denizens within. Thus, the public tends to look with dismay at the work of 'eggheads', and the latter view with disdain the 'low level' of public deliberation. Unfortunately, it has only been slowly and sporadically that the traditional disciplines have made a contribution to national dialogues on abortion, social justice, environmental degradation, the mushrooming of Internet communication, social conflict, gay and lesbian issues, welfare and medicare reform, and so on. When scholars speak out on such issues they are often criticized by their peers for 'selling out,' 'popularizing,' or 'seeking attention.' Yet, as Usher and Edwards (1994) put it, 'disciplines as systematic bodies of knowledge are also regulatory regimes . . . through which power is exercised.' (p. 93).

To the extent that education is about enhancing the quality and efficacy of public deliberation and action, there is much to be said for curricula released from the demands of disciplinarity. In pre-professional education a premium may be placed on liberating the discourses and practices from their disciplinary lodgements. In a Wittgensteinian vein disciplinary discourse may be invited on holiday. Issues of practical public (or private) concern may set the agendas for education. As students confront major issues of the times, they would not be constrained by the tools of a constricted subject-matter. Rather, they would be free to roam across whatever domains are necessary in terms of their goals – ransacking, borrowing, extricating, annexing, combining, reformulating and amalgamating in any way necessary for the most effective outcome. Students working on a problem of local water pollution, for example, might find they require statistical methods, a handful of ecological concepts, historical sources, and a poem for rhetorical impact. As the various vocabularies of relationship are opened for continuous reconstitution, so are we optimally positioned for efficacy across rapidly changing conditions.

Concretizing this view, the Departments of Education in the states of both Connecticut and Maryland (see Baron et al., 1989) have attempted to transform the means of student assessment in grades 9–12. In particular, the aim has been to shift emphasis away from mere regurgitation of accumulated facts (favoured by the 'mind as slate orientation'), and to gear assessment to the means by which students utilize and combine multiple skills in newly challenging contexts and communicate their conclusions to others. Thus, students may work individually or in groups to solve complex, multi-step problems, collect data, analyse, integrate, interpret and report their results to real audiences. As the educators see it, such tasks allow students to 'construct meaning and structure investigations' for particular audiences. The teaching emphasis thus shifts from preparing students for mere repetition of the regimented and standardized discourses to developing skills for confronting complex and ever-changing circumstances outside the educational sphere. These arguments for 'authentic assessment' – related to skills actually needed in the world more generally – are closely related to an emphasis on meaning in practice.

Towards meaning in practice

By traditional accounts, education functions to produce knowledgeable individuals, who either by dint of what they know and/or their rational abilities are equipped for effective action in whatever situations life has to offer. Education is for purposes of mastery and storage of knowledge; subsequent life provides the conditions for its use. Paulo Friere (1972) has voiced one of the most stinging critiques of the resulting mode of education:

> The teacher talks about reality as if it were motionless, static, compartmentalized, and predictable. Or else he expounds on a topic completely alien to the existential experience of the students. His task is to 'fill' the students with the contents of his narration – contents which are detached from reality, disconnected from the totality that engendered them and could give them significance. Words are emptied of their concreteness and become a hollow, alienated, and alienating verbosity. (p. 57)

As advanced above, language acquires its value largely from the way in which it is used by people in specific contexts. The challenge for the educational process, then, is not that of storing facts or theories in individual minds, but generating contexts in which discourse and practice are united, contexts in which dialogues may be linked to the ongoing practical pursuits of persons, communities or nations. In effect, the constructionist would favour a substantial reduction in canonized curricula in which students are required to take courses because they are prerequisites for other courses or a degree. Too seldom is the course material linked to an immediate and practical context of usage, and too often the course material is applicable only within the rarefied and delimited atmosphere of the educational system. Rather, the constructionist would favour practices in which students work together with teachers and others to decide on issues of importance and the kinds of activities that might best allow significant engagement. For example, if students are concerned about ecology, racial tension, abortion, drugs, the rock music industry, the demands imposed by the fashion industry, forms of self-expression and so on, can projects be developed that will generate requisite skills? Can they interact with those engaged in these domains, collect relevant materials, read related books and articles, discuss with each other and ultimately formulate views that can be brought to the attention of parents, police, business leaders, government officials and the like? For the constructionist, then, educational dialogues should be wedded as closely as possible to the circumstances of application. Bruner (1996), has advanced a view of 'knowing as doing'. To this end he argues, that 'on the basis of what we have learned in recent years about human learning, (we do best) when it is particpatory, proactive, communal, collaborative, and given over to constructing meanings rather than receiving them' (p. 84). We are in full agreement.

But in other terms, why should education be preparatory to communal existence rather communal existence determining the contours of adequate education? Reading, writing, mathematics, and laboratory experimentation should not constitute hurdles to be jumped under threat of punishment. Nor are they building blocks for a good life at some point in a distant future. Rather, they might optimally serve as resources for ongoing dialogues and their associated practices. To possess books is much like having additional participants in the dialogue. Mathematics for example, would no longer be the odious medicine it is to many, and which they are forced to swallow even when they cannot articulate the sickness for which it is said to be the cure. Rather, mathematical techniques might become the needed tools for advancing a cause — determining significant perturbations in a phenomenon, assessing costs and benefits, reading demographic charts or effectively communicating the results of one's efforts to others.

To illustrate the possibilities, consider a programme of education carried out in a medical school in Limburgh, The Netherlands. Traditional medical training is premised on an exogenic view of knowledge, holding that practical engagement should await the 'filling of the mind'. Thus, three years of education may precede any significant engagement with the challenges of medical practice. Yet, in the Limburgh experiment the incoming student is immediately placed into apprenticeship with a practising doctor. As problems are encountered within the practical setting, they raise questions that the student cannot answer without inquiring into relevant resources (books, journals, statistical charts). As these resources are sought out and incorporated, the student gains further efficacy as an apprentice, only then to encounter further questions of practical significance which again send him or her back to the necessary resources. When operating at its best, the student is highly motivated to acquire information, and this acquisition is tied to specific contexts of usage. In this sense constructionism favours both community based learning programmes and apprentice processes of education (Rogoff, 1990).

Towards reflexive deliberation

As professional communities coalesce around visions of the real and the good, they tend toward insulation from that which lies outside their boundaries. It is not simply a matter of two cultures – sciences and humanities – but insulation among disciplines within the sciences and humanities and within sub-sectors of these disciplines. (For example, the American Psychological Association now lists over 50 sub-divisions, many of which have their own journals, professional meetings, reputational hierarchies, and so on.) Most important for present purposes, there is little means within a discursive community for questioning its own legitimacy – its strengths, weaknesses, limitations and suppressions. In the sciences, for example, one may easily question the validity of a given piece of research, but the value of research itself is scarcely a matter of debate. Further, there is little means of acknowledging the potentials of alternative world-views. For example, one trained in physiological research has little means of questioning the legitimacy of physiology as a form of truth or recognizing the benefits derived from alternative discourses outside this domain (e.g psychological, spiritual or aesthetic). In effect, physiological discourse (like all others) is self-referring and self-substantiating and in this sense fails to invite alternative forms of articulation into dialogue.

Consistent with the preceding emphasis on moving from authoritative monologue to dialogue in the educational setting, means are required for opening the authoritative languages to reflexive deliberation. That is, the authoritative discourses must be opened to evaluation from alternative standpoints, including both authoritative and informal. By exposing any professional discourse to the concerns of its peers – for example, by considering biological texts in terms of their dominant metaphors (literature) or literary texts in terms of implicit political ideals – we gain perspective on the strengths and weaknesses of the work in question and add dimension to subsequent dialogues. By exposing authoritative discourses to the local and informal standpoints of the community such discourses are again challenged and dialogue enriched. In all cases, the analyst may also gain insight into the strengths and limitations of the standpoint he/she brings to bear.

This concern with reflexive deliberation takes on added dimension in light of longstanding discussions of the 'hidden curriculum', a term referring to beliefs and values that schools teach implicitly. As the hidden curriculum argument suggests, all discursive practices carry with them an associated range of values and practices. Thus, to incorporate a professional discourse (and the modes by which it is taught) is also indirectly to absorb its implicate orderings for cultural life. For example, Bowles and Gintis (1976) have described how working-class students, in particular, are encouraged to be obedient, passive and unoriginal. Apple (1982) has discussed how the production of textbooks and other curriculum materials establishes the values and beliefs of certain groups as 'official' knowledge.

Aronowitz and Giroux (1991) argue that mainstream expectations system-atically exclude members of subordinate groups from academic success and reinforce and justify the values of dominant groups. Similarly, Beyer and Apple (1988) argue that, instead of producing citizens capable of articulating their own views on our collective life, schools produce workers prepared to subordinate themselves to others' judgments.

For most of those concerned with hidden curriculum effects, a strong emphasis has been placed on a pedagogy of critique. Critical reflection serves emancipating functions. Critique is most certainly to be welcomed; it is through this means that otherwise marginalized groups acquire confidence in their own positions. However, two problematic features of such reflexivity are noteworthy: first its exclusive emphasis on critique and second its dedication to liberation values. As proposed in Chapter 3, while critical reflexivity is imperative, it is also delimiting. Critique typically fails to credit the discursive communities under question with internal sensibility – with 'making good sense for good purposes' within their own terms. To presume the evil of the 'hidden curriculum' is to suppress the voices of those who embrace its values. By using critique alone, the potentials of such discourses and practices are suppressed and appro-priation for local purposes discouraged. From the relational standpoint developed here, critique must be supplemented by modes of appreciative inquiry. The point of reflexive deliberation is not to widen the chasm between cultural enclaves, but to enrich the forms of cultural life through processes of inter-weaving.

As also indicated, most critical analyses also favour an alternative, emancipatory agenda. For example, McLaren emphasizes the 'guiding referents of freedom and liberation' (1994: 201). Giroux (1992) argues that we must demystify the official and the hidden curriculum by revealing the evaluative choices implicit in them, and then explore alternatives to these mainstream beliefs and values. Aronowitz and Giroux (1991) argue that we must 'make a firm commitment to cultural difference as central to the meaning of schooling and citizenship' (p. 12), and must 'educate students for the maintenance and defense of the principles and traditions necessary for a democratic society' (p. 34).

From the present standpoint, while such commitments represent valu-able traditions within the culture, they also circumscribe the conversation. They too derive from authoritative communities of knowledge-makers and, thus, tend toward isolation, suppression and self-rationalization. For example, how is the educational process to accommodate those who do not believe in the equality of all voices – ranging from Orthodox Hindus or Catholics to those who would not 'spare the rod'? And what conception of equality should guide our decisions: an equality of opportunity, in which everyone gets a fair chance but those who fail are left behind; or an equality of outcome, in which everyone is guaranteed some degree of success? Facing such diversity, a liberation curriculum runs the same risks of hierarchy and suppression as those institutions under attack.

These limitations have scarcely gone unrecognized. Aronowitz and Giroux (1991) remind us that we should not paternalistically impose 'alternative' views on students and teachers. As Lather (1991) also points out, 'Too often, tied to their version of truth and interpreting resistance as "false consciousness," liberatory pedagogies fail to probe the degree to which "empowerment" becomes something done "by" liberated pedagogues "to" or "for" the as-yet-unliberated' (p. 105). From the present standpoint, there is no means by which a pedagogical practice can escape the criticism that it favours an ethnocentrically circumscribed vision of the good. There is no escaping traditions of relationship. However, because it is within relationships that conceptions of the good and true are generated, then the existence of difference invites the development of new forms of relatedness. That is, forms of interchange must be sought from which disparate groups can forge new and possibly more inclusive orders of the good. In addition to pedagogies of appreciation and critique, then, it is essential to develop modes of creative interchange, practices that will enable creative amalgams to replace conflict and hostility. We shall revisit this issue in Chapter 10.

Toward generative relationships

Traditional views of knowledge as 'within individual minds' favour a distinct division between the teacher and student. The teacher 'knows', and students are thrust into the position of objects to be operated on – minds to be filled with contents or rationalities. From the constructionist standpoint, the individual is not the possessor of contents or rationalities but, rather, participates in them. Knowledgeable and rational statements are not external expressions of the internal mind but are relational achievements. What stands as reason, memory, motivation, intention and the like are the result of coordinated action and negotiation within a community (Billig, 1987; Edwards and Potter, 1992; Myerson, 1994). For the constructionist educator, the primary challenge is that of contributing to generative relationships – relationships from which the student emerges with expanded potentials for effective relating. The student's role shifts from that of an object to be improved to a subject within relationships.

Explorations of relational process in the classroom are now substantial. For example, Edwards and Mercer (1987) have explored the shared meanings within a classroom and the challenge for teachers to make explicit the usually hidden or implicit ground-rules for what is being shared. A fine-tuned analysis of the jointly constructed worlds of teacher and student, especially within the context of assessment, is contained in Grossen's (1988) work. Wortham (1994) demonstrates the ways in which classroom interactions can be swept away by the particulars of the examples under discussion. Walkerdine (1997, 1998) explores the life of students as participants in the discursive regime of the school and demonstrates the capacity of the student for multiple positionings within the discourse. Still other inquiry enables us to see rational thinking as a process *distributed* among participants in a classroom (Salomon, 1996).

Most important, however, is the question of how the focus on relationship may enrich pedagogical process. Rather than a subject-matter or child-centred classroom, how would educational processes be constituted if relationships were primary? In this context one appreciates more fully the limitations of the lecture or teacher's monologic presentation. From the constructionist standpoint lecturers are primarily demonstrating their own skills in occupying discursive positions. While there is some gain to be achieved in furnishing students with models for playing out the role of authority, exposure to models is insufficient to enable them to do the same themselves. To face the issue more bluntly, the very processes necessary for the public production of authority are hidden from student view. The hours of preparation – the re-reading of texts, scanning of notes, exploration of new resources, discussions with colleagues, trial and error presentations in preceding contexts (all of which may be necessary for a consummate lecture) – are essentially removed from student view. Such removal is essential, of course, in sustaining the myth of authority as an individual possession – 'my lecture demonstrates the superiority of *my* mind'. However, these preparatory actions are all immersions within ongoing dialogues within the field, and what one says on the podium are simply localized manifestations of these dialogues. To obscure this range of preparatory participations is not only to sustain a problematic myth, but it is to deny access to the very kinds of processes in which students must engage if they themselves are to communicate with efficacy.

As we shift from the individual to the relationship as the centre of focus, we can again appreciate the work of social constructivists on processes of teacher-assisted learning, semiotic apprenticeship and relations in the zone of proximal development (Becker and Varelas, 1995; Kozulin, 1998; Larochelle, Bednarz, and Garrison, 1998; Wood, Cobb, and Yackel, 1995). All locate the site of learning within the relational matrix. However, perhaps the most visible outcome of constructionist thinking thus far is the emergence of collaborative or cooperative learning (Bleich, 1988; Sharan, 1990). As Kenneth Bruffee (1993) puts it, collaborative learning is a process in which the ongoing exchange among students serves as the primary educational medium. One learns through engaging, incorporating and critically exploring with others. Ideally, through social interchange skills in articulation and responding are developed and new possibilities of world construction are opened. Learning becomes a 'shift in our language-constituted relations with others'. In one inventive display of collaborative learning, author Ken Kesey worked with his creative writing class of 13 students at the University of Oregon to write and publish a collective novel, *Caverns* (Penguin Books, 1989). In other contexts, much the same logic has lead to the production of book-like products (including computer files, video cassettes, films, pamphlets), which themselves can stand as inputs to other groups (parents, city government, community members) or classes. In the same motif, class groups work together in developing positions in a debate, materials to use in teaching others, or communiques to like-minded students in other parts of the world.

Yet, collaborative inquiry may be viewed as but a beginning of exploration into the enormous potential of relationship-centred education. We are thus enriched, for example, by inquiries into forms and potential of dialogue in the classroom (Barbules, 1993; Wells, 1999) and by explorations into the importance of the friendship in teacher–student relations (Rawlins, 2000). Much to be welcomed is also an expansion of the concept of relationship to include more than the social relationships within the class. It is here that the pedagogical innovations fostered by the social constructivists can play a particularly important role. Inspired by Vygotsky's work, the concept of relationship is expanded to include the various tools and physical materials encountered in the educational process. However, there is no principled boundary to the perimeters of relationship. Already we have commented on relationships between the school and community and national agendas. We are only beginning to appreciate the horizons of a fully relational education.

In conclusion

While often contentious, there is nothing within these arguments that favours wholesale abandonment of traditional educational practices. All practices construct the world in their own way, carry values of certain sorts and lend themselves to certain futures at the expense of others. What is being proposed is an alternative to traditional epistemology, one that opens new possibilities for practice. As proposed here, a social constructionist view of knowledge argues strongly for greater democracy in negotiating what counts in educational practice, the local embedding of curricula, the breaking of disciplinary boundaries, the lodgement of disciplinary discourses in societally relevant practices, educational practice in societal issues and a shift from subject and child centred modes of education to a focus on relationships. Many of these emphases are not new to the dialogues on education. And in this sense social constructionism lends strong support to certain existing initiatives. However, in our view we have yet to open the door to the full potentials of a constructionist epistemology.

8

THE ETHICAL CHALLENGE OF GLOBAL ORGANIZATION

In many respects the chaotic crush towards global organizing can be viewed with alarm. In previous centuries it was only the emperor, the Pope, the king or the führer who possessed sufficient power and resources to imagine globalization – the possibility of extending indefinitely the perimeters of influence, ownership, imprimatur and/or self-aggrandizement. With the twentieth-century development of low-cost technologies of communication and transportation, the potential for globalization has become available to virtually all – from youth activists in Tiananmen Square and the winemaker in rural Argentina, to the paper towel manufacturer in a small city. Because of essential needs for an expanding market and low-cost labour and materials, the most aggressive thrust toward globalization has, of course, been that of the business community. And it is the multinational corporation, in particular, that has been subjected to the most intense critique. Globalized business expansion has been variously excoriated for its exploitation of foreign workers (women and children in particular), ruthless destruction of natural resources, disregard for the safety of its working conditions and products, marketing of inessential products and its destruction of local cultures. For a chorus of critics, multinational corporations have been singled out as worst-case examples of ethical consciousness (see Lavipour and Sauvant, 1976; Levitt, 1970; Tavis, 1982; Tugendat, 1972; Vernon, 1977).

Such criticisms have scarcely gone unanswered. Defenders point to the effects of the multinationals in increasing employment opportunities for thousands of otherwise impoverished peoples, creating an entrepreneurial infrastructure in Third World nations, contributing to the democratization of otherwise autocratic nations and even contributing to the end of apartheid in South Africa. Further, in the mushrooming of international voluntary organizations (Cooperrider and Dutton, 1999), commentators point to the potential of globalization for altruistic and life-giving ends. However, much of the argument on behalf of globalization, and particularly in the corporate sector, has remained defensive. Strong attempts are made to generate ethical guidelines and to avoid undesirable publicity (through the development of public relations offices). But the general posture remains one of quiet reserve towards the ethical dimension of globalized expansion.

In the present chapter I wish to open discussion on what I see as a far more promising potential for global organizations. Rather than the apologetic and defensive postures of the past, I believe the time is at hand for global organizations to nurture the potential for ethical leadership. An enormous lacuna in ethical leadership now exists on the international level. I believe that global organizations, and multinational corporations in particular, are now poised for assuming this role. To pursue this argument, I shall first consider the failure of other potential contenders for ethical inspiration. Then, I shall focus on the shift from modern to postmodern forms or organizing. As I shall argue, it is within the postmodern organizing process that we can locate the impetus for reconsidering the ethical potential of the global organization. The ethical potentials of postmodern-organizing are realized most particularly in *relational process*. Finally, I shall demonstrate the ethical potentials of such practices by drawing from recent work in a multinational pharmaceutical corporation.

The ethical challenge of globalization

It is first essential to place the problem of organizational ethics within the global context more generally. This précis will act as a prophylactic against any self-satisfying simplification of good and evil – for example, pitting malignant expansionists against innocent Third World cultures. More importantly, we shall find that the globalizing process itself thrusts issues of the good into unparalleled prominence. To appreciate these points it is important, first, to consider the social origins of ethical presumptions. Virtually any form of social organization embodies an internally shared ontology (a consensus view of 'the real') and ethical sensibility (quotidian commitments to what is collectively deemed worthy and desirable as opposed to improper or reprehensible). Agreements on the nature of reality and on the value of certain activities as opposed to others are essential for the very formation of organizational culture (Weick, 1995); without such agreements the organization would cease to be effective. More generally, beliefs in the good are community achievements (MacIntyre, 1984).

To the extent that organizations are fully integrated into local communities, organizational ontologies and ethics pose little problem. When community constructions of *is* and *ought* are fully reflected in the practices of its businesses, governmental offices, religions and so on the expansion and strengthening of these institutions simply contributes to the shared sense of the good within the community. However, as organizations expand into new territories, so is there a tendency for the reality within the organizational to deviate from the surrounding community. The organizational understanding of the good may come into sharp conflict with local understandings.

In these terms, globalization represents an enormous intensification of ethical conflict. As organizations expand into foreign locales, so do they import alien constructions of the real and the good. From their standpoint, their actions seem reasonable, even commendable; local traditions seem parochial, backward or even reprehensible (surely in need of change). From the local standpoint, however, the ways of life favoured by the globalizing organization often seem invasive, insensitive to local customs and community and even deeply immoral (consider the reaction of Muslim fundamentalists to many Western corporations and products). There is an important sense in which much of the invective directed against the multinational corporation is derived from just this condition – with the corporation evaluated by standards that are largely alien or differentially construed from within as opposed to outside the organization.

In these terms we do not find morally bankrupt organizations seeking world dominion; 'moral bankruptcy' is the epithet of the outsider. Rather, the problem is that of multiple and competing constructions of the good. And, without means of solving these conflicts, we face the problem of deterioration in relations, legal warfare and even bloodshed (consider the bombing of the World Trade Center, the murder of priests in Africa, the ransoming of business executives in Colombia and the Mafia assassination of Russian businessmen).

The problematics of principles and sanctions

From the present standpoint, we find that problems of ethical conduct are not essentially problems of malignant intention. We should not think in terms of the evil practices of the multinationals as against the purity of traditional culture (or vice versa). Rather, ethical problems result primarily from the clashing of community (or cultural) standards of action. As proposed, the rapid shift towards globalization invites an enormous expansion in the domain of ethical conflict. Under these conditions, what resources are available for adjudication, rectification or coordination? How are we to proceed? Perhaps the most attractive alternative is to articulate a set of standards or ideals to which all parties can (or should) aspire. This is the territory of philosophers, business ethicists and human rights specialists concerned with instilling universal goods or values. Yet I find little reason for optimism in this domain. At the outset, after two thousand years of moral philosophy, there is as yet no broad consensus – even in Western culture – on matters of the good. As MacIntrye (1984) characterizes such deliberation, it is both 'interminable and unsettleable' (p. 210). When such standards move across cultures, the conflicts are even more profound. For example, Western principles of women's rights generate harsh antagonism in Islamic culture. Under these conditions, who is legitimated to 'call the ethic' for all? Even multi-nation attempts to hammer out a universal slate of human rights have not been impressively successful. Not only are such platforms resented by governments feeling they are used to undermine their power, but abstract principles seldom dictate specific actions in concrete circumstances (see Gergen, 1994a).

Given the difficulties of establishing universal ethics, most problems of disagreeable conduct are simply treated legalistically. Thus, in the sphere of global organization, international trade commissions, international tribunals, United Nations policies and so on are typically used to prevent egregious violations of situated senses of the good. While such efforts have been useful, they are also limited. By and large, such sanctioning efforts are reactive; they are activated only when problems emerge. In this sense, they are always chasing demons already on the move. There is little opening for positive visions of the future. Further, they generate a schism between 'we' and 'them' – between ruling and assessing organizations on the one hand and those whom they judge. The result in the latter organizations is the emergence of a strategic sensibility: all actions are acceptable so long as they do not arouse the suspicions of the sanctioning body.

In the case of both moral principle and pragmatic sanction perhaps the major problem is that of extrinsic origin. That is, in both cases efforts towards the good originate outside the organization itself. The organization must instil the principles or act according to rules generated elsewhere. They must acquire a special disposition that is not inherent in the routinized activities of the organization itself. If a broadly shared sense of the good is to be achieved, the more optimal solution would lie in the internal practices of the organization – practices valued by the participants in terms of their own sense of mission. It is precisely this set of practices that are emerging in the transition from the modern to the postmodern organization.

Shortfalls of the modern organization

With the field of ethical conflict exponentially expanding, and attempts to instil ethical principles and legislate the good both found wanting, what other sources are available? It is here that I wish to propose that the globalizing organization itself may provide the most promising alternative. I am not speaking here of self-policing organizational policies, of the adoption of specific ethical codes of conduct for the globalizing organization. Such standards would inevitably be 'local', in the sense of representing internal conceptions of the good. Rather, I am speaking of forms of organizational practice which, indeed, are just those practices best suited to the viability of the globalizing organization. Such a proposal may initially seem ironic. After all, it is the globalizing process itself to which we have traced the problem of ethical conflict. However, as I shall hope to demonstrate, such conflict is largely derived from the expansion in a particular form of organization. Ultimately what is required is a transformation in the organizing process itself. Let us turn our attention, then, to contrasting conceptions of the organization.

As we shall discuss in the following chapter, there is now a voluminous literature on the changing nature of the organization in the twentieth century, with much of this commentary focused on the major transformations of recent decades. There are numerous ways of indexing these changes, with terms such as post-industrialization, the information age, chaos management and postmodernism among the more prominent. To sustain coherence with a number of previous offerings (Gergen, 1991; Gergen and Whitney, 1997) I shall use the term *modern* to refer to an ideal form of organization, approximated in varying degree by most major corporations (along with military, educational and governmental establishments) in Western culture for over a century. We may then refer to the emerging processes of organization as *postmodern*. In what follows, then, I shall briefly characterize major features of the modern organization, along with its vulnerabilities – both practical and ethical – within the context of globalization. This will prepare the way for a discussion of the ethical potentials of postmodern organizing.

In brief, the modern organization can first be characterized as hierarchical in form.[1] In the simple case, a single agent takes command (responsibility, control) over a group of subordinates. In expanded form, a policy-making committee, informed by subordinates responsible for collecting rele-vant information, dictates organizational action. In either case, directives flow from top to bottom, information (or feedback) flows in the opposite direction. In this sense, the organization is monological; a single, coherent rationale (strategic plan) dominates all sectors of the organization. The model is also individualist in orientation, with single individuals serving as leaders or followers, assigned responsibilities, subjected to evaluation and rising upwards in the hierarchy (or thrust out) accordingly. The organization itself is also framed in the individualist metaphor, with firm boundaries recognized between what is inside vs. outside the organization. Organizations themselves are typically viewed as locked in a competitive struggle for position in a hierarchy from which they may be discarded.

In the present context, it is also important to point out that the modern organization represents a major incitement to ethical conflict. Although modern organizations internally generate a shared sense of the good and a privately compelling justification for their policies, they do so in relative independence of their social surroundings. As the modern organization becomes globalized it essentially attempts to replicate itself (through its subsidiaries) throughout the world. The monologic rationality and ethical sensibility ideally prevails throughout. In effect, the organization potentially becomes an alien intruder that functions primarily to fortify (and justify) its own hegemonic ends.

It is not simply that the modern organization is flawed with respect to the ethical necessities of a pluralistic world. In my view, as the modern organization globalizes, its capacity for effective functioning is also diminished. In significant degree, such losses result from the availability of the very technologies that have made globalization possible. I refer here primarily of the twentieth century's advances in communication and transportation technology. Through such innovations as the telephone, video recording, the microchip, high-speed computers and satellite transmission, on the one hand, and massive highway systems, rail systems and jet transportation, on the other, it is possible to move information, opinions, persons and products across the globe with ever-increasing speed and efficacy. However, the global expansion of the modern organization is also accompanied by a range of new challenges and adjustments, each of which undermines its viability. Consider the following:

Dispersion of intelligibilities. As the organization expands, a strong tendency toward specialization occurs. The company is divided into functional areas; individuals are hired and evaluated as specialists in different domains (e.g. research, production, marketing). Differing specialties are housed in separate buildings and sometimes in different geographical locations. With further expansion, the organization is reproduced in miniature in other parts of the world. Within each segment, shared conceptions and values develop differentially. Most important, what is obvious, rational and valuable in one part of the organization is seldom duplicated in others. In effect, a multiplication of realities is generated, reducing the intelligibility and the rhetorical efficacy of the singular 'voice from the top'.

Disruption in chains of authority. Because there are few decisions within a functional domain that do not impact on others, and because most major initiatives require the coordinated input from diverse functional specialties, increased reliance must be placed on cross-functional teams. The result is first a blurring of the modern organizational structure in terms of the orderly distribution of responsibilities. The clear assignment of responsibilities to individuals or distinctive functional units is subverted. Further, the command structure is undermined, as unit chiefs lose the power to control and evaluate the work of members operating in multiple-team contexts.

Erosion of rationality. With the availability of high-speed information transmission, information can be rapidly collected from a variety of sources and speedily transmitted across broad networks. Thus decision-makers are confronted with ever-increasing amounts of information relevant to various decisions. Because the organization is increasingly segmented, this also means that there is increasing differentiation in the sources of information available (e.g. economic, political, scientific, cultural). There are more 'kinds' of information to process. And, because information continuously accumulates, new factors are continuously identified and new developments continue to take place. The half-life of available information is reduced accordingly. Yesterday's statistics are all too often a summary of yesterday. Although statistics are the benchmarks most frequently used in strategic planning, few guidelines exist for evaluating when information is useful and when it has outlived its relevance. In effect, not only is reliance on a single centre of rational planning reduced, but the very concept of monologic rationality is thrown into question.

Reduction in centralized knowledge. The same technological advances stimulating global expansion of the organization also mean that centralized authority is progressively cut away from the context of decision-making. Subsidiary decision-makers are more intimately acquainted with the contexts in which they operate; their local knowledge base is richer and more fully nuanced. Further, windows of opportunity are suddenly and unpredictably opened (for example, by a local election, an invention, a shift in interest rates, a merger) and shut. As a result, decisions from a distance – from the spatio-temporal remove of headquarters – prove relatively slow and insensitive. Increased dependency must be placed, then, on local representatives to respond within the context of application.

Undermining of autonomy. Because the media are increasingly important as sources of public information, their power to shape an organization's future is substantially augmented. In effect, media professionals – news analysts, commentators, science columnists, news writers – operate as gatekeepers of national reality. Because their views are typically presumed to be unmotivated – and thus objective – they often seem more authentic than those issuing from the organizations themselves. In this way, organizations lose a certain capacity for autonomous self-direction. Their voice loses authority in the public sphere. Increasingly the views of outside opinion leaders must be taken into account prior to decisions, in effect giving such leaders power to shape the organization's future. The boundary between 'inside' and 'outside' the organization is blurred.

This erosion in autonomy is furthered by the fact that available technologies increase the capacity for various concerned audiences to identify themselves and their goals and to organize action. This is not only true in the case of political parties and governmental offices, but also for various groups which recognize the economic potentials in organizing (e.g. consumer and labour groups), and for various grass-roots interest groups (e.g. environmentalists, feminists, associations of retired people) who now take a keen political interest in global organizations. Not simply passive observers, such groups are actively engaged in information searches and public critique. In effect, the global organization is placed under unprecedented scrutiny, the effects of which may spill into the media at any time. Again, there is a diminution in the capacity of the organization for self-direction.

As we find, the technologies of globalization place the modern organizational structure in jeopardy – with the capacity of central authority to maintain intelligibility, command authority, act rationally, possess superior knowledge and make autonomous decisions all diminishing. As David Freedman (1992) summarizes the case: 'The traditional scientific approach to management promised to provide managers with the capacity to analyze, predict, and control the behavior of the complex organizations they led. But the world most managers currently inhabit often appears to be unpredictable, uncertain, and even uncontrollable' (p. 626). More generally, Bella and Jenkins (1993) observe, 'Highly complex organizational systems are beyond the capacity of any individual or group to grasp, much less control' (p. 170).

Relational process and the ethics of postmodern organizing

As I am proposing, the modern organization is particularly prone to incite problems of ethical conflict. At the same time the twentieth-century process of globalization is accompanied by a decline in the capacity of the modern organization to sustain itself. In effect, ethical conflict is proliferated by a form of organization that ceases to be functional. In this sense, organizations seeking to bolster top-down authority, to control local operations and to be increasingly self-determined are not only operating against their self-interests, but do so at a cost of ethical anguish. Given this condition, we now confront the challenge of envisioning practices of organizing that are at once beneficial for organizational functioning and ethically productive. Can we, then, elucidate processes of organizing that simultaneously benefit the organization and favour a globalized condition of ethical well-being?

It is here that we enter the sphere of postmodern organizational theory. As will be outlined more fully in the next chapter, this literature is undergoing robust development. It is premature to draw confident conclusions regarding ethical potentials. However, the central place occupied by social constructionist dialogues within the postmodern literature does provide some useful leverage. In particular, social constructionist analyses typically favour a situated stance concerning ethical premises. Thus, they stand as bulwark against any monologic articulation of the good. Simultaneously, constructionism places a strong emphasis on relationships as the font of both ontology and ethics. In doing so, the focus shifts from individuals or social structures to processes of ongoing interchange, processes we may characterize as *relational*. In the present context, I wish to propose a conception of *relational process* as a pivotal metaphor for achieving the dual ends of organizational sustenance and ethical well-being. Let us explore.

At the outset, an emphasis on relational process abandons two central features of the modern organization, namely the assumption of self-contained units and of structural solidity. From the relational standpoint, the primary emphasis is not on recognizable units (e.g. headquarters, subsidiaries, the marketing division) and their structural arrangements, but with continuous processes of relationship. By foregrounding relationship we call attention to the forms of coordinated activity from which the very conceptions of headquarters, subsidiaries and marketing division derive. In this sense, there are no single individuals, making autonomous decisions, but processes of relationship out of which actions that we index as 'decisions' become intelligible. An individual, then, is the common locus for a multiplicity of relationships. His/her intelligibility (capacity for reasoned action) is chiefly dependent on participating in processes of relational coordination.

To the extent that parties to a relationship continue to communicate, they will generate an internal domain of intelligibility (a sense of 'the true' and 'the good', as indicated earlier). Thus, as organizations become segmented in various ways – geographically, functionally, hierarchically – so do they generate multiple centres of meaning making. We may configure the organization, then, in terms of a range of *relational nuclei*, each striving to coordinate internal meaning. As internal meanings are stabilized, so is the internal efficacy of the nucleus enhanced. However, as its intelligibilities ossify, so is its capacity for coordination with other nuclei potentially reduced. From the relational standpoint a premium is thus to be placed on avoiding closures of intelligibility, that is, allowing any construction of the true and the good to become sedimented, or simply 'common sense'. Within the nuclei, multiple logics should be encouraged and a healthy appreciation for incoherent potentials prevail. Further, all decisions and policies may be construed as contingent, formalizations of 'the conversation at this moment'. In this way space remains for a continuation of the dialogue and a revisioning of policies and practices.

Finally, most important from the relational perspective, we see that the adequacy of a decision or policy does not rest on the intellectual capacity of the single decision-maker (or decision-making group.) Rather, maximal reliance must be placed on relational processes linking those responsible for the decision or policy to those who will be affected. This is not to recapitulate the modernist presumption that effective decisions should be based on information about target characteristics (e.g. attitudes, motivation, cultural habits, income). Rather, it is to say that 'the targets' should optimally join in fashioning the character of those decisions. The decision-making process, then, should be permeable, interactively embedded within the context of consequence. In effect, relational nuclei within the organization should be multiply enmeshed with other nuclei, engaged in dialogues in which multiple intelligibilities are shared, interpenetrate, modify, concatenate or act with critical reflection on each other. Similar processes of inter-interpolation should characterize relations with various 'target audiences' of concern to the organization.

Outlined here is a vision of the postmodern organizational process, one in which the chief emphasis is placed on relational process. However, we must finally return to our major challenge, that of envisioning globalizing organizations as positive ethical forces. Specifically, in what sense does relational process furnish a basis for ethical promise? On what grounds can it be argued that relational process is intrinsically ethical? The answer to this question can be traced to the earlier proposal that ethics themselves are communal creations; conceptions of the good emerge in the process of relationship. In this sense, an organization in which relational process of the present kind is pre-eminent is also one in which the generative conditions for ethical sensibility are continuously restored. That is, no preconceived conception of the good enters the relationship unchallenged; no voice of the good – developed from afar – remains inviolate. The pre-existing relations offer resources from which participants will surely draw; but the off-stage ethics are not binding within the new context. Conceptions of the good are thus in a state of continuous birth and rebirth within their specific and ongoing contexts of usage.

Towards ethically generative practice

What I am proposing here is essentially a shift from a conception of ethical principles from which proper practices are derived, to forms of *ethically generative practice* – practices that give rise to conjoint valuing and the synergistic blending of realities. By shifting the emphasis to practice, we avoid the endless contestation on the nature of the good, stripped from history and culture. There is no ethical a priori (from which, indeed, springs the very sense of the evil other). Rather, the focus is on developing relational practices which are themselves the sources of the communal sense of the good. Can we offer a blueprint for ethically generative practices, a set of activities that will guarantee the emergence of a collaborative sense of the good? In my view, such a temptation is to be avoided; for to do so would be again to close out the possibility for continuous dialogue. Every practice will necessarily favour certain groups, skills or traditions. Rather than articulating such practices in bold script, we might turn our attention to the locally and contingently effective.

In this context, I wish to share a number of 'stories' growing from extended work with a multinational pharmaceutical company. For several years Mary Gergen and I worked as consultants deliberating with managers around the world concerning optimal management practices for the future. In particular, we asked them to identity what they were now finding to be the most effective communication practices. Would such practices reflect the traditional or modernist conception of optimal communication (stressing centralized authority, top-down flow of policies and the upward flow of information)? Interestingly, the answer was almost univocally in the negative. Repeatedly we were told of management experiences that were relational in character, which emphasized dialogic process, multiple logics and permeable boundaries within organizational spheres and between the organization and its external context. It is this same set of practices that, in my view, possess ethically generative potential. Consider the following:

In one organizational restructuring project, top management avoided the usual 'independent study' of its operations by outside consultants and turned the task over to the organization itself. Fourteen teams, representing all sectors of the company, carried out broadscale interviews, met periodically with other relevant teams to explore the total operations of the company and deliberated on the demands and skills necessary for future success. Finally they all contributed to a seven-volume summary containing their research and recommendations concerning personnel reductions, training and the organization of work. A steering committee, headed by the CEO, eventually adopted some 75 per cent of the recommendations. In effect, virtually all sectors of the company were given voice in moulding the future of the company. The resulting restructuring met with broad approval.

The company was placed under sharp critical attack for its research on genetic engineering. An information campaign, mounted to inform the public of the positive effects of such research, did nothing to dissuade an increasingly vocal organization of dissenters. The company then shifted to a relational orientation, in which they proposed to the opposition that they work cooperatively to create a public exhibition informing the public of their diverse views on these complex and emotionally charged issues. After much active discussion, the various participants agreed on a set of informative exhibits that were subsequently displayed at a city cultural centre. The exhibition was praised for its balance and open design. Company representatives also felt there had been an informative exchange of opinions with the opposition; both sides had developed more differentiated and appreciative views and the public had been exposed to the multiple issues involved.

Pharmaceutical companies in general are placed under close and critical scrutiny by the press. Traditional company policy was to protect internal information and decisions against press intrusion and to plan information campaigns designed to sway the public through the press. However, the relationship thus spawned between the organization and the press was strategic and adversarial. The press became increasingly suspicious and critical. In two countries under study this policy was abandoned in favour of a collaborative relationship with the press. Press representatives were invited to attend decision-making meetings within the company; company representatives met frequently and informally with the press for exchanges of views and information. In both cases, the results proved highly satisfying; distrust and misunderstanding receded.

These several instances are only illustrative of practices with ethically generative potential. Consider as well the development of an international research team, in which young researchers from six nationalities devoted six days to work on issues of mutual understanding and respect; an Asia Pacific Workshop in which representatives of 14 countries met to hammer out business policies for the future; and a meeting of Eastern and Middle European Region representatives to consider future markets. Relational process was also evident in the company's communication with numerous 'target audiences'. In one initiative, for example, the company worked cooperatively with both international and local agencies to develop organ donor programmes; in another, a Third World subsidiary set up a programme to train youth for technical positions within the company.

Importantly, the result of many of these efforts has been an incorporation of outside values into the corporation itself. For example, rather than seeing ecology activists as a threat to profitable enterprises, the chemical division developed an internal programme dedicated to environmental protection; rather than simply letting unused drugs end up in landfills or in the hands of children, French managers took an active role in developing a drug recycling programme; and rather than viewing bioethics as an infringement on research rights, the company took an active role in championing an international policy of bioethics. In effect, external ethical concerns were now incorporated into company policies.

Conclusions

I am proposing here that the globalization of a particular form of organization, termed modern, furnishes the primary incitement to invectives of immorality. Yet, as we also find, the unlimited expansion of this organizational form is detrimental to its own existence. Ethical conflict and a deterioration in organizational efficacy are linked. However, as we scanned the postmodern terrain, we located a range of specifically relational practices that offered promise for both a reinvigorated organization and the coordination of world peoples. Both the instantiation and efficacy of such practices were illustrated in the work of a multinational pharmaceutical company. While there remain myriad questions, there is herein distinct hope for the globalization process. The relational practices of the postmodern organization may serve as a positive force for livable ethics in a multicultural world.

Note

1 See, for example, Berman (1982); Clegg (1990); Crozier, (1964); Frisby (1985); March and Simon (1958); see also Chapter 9 of the present work.

9

ORGANIZATIONAL SCIENCE IN A POSTMODERN CONTEXT

With Tojo Thatchenkery

There is broad agreement that within the Western world the greater part of the last century has been dominated by an interlocking array of conceptions that – retrospectively – may be termed *modernist*. These conceptions, in turn, are related to various techno-material conditions, undergird many forms of institutional life and inform a broad array of cultural practices – for example, within literature, art, architecture and industry. Analysts focus on differing aspects of this period, often using the term *modernity* to emphasize a composite of technological, economic and institutional features (Giddens, 1990; Jameson, 1984) and *modernism* to speak of intellectual and cultural patternings (Frascina and Harrison, 1982; Levenson, 1984). While opinions are widely varied, there is also a general recognition that this interrelated set of modernist beliefs is slowly losing its commanding sense of validity. This consciousness of disjunction is variously indexed by writings on the demise of the cumulative knowledge (Kuhn, 1970), the individual self (Ashley, 1990), coherent identity (Gergen, 1991), objectivity (Marcus and Fisher, 1986), behavioural sociology (Cheal, 1990), empirical psychology (Parker and Shotter, 1990; Sampson, 1989), literary understanding (de Man, 1986), and rational foundations of knowledge (Rorty, 1979). These and other works now provoke broad discussion on the pitfalls and potentials of life in a postmodern context (Gergen, 1991; Lyotard, 1984; Norris, 1990; Pfohl, 1992; Rosenau, 1992; Turner, 1990).

Drawing sustenance from Robert Cooper's (Cooper, 1989; Cooper and Burrell, 1988) volatile critiques of the systemic orientation of modern organizational theory, one pauses to consider organizational science itself. For the very theoretical suppositions under attack in Cooper's work are wedded to a body of interlocking beliefs concerning organizational science as a knowledge-generating discipline. If the theoretical premises are placed in question, so by implication are the metatheoretical commitments from which these premises spring. In the present offering we shall first consider prominent ways in which traditional organizational science is rooted in modernist assumptions, along with several major threats which post-modern thought poses for such assumptions. More importantly, given the waning of the modernist tradition, we must ask what postmodern thought can offer as an alternative conception of organizational science? Can we fruitfully move beyond critical and deconstructive impulses? As we shall propose, a constructionist consciousness, when properly extended, can yield a promising vision of future organizational science. After developing these arguments, we shall explore several significant implications and illustrate their potential.

Modernism and the formation of organizational science

To appreciate the emerging challenge, let us first isolate key presumptions underlying organizational science in the modernist frame. More broadly, this is to articulate a number of the constitutive beliefs that have defined the very character of organizational science – its major forms of research, theoretical commitments and its practices within the workplace. In effect, the implications of these beliefs have been evidenced in virtually every corner of the discipline – from the classroom, to the research site, forms of publication, theoretical content and the practices carried by specialists into organizations themselves. Although there is much to be said about science in a modernist mould, we shall confine ourselves here to several presumptions of relevance to future developments.

The rational agent

As most scholars agree, modernist thought and institutions have impor-tant roots in the Enlightenment (the rise from the 'dark' or 'medieval' ages), a period when the works of philosophers such as Descartes, Locke and Kant were giving sophisticated voice to emerging conceptions of the indi-vidual and the cosmos. Although history has furnished many significant detours (for example, nineteenth-century Romanticism), Enlightenment assumptions have continued into the last century, fuelled to new heights by various scientific and technological advances (attributed to Enlighten-ment presumptions), the growth of industry and prevalence of warfare (both of which increased society's dependency on science and technology) and various philosophic and cultural movements (e.g. logical positivism, modern architecture, modern music).[1]

The Enlightenment was a historical watershed primarily owing to the dignity which it granted to individual rationality. Enlightenment thinkers assailed all forms of totalitarianism – royal and religious. As it was argued, within each individual lies a bounded and sacred principality, a domain governed by the individual's own capacities for careful observation and rational deliberation. It is only *my* thought itself, proposed Descartes, that provides a certain foundation for all else. It is this eighteenth-century valorization of the individual mind that came to serve as the major rationalizing device for the twentieth-century beginnings of organizational science. The effects here are twofold: first, the individual mind of the worker/employee/manager became (and remains) a pre-eminent object of study; and second, knowledge of the organization was (and is) considered a byproduct of the individual rationality of the scientific investigator. On the one hand, if individual rationality is the major source of human conduct, then to unlock its secrets is to gain dominion over the future well-being of the organization. At the same time it is the individual investigator, trained in systematic rational thought, who is best equipped to carry out such study.

More explicitly, these assumptions have been realized in major conceptions of the individual and the organization emerging from organizational study since virtually its inception. For many scholars (see, for example, Clark and Wilson, 1961; de Grazia 1960), Taylorism provided the quintessential modernist model of organizational life. On the one hand it viewed the individual worker as a quasi-rational agent who responds to various inputs (e.g. orders, incentives) in systematic ways. Although shorn of the dehumanizing qualities of early Taylorism, this early orientation is congenial with programmes and practices of the 1960s–1970s, such as job enrichment, job rotation, job enlargement, job design (Hackman and Lawler, 1971) and management by objectives (MBO). More recently, planning-programming-budgeting systems (PPBS) and Total Quality Management (TQM) are often conceptualized as 'input-devices' used to derive the greatest output from employees.

Similarly, the belief in rational agency figures in the conception of the ideal manager, who should effectively plan, organize, coordinate and control the actions of organizational members. Contingency theories (Lawrence and Lorsch, 1967) reveal steps that the individual manager can take in order to create the optimal balance between the organization and environmental conditions. The field of strategic management similarly rests on the assumption of individual rationality (Thompson and Strickland, 1992). For example, expectancy theory (Vroom, 1964), the path–goal theory of leadership (House, 1971) and goal-setting theory (Locke, 1968) are all based on assumptions of individual rationality. The seminal work of Herbert Simon (1957) on 'bounded rationality' – while recognizing limitations in the human capacity to process information – is premised on the assumption of individual decision-making. Management education and training programmes are similarly developed to furnish managers with managerial competencies crucial to producing superior performance (Boytazis, 1982; Lobel, 1990).

In addition to informing the view of the individual worker and the function of the manager, the commitment to rational process has also shaped the contours of macro-organizational theories. It is this topic to which Cooper and Burrell (1988) have largely addressed themselves. As they point out: 'The significance of the modern corporation lies precisely in its invention of the idea of performance, especially in its economizing mode, and then creating a reality out of the idea by ordering social relations according to the model of functional rationality' (p. 96). They illustrate with the work of Bell (1974) and Luhmann (1976). Similarly, cybernetic and general systems conceptions – such as those championed by Boulding, Bertalanffy and Weiner – have contributed to the rational systems perspectives of organizational theory. As Shafritz and Ott (1987) point out, the systems orientation is philosophically and methodologically tied to Taylorism.

Finally, the belief in rational agency undergirds the self-conception of the organizational scientist and the view of his/her role *vis-à-vis* the organization. At base one could argue that organizational theory is the quintessential manifestation of rational thought – rigorous, logical, coherent – and this presumption grants to the professional theorist a heightened value. In the modernist *Zeitgeist* it is the most rational voice that should prevail in the interminable contest of opinions. And it is this implicit claim to reason that has largely provided the justification for organizational consulting: the consultant, by traditional standards, is (or should be) one who – by virtue of scientific training – thinks more clearly, objectively, profoundly and systematically than the layman and is thus deserving of voice within the organization. This logic is amplified by a second modernist belief.

Empirical knowledge

A second legacy of Enlightenment discourse is a strong emphasis on the powers of individual observation. It is reason, in combination with observation, that enables the individual's opinion to count on par with those of religious and royal lineage. This emphasis is played out most importantly in empiricist philosophy over the centuries and has surfaced most vigorously in the last century in forms of logical empiricist philosophy. For logical empiricists (see, for example, Ayer, 1940), only those propositions linked unambiguously to observables are candidates for scientific consideration, and it is only the careful testing of scientific propositions that can lead to increments in knowledge. Within the behavioural sciences these views not only became central rationalizing devices – placing the behavioural sciences, as they did, on equal footing with chemistry and physics – they also stimulated enormous interest in research methodology and statistics.

It is within this soil that organizational science took initial root. One presumed the existence of a concrete organization, an objective entity subject to empirical study. To illustrate, in the premier issue of *The Journal of the Academy of Management*, William Wolf (1958: 14) proclaimed that 'We can describe an organization as a living thing; it has a concrete social environment, a formal structure, recognized goals, and a variety of needs'. Similarly, in his widely cited *Modern organization theory*, Mason Haire (1959) discussed the 'shape' and other 'geometric properties' of an organization, arguing that organizations have bodily properties and growth charac- teristics typical of the biological world. This concrete character of the organization was also evident in Talcott Parsons' contribution to the first issue of *Administrative Science Quarterly* (1956). Here Parsons defined an organization as a 'social system oriented to the attainment of relatively specific types of goals, which contributes to a major function of a more comprehensive system, usually the society itself' (1956: 63). In the same issue of this journal, James Thompson (1956: 102), writing about the task of building an administrative science, placed the major emphasis on 'deductive and inductive methods . . . operational definitions . . . and measurement and evaluation'.

Within this context, it was the responsibility of the organizational scientist to work towards isolating variables, standardizing measures and assessing causal relations within the organizational sphere. Thus, for example, Pugh et al. (1963) proposed to analyse organizational structure in terms of six major variables; in his 'axiomatic theory of organization', Hage (1963) defined eight significant variables (e.g. complexity, stratifi- cation, efficiency, production effectiveness, job satisfaction). Warriner, Hall and McKelvey (1981: 173) have even urged researchers to formulate 'a standard list of operationalized, observable variables for describing organizations'.

At the same time, this celebration of observational process makes its way both into theories of the effective organization and to the positioning of the organizational scientist in the broader cultural sphere. In the former case, an array of organizational theories place a strong emphasis on the necessity for the organization to systematically gather information, facts or data for purposes of optimizing decision-making. Most early theories of rational decision-making, for example, were closely coupled with an emphasis on empirical fact. For instance, Frederick (1963) pointed to the necessity for linking statistical decision theory and other mathematical decision-making strategies to empirical inputs. Rational decisions – whether in organizations or in science itself – are 'primarily a function of available information' (p. 215). The emphasis placed on rigorous observation within the profes- sion, and its reinstantiation within its theories of optimal organizational functioning, also enhances the image of the organizational scientist within the culture. If observational techniques yield information essential to organizational well-being, and the organizational scientist is an expert in rigorous observation, then the scientist's voice is again privileged. By nature of his/her training, the scientist can be an essential aide-de-camp for the aspiring organization.

Language as representation

A third modernist text shapes the contours of organizational science. In comparison to the stories of individual rationality and empirical knowledge, it seems of minor significance. Yet, it is one that proves critical as we move to the postmodern context. The emphasis in this case is on the capacity of language to accurately represent the world, or in effect to 'bear the truth'. So culturally sedimented is the presumption of language as truth bearing that, until recently, it has scarcely been challenged. Its implicit presence, however, is everywhere apparent. At the outset, as organizational scientists we treat language as the chief means by which we inform our colleagues and our culture of the results of our observations and thought. We use language to report on the nature of the world insofar as we can ascertain its character through observation. And it is through observation of the world that we can presumably improve, emend or correct our theories. We may test hypotheses against nature and move ineluctably towards truth in representation. For the profession, words function as carriers of 'truth' or 'knowledge' – whether in journals, lectures, books or the business consultation.

This same belief in the capacity of language to represent the real, when coupled with the belief in reason and observation, also sets the stage for modernist understanding of organizational structure. The effective organization should be one in which various specialty groups generate data (observations) relevant to their particular functions (e.g. marketing, operations, human resources), the results of these efforts being channelled to higher-ranking executives who are informed so as to make rational decisions coordinating these various efforts. In effect, the emphasis on rationality, empiricism and language as representation favour both strong *divisions of labour* (specialization) and *organizational hierarchy* (see, for example, de Grazia, 1960; Rosengren, 1967; the early work of Rushing, 1967 and Thompson, 1960).

The faith in language as truth bearing, coupled with a reliance on reason and observation, also figures in the general assumption of progress in understanding organizations and, thus, of building more successful forms of future organization. If the nature of the objective world is made known through language, others can subject these findings to further test and as their results are again made publicly available (and so on) the inevitable result will be a march toward objective truth. On this view, scientists should acquire increasingly sophisticated knowledge about the nature of the world, be capable of increasingly precise predictions and ultimately be able to build fully effective organizations.

In the formative years of the science, Rollin Simonds (1959) gave voice to this progressive narrative in *The Journal of the Academy of Management*:

> As (the science of business administration) develops . . . there will be more and
> more stress on stating rather precisely cause and effect relationships and on

securing empirical data to substantiate or disprove these statements. Then the results of one investigation may be integrated with another until very substantial evidence is accumulated in support of a set of scientific principles. (p. 136)

In Bell's (1974) terms, modern (post-industrial) society is 'organized around knowledge for purposes of social control and the directing of innovation and change . . . ' (p. 20). Much the same view of scientific progress is projected into theories of organizational learning. Through continued learning the organization will become increasingly adaptive and prosperous.

The postmodern turn

The vast share of contemporary theory and practice in organizational science is still conducted within a modernist framework. However, across many branches of the sciences and humanities – indeed, some would say across the culture more generally – a new sensibility has slowly emerged. As outlined in earlier chapters, this sensibility is predominantly *critical*, systematically dismantling the corpus of modernist assumptions and practices. Such critiques not only threaten the modernist logics, but throw into question the moral and political outcomes of modernist commitments. Yet, while critique is pervasive and catalytic, it has not yet been restorative. While faulting existing traditions, it has left the future in question. How do we now proceed? The question lingers ominously in the wings. In our view, however, there lie embedded within certain forms of critique implicit logics of great potential. Criticism, too, proceeds from an assumptive base, and as its implications are explored, a vision of alternatives unfolds. In terms of positive potentials, we feel the most promising forms of critique are social constructionist in character. In what follows, we shall outline the nature of the critique and their implications for a constructionist vision of organizational science.

From individual to communal rationality

While a faith in individual rationality lies somewhere towards the centre of the modernist world view, postmodern voices turn sceptical. At the extreme, the concept of individual rationality is found both conceptually flawed and oppressive in implication. Its conceptual problems are demonstrated most clearly in the case of literary and rhetorical movements.[2] In major respects, these movements are pitted against the modernist assumption that rational processing lies 'behind' or guides one's 'outward' behaviour. The site of critique in this case is language, which for the modernist furnishes the most transparent expression of individual rationality. As semioticians, literary deconstructionists and rhetoricians propose, language is a system unto itself, a system of signifiers that both precedes and outlives the individual. Thus for one to speak as a rational agent is but to participate in a system that is already constituted; it is to borrow from the existing idioms, to appropriate forms of talk (and related action) already in place. Or, as put forth in Chapter 7, to 'do rationality' is not to exercise an obscure and interior function of 'thought', but to participate in a form of cultural life. As rhetoricians add to the case, rational suasion is not thus the victory of a superior form of logic over an inferior one, but results from the exercise of particular rhetorical skills and devices. In effect, there is little reason to believe that there is a specifically rational process (or logos) lurking beneath what we take to be rational argument; to argue rationally is to 'play by the rules' favoured within a particular cultural tradition.

For many scholars, the implications of such arguments draw attention to the presence of broad and oppressive forces within the culture – appropriating both voice and power by claiming transcendent or culture free rationality. Critiques of the modernist view of individual rationality are most sharply articulated in feminist and multicultural critiques.[3] As the critics surmise, there are hierarchies of rationality within the culture: by virtue of educational degrees, cultural background and other such markers, certain individuals are deemed more rational (intelligent, insightful) than others and thus more worthy of leadership, position and wealth. Interestingly, those who occupy these positions are systematically drawn from a very small sector of the population. In effect, while Enlightenment arguments have succeeded in unseating the totalitarian power of crown and cross, they now give rise to new and more subtle structures of power and domination.

Yet, postmodernist voices also enable us to move beyond critique. For when these various ideas are linked to emerging arguments in the history of science and the sociology of knowledge, an alternative view of human rationality emerges.[4] Consider again the system of language. Language is inherently a byproduct of human interchange. There can be no 'private language' (following Wittgenstein, 1953). To generate a symbol system of one's very own would essentially be autistic. Viable language, then, depends on communal cooperation – the 'joint-action' (in Shotter's, 1984, terms) of two or more persons. Making sense is a communal achievement. Now if being rational is fundamentally an achievement in language (or actions consistent with a given language), as previously suggested, then rationality is inherently a form of communal participation. To speak rationally is to speak according to the conventions of a culture.

From empirical method to social construction

Under modernism observational methods enjoyed an elevated status. The more sophisticated the mensurational and statistical techniques, it was believed, the more reliable and well nuanced the scientific understanding of the phenomenon. From the postmodern standpoint all research is lodged within a forestructure of understanding – a set of orienting assumptions about the nature of the world (what qualities inhere in the object of study) and methodology (as a means of recording these qualities). More generally, our understanding of phenomena are themselves *theory laden*, as are the methods used in their illumination.[5] It is only when commitments are made to a given theoretical perspective (or form of language) that research can be mounted and methods selected. The a priori selection of theories thus determines in large measure the outcomes of the research – what may be said at its conclusion. To illustrate, if the organizational scientist is committed to a view of the individual as a rational decision-maker, then it is intelligible to mount research on information-processing heuristics, to distinguish among heuristic strategies and to demonstrate experimentally the conditions under which differing strategies are effective. If, in contrast, the theorist is committed to a psychoanalytic perspective, and views organizational life as guided by unconscious dynamics, then issues of symbolic authority and unconscious desires become research realities. Projective devices might serve as the favoured research methods. The former research would never reveal a 'repressed wish' and the latter would never discover a 'cognitive heuristic'. Each would find the others' methods similarly specious. To speak, then, of 'the organizational system', 'leadership styles' or 'causal effects' is to draw selectively from the immense repository of sayings (or writings) that constitute a cultural tradition.

The present arguments are well developed in social constructionist scholarship.[6] Such writings are both emancipatory and expository. On the one hand they challenge the taken-for-granted world of the scientist and layman. For example, in questioning the presumption of rational decisions, the distinction between genders or the existence of mental illness they free us from the grip of traditional intelligibilities. They invite alternative formulations, the creation of new and different realities. In their expository role, such writings also attempt to elucidate the processes by which various rationalities and realities are created. They sensitize us to our participation in constituting our world, thus emphasizing our potential for communally organized change in understanding – and thus action.

Language as social action

Because language, for the postmodernist, is the child of cultural process it follows that one's descriptions of the world are not outward manifestations of a mental mirror – that is, reports on one's private 'observations' or 'perceptions'. Scientific reports are not mirrors that reflect our observations of what there is. Yet, if the modernist view of language as a picturing device is eschewed, in what manner can it be replaced? It is in the latter works of Wittgenstein that the major answer is to be located. As Wittgenstein (1953) proposed, language gains its meaning not from its mental or subjective underpinnings, but from its use in action ('language games'). Or, again emphasizing the significant place of human relatedness in postmodern writings, language gains its meaning within organized forms of interaction. To 'tell the truth', on this account, is not to furnish an accurate picture of 'what actually happened', but to participate in a set of social conventions, a way of putting things sanctioned within a given 'form of life'. To 'be objective' is to play by the rules of a given tradition.

More broadly, this is to say that language for the postmodernist is not a reflection of a world but is world-constituting. Language does not describe action but is itself a form of action. To do science, then, is to participate actively within a set of sub-cultural relationships. As scientific accounts are made known to the culture – for example, accounts of organizations as information systems or managers as information processors – they enter the stock of cultural intelligibilities. They shape our modes of understanding and thus our related forms of conduct. To treat the organization as an information system and managers as ideally guided by a rational calculus is to favour certain forms of cultural life and to undermine or prevent others. We shall return to the implications of this view shortly.

With this relational view of language in place, modernism's presumption of the unending accumulation of knowledge is thrown into question (Lyotard, 1984). Because scientific theory is not a map of existing conditions, then research does not function as proof of scientific accounts. Scientific research may lead to technical accomplishments, but it does not establish the truth of our descriptions and explanations. As research operates to displace one scientific theory with another, we are not moving ineluctably 'forward' on the road to truth; we are – as many would say – replacing one way of putting things with another. Again, this is not to deny that scientific research enhances our capacities for certain kinds of prediction and generates new forms of technology. However, it is to question the accompanying descriptions and theoretical explanations as truth telling.

To appreciate the positive implications of this condition, consider the monologic thrust of traditional science. Scientific research typically functions to narrow the range of descriptions and explanations – to winnow out the false, the imprecise and the inconsistent forms of language and to emerge with a single best account – that which best approximates the 'objectively true'. For the postmodernist the results of this effort toward univocality are disastrous in implication. The culture is made up of a rich array of idioms, accounts and explanations, and these various forms of talk are constitutive of cultural life. To eradicate our ways of talking about love, commitment, family, justice, values and so on would be to undermine ways of life shared by many people. In its search for the 'single best account', science operates as a powerful discrediting device – revealing the 'ignorance' of the layman in one sector after another. Love is shown to be a myth, families are formed out of the requirements of 'selfish genes', values are merely the result of social influence, and so on. We are invited, then, to replace the scientific emphasis on 'the single best account' with a multiplicity of constructions. Or in short, totalitarianism is replaced by pluralism.

Towards a postmodern organizational science

As we find, postmodern critique operates as a major form of de-legitimation. In the scientific sphere it contributes to a loss of confidence in rational theory, the safeguards of rigorous research methods, and the promise of a steady increase in objective knowledge. As Burrell and Morgan (1979) maintain, there is a loss in the presumption of an obdurate subject-matter – an object of study that is not constituted by the perspectives of investigators themselves. When translated into the sphere of organizational life, the outcome of such arguments is a threat to longstanding assumptions of effective leadership, the scientifically managed transformation of organizations, the promise of steady growth in organizational efficacy and the capacity of organizational science to produce increments in knowledge of organizational functioning. These are indeed momentous transformations, and if current discussions continue unabated we may soon confront a major evolution in the concept and practice of organizational science.

Yet, while the vast majority of scientists and practitioners may see these emerging threats as tantamount to nihilism, in the present attempt we have also located a reconstructive theme. In particular, we have emphasized the replacement of individual rationality by communal negotiation, the importance of social processes in the observational enterprise, the socio-practical function of language and the significance of pluralistic investments in the conception of the true and the good. In short, we have derived a rough outline for a *social constructionist* view of the scientific effort, a view that is congenial to many of the postmodern critiques but that enables us to press beyond the critical moment.

In this final section we turn, then, to the possible contours of a positive organizational science within a postmodern context. This task is informed by a range of writings which have already introduced postmodern thought into organizational science – namely the *Organization Studies* series on postmodernism and organizational analysis edited by Cooper and Burrell in 1988. Other writers such as Boje (1992), Clegg (1990), Gergen (1992), Ogilvy (1990) and Parker (1992) have also made significant contributions to wedding postmodernist thought to management discourse. In 1992 the topic of postmodernism figured in the annual meetings of the Academy of Management (Boje, 1992; Boland and Tenkasi, 1992; Clegg, 1992; Gephart, 1992; Hetrick and Lozada, 1992; Nielsen, 1992; Thachenkery and Pasmore, 1992a). These inquiries are also complemented by an impressive array of related work in organizational analysis (Bradshaw-Camball and Murray, 1991; Calas and Smircich, 1991; Hassard, 1991; Lee, 1991; Martin, 1990; Morgan, 1990), the social construction of leadership and organization (Chen and Meindl, 1992; Srivastva and Barrett, 1988; Yakhlef, 1992) meaning-making in organizations (Cooperrider and Srivastva, 1987; Weick, 1995; and a special issue of *Organization*, vol. 4, no. 2). In an attempt to integrate various strands of this work, and simultaneously elaborate on the potentials of organizational science in a constructionist mode, we focus on four areas of special significance: research, critique, generative theory, and organizational action.

The place of research technologies

Within the modernist frame the technologies of empirical research (e.g. experimentation, simulation, attitude and opinion assessment, participant observation, trait testing, statistical evaluation) were largely used in the service of evaluating or supporting various theories or hypotheses about behaviour in organizations. Under postmodernism, methodology loses its status as the chief arbiter of truth. Research technologies may produce data, but both the production and interpretation of the data must inevitably rely on forms of language (metaphysical beliefs, theoretical perspectives, conceptions of methodology) embedded within cultural relationships. Thus, research fails to verify, falsify or otherwise justify a theoretical position outside a commitment to a range of culturally embedded assumptions.

At the same time, there is nothing about postmodernism that argues against the possibilities of using empirical technologies for certain *practical* purposes. To be sure, there is widespread scepticism in the grand narrative of progressive science. Such scepticism however, is often called into question by virtue of the obvious fact that we can do things called 'transmitting information', 'automating production' and 'quality control' that we could not do in previous centuries. Yet, it is not technological capability (or 'knowing how') that is called into question by postmodern critique, but the truth claims placed upon the accompanying descriptions and explanations (the 'knowing that'). In this sense, organizational scientists should not be dissuaded by postmodernist arguments from forging ahead with methodological and technological developments. First and foremost, within certain limits the *methodologies of prediction* remain essential adjuncts to the organization. The prediction of team vs. individual production on a particular assembly line, management turnover in a specified company and white-collar theft in a particular bureaucracy, for example, may be very useful contributions in a field of conventionally accepted realities. In the same way, we may continue to employ what may be termed *methodologies of sensitization*, that is, methods that bring new and potentially useful ideas into deliberation. Research methods such as experiments and interviews may very well produce results that sensitize us to alternative interpretations of the world. So long as one does not objectify the terms of description and is mindful of the valuational implications of such work, then such methods are welcomed by constructionist arguments.

While postmodern critique undermines the function of research in warranting truth, and shifts the empirical emphasis to more local and practical concerns, it also invites a broad expansion in the conceptualization of research. Rather than being used to buttress the theoretical forestructures of various scientific enclaves, research technologies can serve a variety of *social* functions. Many organizational researchers have already begun to mine the potentials of this view. For example, Gareth Morgan (1983: 12–13) has spoken of scientific research as a 'process of interaction . . . designed for the realization of potentialities'. Argyris et al. (1985) and Schon (1983) have argued for the inextricability of research and social action. It is within this vein that participatory action research (Reason & Bradbury, 2001; Torbert, 1991) operates to collapse the traditional roles of the researcher and researched to *realize the potentials of local knowledge*.

Yet, these are not the only functions of research within a constructionist frame. Various research strategies may also be used to *give voice* to otherwise marginalized, misunderstood or deprivileged groups. Thus far scholars have occupied themselves primarily with exploring the ways in which various voices are silenced. For example, Calas and Smircich (1991) have used feminist deconstructive strategies to expose rhetorical and cultural means by which the concept of leadership has been maintained as a 'seductive game'. Martin (1990) has looked at the suppression of gender conflicts in organizations, showing how organizational efforts to 'help women' have often suppressed gender conflict and reified false dichotomies between public and private realms of endeavour. Mumby and Putnam (1992) have demonstrated the androcentric assumptions underlying Simon's concept of 'bounded rationality. And Nkomo (1992) has analysed how the organizational concept of race is embedded in a Eurocentric view of the world. While this form of analysis is essential to a postmodern organizational science, innovative practices or methodologies are also required to bring forth the marginalized voices in the organization. Practices are invited that enable the unspoken positions to be expressed and circulated and to enter actively into decision-making processes.

Finally, in the broadened conception of research, methods may be sought to *generate new realities*, to engender perspectives or practices as yet unrealized. Thus far, the most favourable technologies for achieving these ends take the form of dialogic methods (for a range of illustrations see Cooperrider and Srivastva, 1987; Kilmann et al., 1983; Reason and Rowan, 1981; Schein, 1993; Senge, 1990) Dialogic methods often enable participants to escape the limitations of the realities with which they enter and, working collaboratively, to formulate modes of understanding or action that incorporate multiple inputs. As Covaleski and Dirsmith (1990) suggest, dialogic research often facilitates the generation of unforeseen relationships. Particularly promising is movement toward 'appreciative inquiry' (Cooperrider et al., 1999), practices which enable organizations to share positive stories of the past and to use these in developing together ideal forms of the future.

Towards dialogic reflection

Cultural life largely revolves around the meanings assigned to various actions, events or objects; discourse is perhaps the critical medium through which meanings are fashioned. And, because discourse exists in an open market, marked by broadly diffuse concatenations, recombinations and transformations, patterns of human action will also remain forever in motion – shifting at times imperceptibly and at others disjunctively. This means that the efficacy of our professional technologies of prediction, intervention and decision-making are continuously threatened. Today's effective technology may be tomorrow's history. In this sense, prediction of organizational behaviour is akin to forecasting the stock market; with each fresh current of understanding the phenomenon is altered.

In this sense we may see organizational science as a generative source of meaning in cultural life – in its descriptions, explanations, technologies and its services to organizations. And, in generating and disseminating meanings, so does the science furnish people with implements for action. Its concepts are used to justify various policies, to separate or conjoin various groups, to judge or evaluate individuals, to identify oneself or one's organization, and so on. In effect, organizational science furnishes pragmatic devices through which organizational/cultural life is carried out. From this standpoint, two vistas of professional activity become particularly salient. Here we consider ideological and social critique; we then turn to the challenge of creating new realities.

Within modernist organizational science there was little justification for moral or political evaluation of the science itself. The discipline attempted to provide value neutral knowledge and assessments; if this knowledge was used for unethical or untoward purposes this was not the concern of the science qua science. Thus at the present juncture scientific training provides very few resources for moral or political evaluation. Organizational science has specialized in a language of 'is' rather than 'ought', a discourse of rational judgment as opposed to humane concern (Cooperrider and Srivastva, 1990; Jacques, 1992; Peck, 1992). Yet, with the postmodern emphasis placed on the pragmatics of language, organizational science can no longer extricate itself from moral and political debate. As a generator and purveyor of meanings, the field inherently operates to the benefit of certain stakeholders, activities and forms of cultural life – and to the detriment of others. Two forms of critical analysis are especially important.

At the outset, organizational science can appropriately develop a literature of *self-critique*. Required are debates on the cultural implications of its own constructions. With the benefit of the various intellectual movements described above, this form of self-reflection is already under way (see, for example, Cooper, 1989; Kilduf, 1993; Pfeffer, 1982; Thompson, 1993). To illustrate, Boyacigiller and Adler (1991) show how American values regarding free will and individualism affect conceptualizations of organizational behaviour. The American cultural assumption that individuals are (or should be) in control of their actions, contrasts with the beliefs of cultures emphasizing communal commitment. The works of feminist scholars cited above, along with those representing various ethnic and political standpoints, also contribute valuably to critical self-reflection.

Critical-emancipatory (Alvesson & Willmott, 1992; Willmott, 1997) and radical humanist (Atkouf, 1992) writings further extend the horizons. The postmodern transformation not only furnishes a strong warrant for such work, but invites a vigorous expansion of these efforts.

Simultaneous to the appraisal of its own practices, organizational science may appropriately direct its concerns to the forms of *organizational structure and practice* within the culture – or the world. What is to be said in praise of contemporary organizational arrangements and in what ways are they deficient? This is not simply to extend the modernist quest for the most efficient, productive and profitable organizational structure and practices. Rather, it is to generate reflection on the 'organization' as a form of cultural life. To what extent are existing modes of organization desirable, for whom and in what ways? In certain degree, comparative studies of organizational life carry with them such valuative standpoints. For example, Allen, Miller and Nath (1988) argue that in countries where individualism is highly regarded, actors tend to view their relationship with organizations strategically, whereas in collectivist cultures the individual feels more in harmony with the organization and the environment. There is a strong belief in The American system in the power of the individual to make a difference, which is consistent with the fact that the average American CEO earns 160 times more than the average American worker, whereas in a more collectively oriented culture such as Japan, the corresponding differential is under 20 (Crystal, 1991). While such explorations sensitize the reader to possible biases in the taken-for-granted world of organizational life, in fact they serve as subtle criticisms of Western modes of life.

The construction of new worlds

As ventured in Chapter 3, there are significant limits to critical appraisal, and more positive vistas must be opened. We turn our attention, then, to one of the most significant and potentially powerful byproducts of organizational science – its languages of description and explanation. As concepts, metaphors, narratives, images and the like are placed in motion within the culture, they are often absorbed into ongoing relations. Such relations thereby stand to be transformed. This possibility invites the scientist to use his/her intellectual talents for purposes of creating new cultural realities. Within the modernist era, the organizational scientist was largely a polisher of mirrors. It was essentially his/her task to hold this mirror to nature. For the postmodernist such a role is pale and passive. Rather than 'telling it like it is', the challenge for the postmodern scientist is to 'tell it as it might become' (see Chia, 1996, on the concept of 'becoming realism'). What is needed are scholars willing to be audacious, to break the barriers of common sense by offering new forms of theory, of interpretation or intelligibility. The concept of *generative theory* (Gergen, 1994a) is apposite here. Such theory is designed to unseat conventional assumptions and to open new alternatives for action. Through such theorizing, scholars contribute to the forms of cultural intelligibility, to the symbolic resources available to people as they carry out their lives together.

Generative theorizing is already evidenced in the steadily increasing number of contributions drawing from postmodern analytics to forge new ways of conceptualizing (and challenging) organizations themselves. In these instances theorists typically view bureaucratic, hierarchical and rationally controlled organizations as constituted and sustained by the particular range of modernist discourses (both in the academy and the market). As outlined in Chapter 8, because of radical changes in the technological ethos, information availability, economic globalization and the like the modernist organization is no longer viable. The new wave of postmodern and constructionist discourses are then employed as means of describing and creating what is often called the *postmodern organization*. Much of this work is foreshadowed in Cooper's (1989) critique of systemic organization, and on language as an active force in simultaneous processes of organization/ disorganization. Useful compilations of these resources have been made by Reed and Hughes (1992) and Boje, Gephart and Thatchenkery (1996). Importantly, this work also carries on a dialogic relationship with the marketplace and in this way acquires a constitutive capability (see, for example, Berquist, 1993; Morgan, 1993; Peters, 1992).

To illustrate, consider the sweeping moves toward globalization currently occupying the business community (see, for example, Bartlett and Ghoshal, 1991; Cooperrider and Pasmore, 1991; Weick and Van Orden, 1990). From the present perspective, organizational science should not strive towards a single best, most rational and empirically grounded theory – a grand or totalizing narrative. Rather, a variety of theoretical perspectives is invited. Views of globalization as a 'post-Fordist model of accumulation' (Albertsen, 1988) or 'flexible accumulation' (in Harvey's, 1989, terms) should stand alongside accounts of the global organization as 'post-Copernican' (Peters, 1992) in its existence within a network of collectivities. We may also strive toward new forms of articulation, as in the concept of *systase* (Gebser, 1985). In contrast to the system, the systase is an organization without an absolute centre, around which order – as a 'patchwork of language pragmatics that vibrate at all times' (Lyotard and Thebaud, 1985: 94) – is continuously being established and threatened. At the same time, these overarching conceptualizations require supplementation by accounts at the more concrete level of action. In pursuing this line of argument Joseph (1994) cites the evolution of a transnational non-profit organization that went global during the 1970s. By the 1980s it became clear that their universal model of socio-economic-cultural development could not be applied across cultures. What was needed was a reorganization whereby each local organization autonomously pursued its own model of development. As a result the organization developed a remarkable competency to function as an international network of locally disparate organizations.

The challenge of generative theory must also be qualified in three ways. First, organizational science has already produced a vast range of theory. From the postmodern perspective these myriad formulations are not a deficit – an indication, in modernist terms, of the pre-paradigmatic and non-cumulative character of the science. Rather, each of the existing theories represents a discourse potentially available for many purposes in a variety of contexts. Generative efforts may include, then, reinvigorating the theories of the past (cf. Chia and King, 1998; Morgan, 1993), redefining or recontextualizing their meanings so as not to be cast from the repository of potentials (see Kostera, 1997, on 'creative reconstruction'). Second, the move toward generative theory should be maximally sensitive to issues of *use-value*, that is, how and whether a given form of language can be absorbed into ongoing relationships (see Colville, Waterman, and Weick, 1999). As Argyris (1996) has put it, the field must press towards the creation of 'actionable' discourses. When written in an argot suitable only for highly sophisticated scholars, professional writing may be greatly circumscribed in terms of market-place utility. There is a great need, then, for the rhetorical enrichment of professional writing (see also Chapter 4).

Organizational action

A final feature of postmodern organizational science extends the preceding logic. Our concern in this case is with scientists as active agents within organizations themselves, serving, for example, as consultants, evaluators, board members and so on. In our view, it is this context in which the above emphases on the multiple functions and forms of research, critical reflexivity and generative theorizing become most fully realized. At the same time, we view this relationship as principally dialogic, as a site not only for academic discourse and practice to percolate outwards, but for the discourses and practices of the organization to filter into the academy.

Rather than theorizing this relationship further, it may be useful to explore a single case attempting to realize many of these proposals in practice. The account will help to demonstrate the potentials and limitations of these proposals when activated in an organizational setting. In the preceding chapter a consultation was described in which the Gergens' services were enlisted by a multinational pharmaceutical company. As the problem was described, the organization had expanded into some fifty different countries and was now experiencing considerable difficulty in communicating and coordinating actions effectively. Individuals across the various functions, and across nations, failed either to understand or appreciate each other's perspectives and decisions. Tensions were especially intense between the parent company and the foreign subsidiaries; each tended to be critical and mistrustful of the other's actions.

From a modernist standpoint, it would be appropriate at this juncture to launch a multifaceted research project attempting to determine precisely the origins of the problem, locating the specific conditions, structures or individuals responsible and, based on the results of such study, to make recommendations for an ameliorative plan of action. From a postmodern constructionist standpoint, however, there are good reasons for rejecting this option. Not only is 'the problem' continuing to change while the research and intervention are being carried out, but the very idea that there is a single set of propositions that will accurately reflect the nature of the condition (or its 'causal' underpinnings) is grossly misleading. Further, to warrant this interpretation with empirical data, and to present the inter-pretation as authoritative (as truth beyond perspective), is to perpetuate a bad faith relationship with the organization. Competing realities are suppressed in the name of 'scientific authority'.

Given these and other problems with the modernist orientation, we first established a series of *generative dialogues* in which we, the consultants, served a collaborative role. Interviewing various managers at various levels of the organization, both in the parent company and subsidiaries, we explored their views on various relationships within the organization. Our attempt was not to locate and define 'the problem' with ever-increasing accuracy, but to elicit discursive resources that would enable the managers to remove themselves from the daily discourses of relationship and to consider their situation reflexively. The hope was, on the one hand, to loosen the sedimented realities giving rise to 'the problem' and to multiply the voices that could speak to the issues and thus the range of options for action.

Although these discussions ranged broadly, two forms of questioning were common across all: first, we asked the participants to describe instances in which communication and coordination were highly effective. Drawing from Srivastva and Cooperrider's (1990) work on appreciative inquiry, our hope was, first, to deconstruct the common sense of failure ('we have a serious problem') and, second, to secure a set of positive instances that might serve as model practices (sources of reconstruction). However, we also inquired about areas in which the managers felt there were specific problems in communication and coordination. The point here was to tap common constructions of deficit within the organization that might be used to generate further dialogues (e.g. a rationale for 'we need to talk').

The second phase of the project served to *introduce conceptual resources*. Given the reasoning developed above, we see theoretical discourse (when properly translated) as having catalytic potential within the field of practice. By introducing new metaphors, narratives or images new options for action can be opened. It was essential, however, that these resources reflect the preceding dialogues – that they blended organizational realities with scholarly deliberation. We thus sent letters to each of the participants summarizing their comments. These summaries were crafted in terms central to postmodern organizational theory. On the one hand, the managers' accounts were used to illustrate shortcomings of the modernist organization – its hierarchies, singular logics, clear separation of boundaries, individualistic views of leadership, and the like.

Further, positive cases were often linked to postmodern conceptions of organization, including, for example, participatory performance, interactive decision-making, reality creation, multicultural resources and coordinating interpretations. In effect, by instantiating a set of concepts and images with ongoing practices from the organization, we hoped that the theoretical resources could be appropriated for conversational use within the organization.

In a third phase we attempted to *broaden the conversational space*. That is, after securing permission from the various participants, we shared the contents of their interviews with other managers. These documents were circulated broadly in an attempt to (1) enrich the range of conversational resources available to the participants, (2) furnish a range of positive images for future use, (3) provide a range of problems that might invite further discussion, and (4) inject into the discussions a common language (benefiting from postmodern organizational theory). We cannot ascertain at this juncture whether useful discussions are indeed occurring; this would be a subject of further dialogue. And it would surely be cavalier to suppose that these various moves are sufficient for altering the corporate culture at large. At a minimum, management training would be desirable along with alterations in corporate communication structures. However, these various interchanges did inject into the organization a variety of constructionist assumptions, suggested new forms of organizational practice (technology) and reflexively enriched our own theoretical orientation – all functioning to invite new and transformative conversations.

In conclusion: towards catalytic conversation

The present chapter has first isolated an interrelated set of assumptions central to organizational science. These modernist assumptions were then placed at risk through a consideration of postmodern critique. We then moved beyond critique to offer an alternative vision of organizational science, one that places a major emphasis on processes of social construction. From this latter perspective we outlined a rationale for what we see as a vitally expanded and enriched conception of organizational science.

Yet, these views should scarcely be considered fixed and final. On the contrary, the very conception of a science in the postmodern context is one that emphasizes continuing interchange, continuing reflection and transformation. The present account is thus the beginning of a conversation rather than a termination. Not one of the present arguments is without its problems. For example, Jean François Lyotard has criticized contemporary science for its abdicating concern with knowledge as an end in itself. As he sees it: 'knowledge is . . . produced in order to be sold, it is . . . consumed in order to be valorized in a new production. Science becomes a force of production, in other words a moment in the circulation of capital' (1984:

4–5). Is the present search for the utility of a postmodern organizational science not subject to the same critique? Is there a more promising alternative? There are further questions including, for example, the implicit regime of values contained within this analysis, the possibilities of infinite regress in argumentation and the intellectual and cultural dangers of relativism. Let the dialogue continue . . .

Notes

1 For a brief but relevant summary of these cultural underpinnings, see Gergen (1991). For more detailed accounts see Berman (1982), Frisby (1985) and Randall (1940).

2 See especially Derrida (1977), Norris (1983) and Simons (1990).

3 For feminists illustrations see Grosz (1988) and Harding (1986); for an African-American critique of scientism see West (1993).

4 Major contributions to this literature include Barnes (1974), Feyerabend (1976), Knorr-Cetina (1981), Kuhn (1970) and Latour and Woolgar (1979).

5 The classic arguments to this effect are those of Kuhn (1970) and Feyerabend (1976).

6 In the organizational arena see especially Astley (1985), Morgan (1998), Thatchenkery (1992) and Whitley (1992).

PART III

SOCIAL CONSTRUCTION AND CULTURAL CONTEXT

10

FROM IDENTITY TO RELATIONAL POLITICS

Social construction and identity politics form a pair of star-crossed lovers, entwined in a relationship suffused with passion, provocation and perfidy. No easy relationship this, but one in which deep intimacy has given birth to an enormously influential array of movements across the land. As I presently see it, however, the fecundity of this union is rapidly diminishing. The tensions between these otherwise intimates have burst into bitterness. Their love-children now tread very mean streets – with damaging counter-critique, derision, disregard and disaffection on every darkened corner. And with identity politics under siege, social constructionism now seems a suspicious ally – if not indeed an assassin. Can identity politics sustain its course successfully, and should its relationship with social construction be maintained? In what follows I shall propose that identity politics cannot continue successfully in its existing modes of action and that, indeed, we find a movement struggling toward reformation. Similarly, constructionist dialogues have entered a new phase of development. This turn in constructionist endeavours can and should play a key role in the future evolution of identity politics. We are poised, then, for a rekindling of the passions in what I will call a *relational politics*.

Although the phrase 'identity politics' has served many different purposes, for the present I will take it to stand for a mode of political activism – typically though not exclusively initiated by groups excluded from traditional mainstream politics. Such marginalized groups generate a self-designated identity (group consciousness) that is instantiated by the individual identities of its constituents. Identity politics differs from many social movements, such as left-wing or fundamentalist Christian activism, in that the constituents of the former – such as women, Afro-Americans, gays – are politically marked as individuals. Politics and personal being are virtually inseparable. This inseparability is owing largely to perceptions of the natural. One may by virtue of reason or impulse join the National Rifle Association or the Praise the Lord Club. Not so with being a Native American or a black Muslim. One simply is, by virtue of nature, tradition or thrown condition, an Asian-American, a lesbian or a member of the lower class. It is largely by virtue of the 'natural' condition of its members that the groups lay claim to certain inalienable rights – for example, equal opportunities, equal treatment, freedom to practice, participation in democratic governance.

Why a love affair between identity politics and social constructionism? There are many reasons. Among them, the generalized shift toward social construction in the academy furnished a powerful justificatory basis for political and moral activism. For the better part of the century, the academy basked in what it believed to be an ideological non-partisanship (see, for example, Bell's *The end of ideology*). Epitomized by the positivist–empiricist stance in the natural and social sciences, it was held that the function of inquiry is to determine what is objectively true. Moral and ideological commitment obfuscate the quest, as it was said, yielding bias and misinformation ('proper scholarship is about truth, not the good'). However, as constructionist critique challenged claims to objectivity – truth beyond cultural standpoint – so did it eradicate the is–ought divide. Not only did the discourses of truth, objectivity and rationality cease to be commanding rhetorics, but their claimants seemed guilty of either ignorance (lack of reflection on implicit ideology) or exploitation (masking self-serving ideology in the cloak of neutrality). The constructionist assault, then, led to a slow deterioration of authority, with the simultaneous liberation of politically and morally invested inquiry. If one's professional work is inevitably political, as constructionists reason, then the academician is furnished with a new and inspiring telos. Rather than generating knowledge that may or may not be used by those making decisions for the society – as the pure scientists envisioned their goal – the knowledge-generating process becomes itself a means of creating the good society. (Women's Studies, Black Studies and Queer Studies are exemplary of this impulse.)

Not only did constructionism thus help to incite the political impulse, but it has also generated a powerful set of implements for societal critique. As outlined in preceding chapters, constructionist inquiry has demonstrated how claims to the true and the good are born of historical traditions, fortified by social networks, sewn together by literary tropes, legitimated through rhetorical devices and operate in the service of particular ideologies to fashion structures of power and privilege. For the sophisticated constructionist, there are no invulnerable or unassailable positions, no foundational warrants, no transcendent rationalities or obdurate facts in themselves. Most important for the present, many of these modes of deconstructing the opposition are 'street ready'; they can be (and are) paraphrased easily in the daily argots of political activism.

The unravelling of identity politics

You will not be mistaken if you recognize in these remarks a soupçon of nostalgia. These have been times of dizzying excitement, crashing idols, scintillating discussion and epiphanies of virtue. I scarcely think the implications are yet fully explored nor their action potential exhausted. However, in my view the enormous force of identity politics, aided and abetted as it has been by constructionist dialogues, has begun to subside. In large measure, this deterioration of efficacy can be understood in terms of cultural change, change which can in part be traced to the influence of identity politics itself. To take a constructionist stance in this analysis, and extending the arguments of Chapter 3, let me focus only on the rhetoric of identity politics.

At the outset, the prevailing rhetoric has been of little influence outside groups of the already committed. For the targets – those most in need of 'political education' – such rhetoric has more often been alienating or counter-productive. By and large, identity politics has depended on a rhetoric of blame, the illocutionary effects of which are designed to chastise the target (for being unjust, prejudiced, inhumane, selfish, oppressive and/or violent). In Western culture we essentially inherit two conversational responses to such forms of chastisement – incorporation or antagonism. The incorporative mode ('Yes, now I see the error of my ways') requires an extended forestructure of understandings (i.e. a history which legitimates the critic's authority and judgment, and which renders the target of critique answerable). However, because in the case of identity politics there is no pre-established context to situate the target in just these ways, the invited response to critique is more typically one of hostility, defence and counter-charge.

Such antagonistic replies are additionally invited by virtue of the differing discourse worlds of the critic as opposed to target. What are viewed as 'exploitative wages' on the one side are branded as 'just earnings' on the other; 'prejudicial decisions' on the one side are excoriated as 'decisions by merit' on the other; attempts to combat 'exclusionary prejudices' are seen as disruptions of 'orderly and friendly community'; 'rigid parochialism' for the critic is understood as 'love of enduring traditions' by the target. Under such conditions those targeted by the critiques are least likely to take heed and most likely to become galvanized in opposition. As Mary Ann Glendon argues in *Rights talk*, the rhetoric of rights 'polarizes debate; it tends to suppress moral discussion and consensus building. Once an agenda is introduced as "right," sensible discussion and moderate positions tend to disappear.'

It should be added that this antagonistic animus is not limited to the relationship of critic to target but, rather, has carried over into many of the political movements themselves. With the rhetoric of blame a favoured option for dealing with others, it also becomes a hammer for fixing what is wrong within the political movements. Any movement that targets the culture as guilty of suppressing voices will soon find that within its own ranks some voices are more equal than others. In the thrust towards economic equality women turn on men for their patriarchal disposition; in the drive towards gender equality, white women are found guilty of silencing the black voice; the educationally privileged guilty of elitist and exclusionary language; the straight for politics inimical to the lesbian; and so on. To illustrate, prominent black intellectual Patricia Hill Collins (1990) writes of the necessity for a specifically black feminist movement. However, she also advocates a 'critical posture toward mainstream, feminist, and Black scholarly inquiry' more generally (p. 12). Here she joins other prominent black thinkers, along with a cadre of Hispanic, Native American and Asian American women in challenging feminism for its implicit racism and its overarching concern with white, middle-class women's issues.

Not only is the dominant rhetoric of identity politics divisive in its effects, there are important respects in which it has lost its efficacy by virtue of its profusion. The rhetorics of rights, for example, has travelled weightlessly across contexts of contention. Where the most celebrated battles for equality were fought within the domains of class, race and gender, the forms of rhetoric have become available to all who suffer. Rapidly the big three were joined by Native Americans, Asian Americans, Hispanics, the aged, the homeless, ex-mental patients, the disabled, gay and lesbian enclaves, along with advocates for the rights to life and children's rights. We also find litigation based on claims to a right to higher education, death-row inmates' rights to reproduce, and women's rights to urinate in any public facility. As Amitai Etzioni (1993) proposes: 'The incessant issuance of new rights, like the wholesale printing of currency, causes a massive inflation of rights that devalues their moral claims'. Glendon (1991) adds that rights talk contains the 'unexpressed premise that we roam at large in a land of strangers, where we presumptively have no obligations toward others except to avoid the active infliction of harm'. Other critics are far more scathing. National columnists have even spoken of 'the rights babble'.

Finally, given its relatively longstanding presence in cultural life, there has been ample time for the development of effective counter-rhetorics. As Hirschman (1991) points in the *The rhetoric of reaction*, discursive attempts to thwart social change have a rich history. However, the past several decades have stimulated a new range of self-insulating rebuttals. There is, for example, the redoubt of 'victimization' – which proposes that claims to being a victim of oppressive circumstances are merely excuses to cover failures of inaction or irresponsibility. Reactionary critic, Charles

Sykes (1992), proposes that we have become a 'nation of victims', and that the rhetoric of rights and blame is responsible for a 'decay in the American character'. In his volume, *The abuse excuse*, Alan Dershowitz claims that we have become a nation of 'sob stories'. One of the most powerful rebutting rhetorics, owing to the fact that it has been appropriated from identity politics itself, is that of political correctness. So trenchant are the minorities' critiques of established policies and practices that, for the target, they take on a tyrannical demeanour – thus violating *their* rights to tradition and voice. As one commentator recently noted, it may be one of the first times in the nation's history in which both sides of political debate lodge their defence in civil liberties. Finally, as anti-liberalist critics such as Michael Sandel (1982) have begun to dismantle the justification of individual rights, the way has been paved for a rhetoric of responsibility to replace that of rights. It is this latter rhetoric that has enabled the Communitarian movement to gain such high cultural visibility.

The constructionist conundrum

If identity politics were not sufficiently embattled by the vicissitudes of cultural history, it has also begun to feel a certain suffocating presence from its constructionist paramour. For, while social constructionism supplies vibrant discursive resources for building internal strength and undermining the opposition, it also plays havoc with central tenets of identity politics. In particular, as outlined in Chapter 1, constructionism offers strong arguments against the realism, essentialism and ethical foundationalism endemic to much of the discourse of identity politics.

In the first instance, the social critiques developed within identity politics are typically lodged within a realist discourse, a discourse which privileges its critique with the capacity for truth beyond perspective. In characterizing the barriers of class, the glass ceiling, homophobia, the effects of pornography on rape and the embryonic fetus as a human being, for example, claims are being about the state of nature independent of our interpretive proclivities. For the constructionist, of course, such claims are not so much reflections of nature as the outcome of social process. The descriptions are inherently positioned both historically and culturally, and myriad alternatives are both possible and creditable from other societal locations. The realist posture is all the more ironic, the constructionist reasons, because such critiques are often coupled with a deconstruction of the opposition's objectivity. The constructed character of the dominant discourse is used by the identity politician to pave the way for the marginalized alternative, with the latter position then treated as if transparent.

Closely related to a problematic realism is the essentialist presumption implicit in much identity politics. To make claims for the rights of women, children, the aged, the poor, the insane and so on typically implies the existence of an essential entity – a group unified by its distinctive features. The group name is treated as referential – derived from characteristics existing in nature, independent of the name itself. For the constructionist, of course, reference is preeminently a social achievement and thus inherently defeasible. The reality of history, ethnicity, class and so on is generated within contemporary cultural life, and could be otherwise. As Henry Louis Gates (1994) proposes, blackness is 'not a material object, an absolute, or an event', but only 'a trope'. And lodging the argument in social process, he goes on: 'Race is only a sociopolitical category, nothing more'. As this socio-political category is applied to individuals it also acts as a reductive agent, circumscribing one's identity and reducing one's potential to be otherwise. In his *Reflections of an affirmative action baby*, Stephen Carter proposes that such labels operate as problematic stereotypes, covering over complexities and generating misleading social policies. (See also Calhoun, 1994.)

Finally, constructionist thought militates against the claims to ethical foundations implicit in much identity politics – that higher ground from which others can so confidently be condemned as inhumane, self-serving, prejudiced and unjust. Constructionist thought painfully reminds us that we have no transcendent rationale upon which to rest such accusations and that our sense of moral indignation is itself a product of historically and culturally situated traditions. And, the constructionist intones, is it possible that those we excoriate are also living within traditions that are, for them, suffused with a sense of ethical primacy? As we find, then, social constructionism is a two-edged sword in the political arena, potentially as damaging to the wielding hand as to the opposition.

The relational turn in social construction

As many propose, identity politics is reaching an impasse. No longer does it seem an effective means of securing voice, dignity and equality. More positively, however, I see significant signs of transformation in both identity politics and in social constructionism. In the former case, for example, left-wing activist Todd Gitlin (1993) despairs of what has become of identity politics, the proliferation of which, he says, 'leads to a turning inward, a grim and hermetic bravado celebrating victimization and stylized marginality' (p. 173). Black intellectuals, Cornel West, Toni Morrison and Henry Louis Gates, have also turned critical towards the past political postures and now resonate with many others seeking an evolution in identity politics. Let me, then, describe what I feel to be a central outgrowth of contemporary constructionist thought. We may then consider how this movement lends itself to a re/visioned political agenda.

Since their emergence as a self-conscious force (most prominently in the 1970s), social constructionist writings have largely been deconstructive in their aims and effects. By demonstrating the social, linguistic, rhetorical, ideological, cultural and historical forces responsible for generating the world of knowledge – both professional and everyday – they have challenged all claims to authority, truth, rationality and moral superiority. As described in Chapters 2 and 3, they have been highly effective forces for extending rights for negotiating the real and the good. And, while this enterprise must and should continue, alone it is insufficient. It is insufficient in part because its primary role is symbiotic: critique remains dormant until the fools begin to dance. At the same time, as constructionist discourse is placed into orbit, as it begins to insinuate itself into the ways we describe and explain, so does it invite alternative forms of action – new patterns of relationship. In certain respects, these patterns represent dislocating alternatives to traditions of centuries duration. In effect, constructionism harbours enormous revolutionary potential for our cultural forms of life. In the exploration of this potential, constructionist inquiry moves from a symbiotic to a productive posture – from deconstruction to reconstruction.

I have said much about these positive outcomes in an earlier work (Gergen, 1999) and, indeed, the preceding pages amply illustrate the vision in motion. However, for present purposes, I wish to focus on only one emerging development, namely that of relational theory and practice. Constructionist dialogues consistently underscore the significance of relationship as the matrix from which meaning is derived. It is in the generation of coordinations – of actions, words, objects – that human meaning is born. All that we take to be true of nature and of mind, of self and others, thus finds its origins within relationship. Or, in Martin Buber's (1970) terms, 'In the beginning is the relationship'. It is this line of reasoning that has played a spirited counterpoint with the conceptual movement from individual to relational selves (Chapter 2) with the therapeutic movement away from exploring individual minds and toward co-constructed realities (Chapter 6), pedagogic practices of collaborative education (Chapter 7), and those practices of the multi-national organization in which we found ethical potential (Chapter 8). This turn in constructionist thought is not towards the enunciation of a new truth, that of relationship; rather, this turn in sensibilities opens a new space for innovation and transformation.

Towards relational politics

If we extend the relational metaphor what are the implications for identity politics? In my view the potentials are substantial. Indeed, I believe that we find here the seeds for both revitalization and transformation of the most profound variety. Let me cast such a transformation in terms of *relational politics* – a politics in which the self/other, we/them binaries are replaced by a realization and appreciation of the significance of relational process. It is in those practices that break free from the parochial coagulation of meaning, and set disparate discourse into common orbit that we shall locate the source of viable social change. I am not speaking here of a mere fantasy, another grand but unworkable design hatched in the ivory tower. Rather, I believe that relational politics are already in evidence – not altogether self-conscious, but struggling in multiple sites towards common intelligibility. Here I wish to touch on only three specific sites of development: the re-visioning of self and other, discursive practice and social action.

Re-theorizing self and other

To an important degree, identity politics is a descendant of Western, individualist ideology. The group replaces the individual as the centre of concern but the discourse of individuality is not thereby disrupted. Rather, the group is treated discursively in much the same way as the individual: imbued with good and evil intent, held blameworthy, deemed worthy of rights, and so on. In spite of the shift towards the social, we thus inherit the problems of individualism yet once again – simply one step removed. Rather than a society of isolated and alienated individuals – a potential war of all against all in the individualist sense – we have a battlefield of antagonistic groups. As James Hunter (1991) has put it, we are now engaged in 'culture wars'.

Advocates of identity politics have become keenly aware of the problematics of separation. As they point out, the dominant culture is already prone towards objectification of the Other. In du Preez's (1980) terms, the other is forced into *identity traps* that confirm the dominant culture's sense of superiority and self-righteousness. It is in this light that we can understand the attempt by black intellectuals to blur the boundaries of ethnic, sexual and political identity. For example, in his volume, *Race matters*, Cornel West warns against the delineation of a distinct black culture and seeks a 'frank acknowledgment of the basic humanness and Americanness of each of us'. Similarly, Stanley Crouch, in *Notes of a hanging judge*, argues that politics must involve African-Americans 'not as outsiders' – a distinct group unto itself – but as participants in broad-ranging enclaves of society, for example as 'voters, taxpayers, and sober thinkers'. In a similar vein, Todd Gitlin (1993) speaks of *commonality politics*, oriented around understanding differences 'against the background of what is *not* different, what is shared among groups' (p. 173).

These are salutary invitations to subvert the traditional self/other binaries. The constructionist shift towards relationship offers resources for moving further. We confront the possibility of developing intelligibilities that go beyond the identification of separable units – I vs. you, we vs. them – and that may create the reality of a more fundamental relatedness, the palpability of inseparability. It is here that the preceding discussion of relational selves (Chapter 2) is particularly apposite. As we reconceptualize thought, memory, emotion and so on as relational constellations, the distinction between self and other is blurred. The tendency to view the social world as constituted by individual units – whether selves or groups (and by implication ethnicities, classes, institutions and nations) – gives way to a conception of relational process. The chief concern shifts to the processes by which what we take to be units (selves, groups and so on) come into being. The focus is not on the dancers but the dance.

Although much has been said about relational theory in earlier chapters, these efforts are in their infancy. Also exciting are Davies and Harré's (1990) conception of self-positioning, Taylor's (1989) 'webs of interlocution', Mitchell's (1993) 'ambiguity of authenticity', and Baudrillard's (1988) selves as terminals of multiple networks. Additionally compelling are circulating images of selves as *multiple-partials*, that is, as constituted by multiple facets, each reflecting a different domain of human relationship and each representing but a partial aspect of the whole. Here Connolly's (1991) volume, *Identity/difference*, and Judith Butler's *Gender trouble* come to mind. In each case we find a rich range of images that could substantially alter our interpretation of social life. As the reality of relationship becomes increasingly intelligible we find substantial implications for future deliberation on identity politics. To briefly scan the horizons, we are invited to consider the possibility that:

- There is no natural (biological, genetic) basis for inter-group antagonism (as socio-biologists, ethologists and Freudians are wont to argue). Violence is a meaningful integer in a relational dance; this dance is rooted in historical convention and is subject to change both on the grass-roots and policy levels.
- Prejudice does not originate in the individual mind. Prejudicial action is a meaningful move within a variety of cultural scenarios. As the scenarios unfold, so is prejudicial action invited. Because of our participation in the culture (including its mass media) all of us are capable of such actions. By the same token, we are all capable of loving, caring and societally responsible action. All actions, in effect, are byproducts of existing relational forms.
- Identity – whether individual or group – is not derived from the nature of the world. (There are no necessary or natural distinctions among persons or groups.) Rather, identity is a relational achievement. Individuation (or unitization) is only one of many ways in which we might describe or explain the world. And such forms of discourse obscure the domain of human connection.
- There is no means of ultimate victory (politically, economically, militarily) if winning means eradication of the other (or the other's position). To condemn, excoriate or wage war against a constructed other in our society is inherently self-destructive; for in a fundamental sense we are the other. We are born of our relationship and derive our sense of identity from relationship.
- Societal transformation is not a matter of changing minds and hearts, political values or the sense of the good. Rather, transformation will

require unleashing the positive potential inherent in relational process. In effect, we must locate a range of relational forms that enable collective transformation as opposed to alienated dissociation. This latter point will become amplified in what follows.

Towards relational discourse

In addition to the development of relational conceptions of self and other, relational politics invites the exploration of alternative modes of talking/acting with others – and particularly those with whom we otherwise disagree. This is not because we require prettier, sharper or more sophisticated words in which to wrap the case. I am not speaking here of 'knock-down arguments' or a 'better spin'. Rather, discourse is important because it is itself constituent of relationship. As social action, discourse is a means by which relationships are fashioned; a shift in mode of speaking or writing stands as an invitation to alter the character of relationship. Here and in previous chapters we have glimpsed some of the ways in which traditional rhetorics – for example, claims to truth, claims to moral authority and critical attack – function to alienate, antagonize and escalate conflict. An effective relational politics requires, then, a poetic leap into new forms of discourse and, more specifically, forms that invite broader opportunities for mutual sustenance. Or, as David Goldberg (1993) puts it, what is required is a new range of *incorporative metaphors*, not in this case for purposes of theoretical development, but serviceable in the hurly-burly of daily interchange.

It is in this context that a number of colleagues have joined Sheila McNamee and me (McNamee and Gergen, 1999) to explore the potentials of *relationally responsible* discourse. As reasoned in this case, if we place a value on the process of meaning-making – essentially that process without which there would be no domain of political value – then our attention is drawn to forms of discourse that sustain as oppose to subvert this process. In what ways can we speak, it is asked, such that our capacities for the productive (as opposed to destructive) generation of meaning are sustained? In our view one major discursive ritual that often destroys the grounds for sustained interchange is that of individual blame. The discourse of blame functions much like criticism (see Chapter 3), in that the target is typically degraded, set apart from the community of the good and thus alienated from it. In the process of blame, the vast sea of complexity in which any action is submerged is denied and the single individual serves as its sole origin. To be relationally responsible is to locate alternative forms of discourse that can serve as replacements for the ritual of blame and recrimination. How else can we talk, such that we might alter or terminate the unwanted action but simultaneously sustain a relationship of mutual respect?

Consider but a single possibility, the crafting of conjoint relations (McNamee and Gergen, 1999). As we saw, there is increasing interest in moving away from rhetorics of antagonism and separation to articulate visions of unity. The discursive shift from *I* vs. *you* to *we* has enormous consequences for political process. The construction of separation gives way to one of shared investments. The practical question, then, is how to conversationally craft conjoint relations. All units of social life – from the individual person to the community and nation-state – are relational constructions. They typically require conversational coordination to bring them into recognition as units. Thus, wherever there is antagonism – the recognition of *I* vs. *you* – we confront the opportunity of creating a transcendent discourse of the *we*. To replace the ritual of blame, a relationally responsible inquiry might be launched into how the untoward act has been jointly achieved. How did we *together* create a situation in which an intolerable act has resulted? Not only does such inquiry enable participants to remain creatively connected, but so are new lines of inquiry opened. It is not simply that the single individual must 'correct his ways', but rather, there is an exploration of cooperative opportunities.

Let me illustrate in a homely way. Several years ago my wife, Mary, and I were driving on a dangerous cliff-side road in southern Europe. The rain was unrelenting, visibility was minimal, the traffic was treacherous, and we were late for an appointment. We were both highly tense, and as my driving was less than flawless, Mary became increasingly critical and I became increasingly irritated and resentful of her blame. Soon it was not only the road we had to fear but ourselves. After a breathtaking near-collision, I pulled the car over to the side of road so we could collect ourselves. Here we decided to reconceptualize the drive. Rather than defining me as 'the driver' and her as the 'endangered passenger' we decided it would be better to share the roles. WE would drive and WE would criticize together. She became an added pair of eyes on the road, I developed a self-critical posture. The results were gratifying: not only did we avoid shredding our relationship but we lived to tell the tale.

On a more general scale, however, with the flourishing of a discourse of conjoint relations we confront the possibility that political parties could desist in blaming each other for various governmental or social failings. As many see it, the ritual of mutual recrimination has undermined the potentials for effective policy making at the national level. Virtually all preferences in one political party are automatically targets of critique by the opposing party; virtually all claims to achievement are degraded; all failings are traced to origins in the opposition. With the shift towards conjoint realities, we open a space for alternative conversations. How have 'we together' created the conditions of failure; how have these achievements been jointly wrought and is it possible that differing preferences can be conjoined in new and creative ways? A relational politics need not obscure or eradicate differences; however, there is much to be gained by seeing these differences as derived from relational process as opposed to independent origins. We have scarcely tapped the possibilities for 'actionable' vocabularies of relational responsibility; the future remains open. Let us finally turn to more direct forms of political action.

The politics of relational practice

A transformation in theoretical resources and discursive practices is scarcely sufficient. What are most acutely needed are innovative forms of political action. In my view one of the most significant innovations derived from the identity politics movement was to broaden extensively the arena of the political. In particular, political practice ceased to be reserved for the arena of politics formally considered – campaigning, voting, office holding, etc. – and it ceased to be hierarchical – the flow moving from the top echelons down to the grass roots. Rather, the doing of politics became everyone's business from the arenas of the local and the immediate – into the streets, the classrooms, business, and so on. Further, as we have slowly learned – particularly from feminist activists – there are no everyday activities that are not political in implication – from the cartoons our children watch to our purchase of shampoo and shirts. In this sense, political action does not require either aggressive championing of specific agendas or party partisanship to be effective. It seems to me that the future of relational politics might promisingly be shaped by conjoining these realizations: we may view relational politics as *defused* (in terms of a reduction in aggressive or hegemonic pursuits) and *diffused* (in terms of an expansion into all forms of relationship). Politics in the relational mode may be subtle, fluid and unceasing – not the work of specific groups on specific sites identified as 'political', but the work of us all, in all relationships.

My special concern here is with forms of practice informed by or congenial with the relational turn in constructionist theory. How can we move from argumentation, agitation and litigation to ordinary but unceasing forms of mutually sustaining activity? What forms of practice may be generated that move away from isolation and insulation and towards the cross-fertilization of identities, the intermingling of practices, the interweaving of selves and ever-broadening forms of coordinated action? I do think such practices are possible and, indeed, there are numerous instances of just such innovation. Some of these have been described in previous chapters of this book – especially those on therapy, education and writing. For example, the constructionist move in therapy (Chapter 6) has successfully shifted the focus from defective individuals to relational processes. The shift is away from who or what is defective to how it is we come to interpret life patterns as defective and what alternative forms of construction may enable relations to proceed more congenially. Therapy, then, is not intent on locating evil (disease, dysfunction) and correcting it, but on coordinating meanings within relationships such that the discourse of evil is rendered obsolete. In the case of education (Chapter 7) we discussed newly emerging practices of collaborative learning, critical reflection, polyvocal literacy and dialogic evaluation. And in the case of academic writing (Chapter 7) we were drawn to forms of representation that strengthened relationships. I see such practices as relational politics in action.

There is no inherent limit to the forms of action that can be generated in the service of relational politics. Every form of human coordination offers opportunities for innovation. However, a few concerted attempts – among them some favourites – will round out the discussion.

COMMUNITY FOCUSED INSTITUTES   I am deeply impressed by the activities of many therapeutically oriented institutes to move outwards into community work – not in the name of a specific political advocacy, but for purposes of crossing boundaries of divided discourse and value. Prominent, for example, is the work of Sallyann Roth and Laura and Richard Chasin and their colleagues at the Public Conversations Project.[1] (Chasin and Herzig, 1994), where the attempt has been to bring together leaders from warring ideological camps – for example, pro-choice and pro-life, or straights and gays. The purpose of these interchanges is not to champion one cause over the other, not to impugn the intelligibility of either tradition, nor to dismiss the conflict. Rather, by suppressing various forms of divisive rhetoric, and simultaneously giving voice to narratives of lived experience ('my experience with abortion', 'what it is like for me to be gay'), the attempt is to open a way of incorporating the other, of appreciating the situated character of the perspectives in question. No, the ideological conflict is not thereby dissolved, but the outcome appears to be a far more humane mode of relating to the other. I also think here of the impressive work of Fred Newman and Lois Holzman (Newman and Holzman, 1996, 1997) and their colleagues at the East Side Institute in Manhattan. Going far beyond therapeutic practice the institute helps ghetto youth to organize talent shows, offers public dialogues between blacks and Jews and has run a multi-racial elementary school in Harlem. Even those who seek treatment in therapy are encouraged to join others in organized political action, and specifically action that might alleviate the conditions responsible in creating their problems.

APPRECIATIVE INQUIRY   In the domain of organizational management, David Cooperrider (1999) and his colleagues at Case Western Reserve have developed a form of organizational intervention called *appreciative inquiry*. When organizations confront conflict – between management and workers, men and women, blacks and whites and so on – appreciative inquiry shifts the focus away from problem talk: who is to blame, what is the root of the disagreements, and how can the conflict be resolved. All such talk contributes to the objectification of 'the problem.' Rather the attempt is to work with the organization to locate stories of desirable or ideal relations – cases in which groups work well and effectively with each other. Further, as these appreciative narratives are brought into public consciousness, the organization is brought into discussion of the kind of future they might build around such cases. In the very process of instancing the positive, and forging an image of a desirable future, the divisive constructions lose their suasive capacity. This orientation to positive collaboration has also been extended to processes of community building, inter-religious integration, education, elder care, police training and more.[2] And, under the direction of Bliss Browne and her colleagues, citizens of Chicago are being united to create a new future together. Their programme, Imagine Chicago, has fostered appreciative and growth directed dialogue not only within numerous Chicago communities, but across diverse economic and ethnic groups.[3]

These relational innovations have been party to constructionist dialogues. However, there are additional movements of note, which are not so much informed by relational conceptions as they are congenial. Here I would include the enormous growth over the past decade of *private voluntary organizations* – grass-roots organizations devoted to humane and life-giving practices. There are now some 30,000 of these organizations operating on a transnational basis, coordinating participants from around the globe in reducing hunger, curing disease, controlling AIDS, saving the environment, helping children to survive, and so on. As Cooperrider and Dutton (1999) propose, there are 'no limits to global cooperation'. The mushrooming of *virtual communities* also represent a potential contribution to relational politics. There are now almost five million users of the Internet, a large proportion of whom take part in small, loosely linked communities of meaning. Cutting across racial, ethnic, age, gender, geographical and religious lines, such communities enable dialogue on innumerable issues, both profound and personal.[4] I am also impressed with the attempt towards full ecumenicalism among world religions – as realized, for example in the recent Parliament of World Religions. This meeting, in Chicago, brought together 8,000 people from 150 faiths around the globe into mutual inquiry. In each of these cases, the signifiers cross boundaries and begin to play in new arenas.

In conclusion

I do not wish to suggest in these proposals that we should abandon the existing tradition of identity politics, the discourses of oppression, justice, equality, rights and so on, nor the *in your face* activism that we have come to know so well. The point is not to eradicate existing vocabularies of action. Rather, my hope is that we are now participating in the generation of a new vocabulary, a new consciousness and a new range of practices – a relational politics that will be incorporative, pervasive, collaborative and unceasing. As lesbian feminist Shane Phelan (1989), proposed, 'identity politics must be based not only on identity, but on an appreciation for politics as the art of living together' (p. 170). Relational politics is precisely the attempt to realize this art.

Notes

1 Also see http://www.publicconversations.org/

2 See, for example, Hammond (1996) and www.TAOS.ORG. For ongoing discussion of these applications and extensions, consult the newsgroup by writing to Jack Brittain (mgtjwb@business.utah.edu).

3 See www.imaginechicago.org

4 Limitations to Internet coordination will be treated in the subsequent chapter.

11

TECHNOLOGY, SELF AND THE MORAL PROJECT

One of the central challenges for any culture is that of securing an acceptable, if not virtuous, mode of collective life. In effect, every culture is challenged by what we may loosely term a *moral project*. At least since the Enlightenment, we in Western culture have wished to answer this challenge by some means other than force of arms. Rather, in place of this crude form of control we have generally wished to link institutional order to a rational scaffold. That is, we have sought to construct an intelligibility that can be shared by all, an image of a moral life and how it is to be achieved. For over three centuries hopes for the moral society have rested on two major and conflicting intelligibilities, the one centring on the individual moral agent and the other on the community. These two fulcra of moral action serve as the chief focus of the present offering. Can they remain substantial and serviceable in the twenty-first century? Are there hopeful alternatives?

Here let us suppose that forms of moral intelligibility are neither developed nor sustained in a vacuum. Their genesis and possible demise depend importantly on existing conditions – both material and cultural. Whether a system of religion flourishes, for example, will depend on existing institutions of education, the economy, government ideology and so on. In this light let us consider one of the major transformations of the twentieth-century, namely in the *technologies of sociation*. From the telephone, automobile, mass transportation systems and radio early in the century, to the jet plane, television, Internet, satellite transmission, fax and cellular phone in the latter, low-cost technologies have dramatically expanded and intensified the domain of social connection. Whether we speak in terms of the 'information age, the 'globalization process' or a 'new world order', we find that daily life is marked by a steady expansion in the range of opinions, values, perspectives, attitudes, images, personalities and information to which we are exposed.[1]

Thus the central question posed by the present analysis: within the emerging technological context can the traditional conceptions of self and community remain viable bases for moral order? As I shall propose in what follows, this technological transformation is significantly undermining the potentials of both individualism and communalism to secure a morally viable society. What are required in the emerging condition are new forms of intelligibility and associated institutions. After considering the erosion of our longstanding traditions, I shall extend a theme common to the preceding chapters and outline the emerging potentials of *relational being*.

The self: death by technology

Drawing from early Greek, Judaic and Christian traditions, but most fully articulated within the course of the Enlightenment, we have traditionally viewed the single individual as the atom of the moral society. Whether we speak in terms of psyche, soul, agency, rational deliberation or conscious choice, we generally hold that moral action is derived from particular conditions of individual mind. Thus philosophers seek to establish essential criteria for moral decision-making, religious institutions are concerned with states of individual conscience, courts of law inquire into the individual's capacity to know right from wrong and parents are concerned with the moral education of their young. The general presumption is that the virtuous mind propels meritorious conduct, and that with sufficient numbers of individuals performing worthy acts we achieve the good society. It is this view that continues to inform much scholarly and scientific theorizing. It is inherent in Kohlberg's (1981) proposal for the epigenesis of moral thought, along with the appeals of Buber (1970) to treat the other as *thou*, and Levinas (1981) to respond to the face of the other within oneself. As long held, it is the individual on whom we must rely to achieve moral order.

Yet, let us consider the conception of self in terms of technological context. Here Walter Ong's (1982) classic analysis of the shift from oral communication to print technology is helpful. As Ong proposed, the shift from an oral to a print culture significantly altered the common forms of thought. Thus, for example, in oral societies people were more likely to depend on recall, concrete as opposed to abstract categories, and redundancy as opposed to precision. Yet, there is an important sense in which this fascinating thesis is insufficiently realized. While Ong wished to trace forms of mental life to cultural context, he had no access into mental conditions themselves. That is, the analysis tells us not about mental life itself but about changes is our beliefs about mental process. To extend the implications of Ong's analysis, we may ask whether the importance of individual minds – or the mind as a domain of signal importance – was not vitally enhanced by the expansion of print media. In an oral society, where the determination of the real and the good grows from face-to-face negotiation, there is little reason to launch inquiry into the speaker's private or mental meaning. Through words, facial expressions, gestures, physical context and the constant adjustments to audience expression, meanings are made transparent. However, when print allows words to spring from the face-to-face relationship – when printed discourse is insinuated into myriad contexts separated in time and space from its origins – then the hermeneutic problem becomes focal. That is, we begin serious speculation about 'the mind behind the words'. And with such questions as 'what did he intend?', 'what was his meaning here?', we create the reality of mind as the origin of action.[2]

Given the potential dependency of conceptions of self on technological conditions, let us consider our contemporary ethos. In particular, what is to be said about the increasing insinuation of the technologies of sociation into our lives and the effects on our beliefs in individual minds? In my view this technological transformation is slowly undermining the intelligibility of the individual self and its function as a source of moral action. The reasons are many and cumulative; I limit discussion here to several concatenating tendencies.[3]

Polyvocality

By dramatically expanding the range of information to which we are exposed, the range of persons with whom we have significant interchange and the range of opinion available within multiple media sites, so do we become privy to multiple realities. Or more simply, the comfort of parochial univocality is disturbed. From the spheres of national politics and economics to local concerns with education, environment or mental health we are confronted with a plethora of conflicting information and opinion. And so it is with matters of moral consequence. Whether it is a matter of Supreme Court nominees, abortion policies or affirmative action, for example, one is deluged with conflicting moral standpoints. To the extent that these standpoints are intelligible, they also enter the compendium of resources available for the individual's own deliberations. In a Bakhtinian vein, the individual approaches a state of radical polyvocality.

If one does acquire an increasingly diverse vocabulary of deliberation, how is a satisfactory decision to be reached? The inward examination of consciousness yields not coherence but cacophony; there is not a 'still small voice of conscience' but a chorus of competing contenders. It is one's moral duty to pay taxes, for example, but also to provide for one's dependents, to keep for oneself the rewards of one's labour and to withhold monies from unjust governmental policies; it is one's moral duty to give aid to starving Africans, but also to help the poor of one's own country, to prevent population growth and to avoid meddling in the politics of otherwise sovereign nations. Where in the mix of myriad moralities is the signal of certitude?

If immersion in a panoply of intelligibilities leaves one's moral resources in a state of complex fragmentation, then in what degree are these resources guiding or directing? Or more cogently for the present analysis, if 'inward looking' becomes increasingly less useful for matters of moral action, does the concern with 'my state of mind' not lose its urgency? The more compelling option is for the individual to turn outwards to social context – to detect the ambient opinion, to negotiate, compromise and improvise. And in this move from the private interior to the social sphere, the presumption of a private self as a source of moral direction is subverted. If negotiating the complexities of multiplicity becomes normalized, so does the conception of mind as moral touchstone grow stale.

Plasticity

As the technologies of sociation increase our immersion in information and evaluation, so do they expand the scope and complexity of our activities. We engage in a greater range of relationships distributed over numerous and variegated sites, from the face-to-face encounters in the neighbourhood and workplace, to professional and recreational relationships that often span continents. Further, because of the rapid movement of information and opinion, the half-life of various products and policies is shortened and the opportunities for novel departures expanded. The composition of the workplace is thus in continuous flux. The working person shifts jobs more frequently, often with an accompanying move to another location. In the early 1990s one in three American workers had been with their employer for less than a year and almost two out of three for less than five years.

As a result of these developments, the individual is challenged with an increasingly variegated array of behavioural demands. With each new performance site, new patterns of action may be required; dispositions appetites, personae – all may be acquired and abandoned and reappropriated as conditions invite or demand. With movements through time and space, oppositional accents may often be fashioned: firm here and soft there, commanding and then obedient, sophisticated and then crude, righteous and immoral, conventional and rebellious. For many people such chameleon-like shifts are now unremarkable; they constitute the normal hurly-burly of daily life. At times the challenges may be enjoyed, even sought. It was only five decades ago when David Riesman's (1953) celebrated book, *The lonely crowd*, championed the virtues of the inner-directed man and condemned the other-directed individual for lack of character – a man without a gyroscopic centre of self-direction. In the new techno-based ethos there is little need for the inner-directed, one-style-for-all individual. Such a person is narrow, parochial, inflexible. In the fast pace of the technological society, concern with the inner life is a luxury – if not a waste of time. We now celebrate protean being. In either case, the interior self recedes in significance (see, for example, Lifton, 1993).

The loss of authenticity

Let us consider a more subtle mode of self-erosion, owing in this instance to the increasing inundation of images, stories and information. Consider here those confirmatory moments of individual authorship, moments in which the sense of authentic action becomes palpably transparent. Given the Western tradition of individualism, these are typically moments in which we apprehend our actions as unique, in which we are not merely duplicating models, obeying orders or following conventions. Rather, in the innovative act we locate a guarantee of self as originary source, a creative agent, an author of one's own morality. Yet, in a world in which the technologies facilitate an enormous sophistication in 'how it goes', such moments become increasingly rare. How is it, for example, that a young couple, who for twenty years have been inundated by romance narratives – on television and radio, in film, in magazines and books – can utter a sweet word of endearment without a haunting sense of cliché? Or, in Umberto Eco's (1983: 67) terms, 'how can a man who loves a cultivated woman say to her: '"I love you madly," when he knows that she knows (and that she knows that he knows), that these words have already been written by Barbara Cartland?' In what sense can one stand out from the crowd in a singular display of moral fortitude and not hear the voices of John Wayne, Gary Cooper or Harrison Ford just over one's shoulder?

Should one attempt to secure confirmation of agency from a public action – political remonstrance, religious expression, musical performance, and the like – the problems of authenticity are even more acute. First, the existing technologies do not allow us to escape the past. Rather, images of the past are stored, resurrected and re-created as never before. In this sense, the leap from oral to print memory was only the beginning of a dramatic technological infusion of cultural memory. Thus, it becomes increasingly difficult to avoid observations of how any notable action is historically prepared. To perform publicly is to incite incessant commentaries about how one is, for example, 'just like the 60s', 'has his roots in Billy Sunday revivalism' or 'draws his inspiration from Jimi Hendrix'. Should the public demonstration gain media interest there is also a slow conversion from the authentic to the instrumental. That is, what may have once seemed spontaneous is now converted to a performance 'for the media' and its public. Indulgence in political passion, for example, becomes muted by the attentions one must give to wardrobe, voice projection and facial expression. One cannot simply 'play the music', but must be concerned with hairstyling, posture and girth. In a world in which the local is rapidly transported to the global, the half-life of moral authenticity rapidly diminishes.

Transience

To the extent that one is surrounded by a cast of others who respond to one in a similar way, a sense of unified self may result. A person may come to understand, for example, that he is the first son of an esteemed high-school teacher and a devoted mother, a star of the baseball team and a devout Catholic. This sense of perdurable character also furnishes a standard against which the morality of one's acts can be judged. One can know that 'this just isn't me', that 'If I did that I would feel insufferable guilt'. However, with the accumulating effects of the technologies of sociation, one now becomes transient, a nomad or a 'homeless mind' (Berger, Berger, and Kellner, 1973). The average American now moves over 11 times during the lifespan, with steadily increasing job opportunities in the global sphere. The demand for distant travel – both professional and leisure – has created an exponential increase in the annual number of air travellers. And, one must add as well the dimension of virtual travel – the enormous numbers of hours devoted to television, email or the web. In each case, we may psychologically span continents and cultures for hours at a time. In effect, the continuous reminders of one's identity – of who one is and always has been – no longer prevail. The internal standard grows pallid and, in the end, one must imagine that it counts for little in the generation of moral action.

There is a more subtle effect of such techno-induced transience. It is not only a coherent community that lends itself to the sense of personal depth. It is also the availability of others who provide the time and attention necessary for a sense of an unfolding interior to emerge. The process of psychoanalysis is illustrative. As the analyst listens with hovering interest to the words of the analysand, and these words prompt questions of deeper meaning, there is created for the analysand the sense of palpable interiority, the reality of a realm beyond the superficially given or, in effect, a sense of individual depth. The process requires time and attention. And so it is in daily life; one acquires the sense of depth primarily when there is ample time for exploration, time for moving beyond instrumental calculations to matters of 'deeper desire', forgotten fantasies, to 'what really counts'. Yet, it is precisely this kind of 'time off the merry-go-round' that is increasingly difficult to locate. In the techno-dominated world, one must keep moving, the network is vast, commitments are many, expectations are endless, opportunities abound and time is a scarce resource. It is no longer convenient to possess 'inner depths'.

Commodification of self

These arguments are closely tied to a final technology-induced shift in cultural understanding. Because the technologies of sociation enable information to be disseminated widely at a low cost, popular entertainment has become a major industry. Critical to the entertainment industry are individual performers – individuals who, because they are entertaining, command a broad audience and vast remuneration. In effect, 'the self' becomes available as a saleable commodity. The individual performer may alter his/her name, spouse and lifestyle in order to increase fame and income. As the entertainment industry increases, and television channels become more numerous, the demand for 'characters' becomes ever wider. Increasingly the common person – owing to a peculiar passion, unique story, act of heroism or stupidity or possession of 'inside information' – becomes a potential candidate for fame and fortune.

On a more subtle level, the potentials of persons to reconstruct themselves in multiple contexts also lends itself to a sense of 'self for sale'. In a continuous, long-term, face-to-face relationship one need seldom ask 'what do I want to get from this relationship' and 'how must I behave in order to get it'. It is primarily when one is parachuting in from an alien context that such questions are asked. Given one's polyvocal potentials, one is thus sensitized to the possibility of fashioning a profitable self – one that will garner the rewards of effective integration. Selling one's persona for the entertainment industry bears close kinship to the instrumental attitude resulting from moving across a complex terrain of relations in everyday life. In each case there is a growing consciousness of self as commodity. Being 'true to self', achieving depth of character or finding one's identity all become old encomiums from the past – but no longer profitable.

Each of these tendencies – toward polyvocality, plasticity, repetition, transience and commodification – functions so as to undermine the long-standing presumption of a palpable self, personal consciousness as an agentive source or interior character as a touchstone of the moral life.[4] Yet, while lamentable in certain respects, the waning intelligibility of moral selves is much welcomed in other quarters. Both intellectually and ideologically the concept of the self as moral atom is flawed. On the conceptual level, it is not simply that the conception of moral agency recapitulates the thorny problems of epistemological dualism – subject vs. object, mind vs. body and minds knowing other minds. These issues are quite familiar from preceding chapters. But more specifically, the very idea of an *independent* moral decision is uncompelling. How, it is asked, could moral thought take place except within the categories supplied by the culture? If we subtracted the entire vocabulary of the culture from individual subjectivity, how could the individual form questions about justice, duty, rights or moral goods? In Michael Sandel's (1982: 179) terms: 'To imagine a person incapable of constitutive attachments . . . is not to conceive an ideally free and rational agent, but to imagine a person wholly without character, without moral depth.'

These conceptual problems are conjoined to widespread ideological critique. Alexis de Tocqueville's (1969: 506) observations of nineteenth-century American life set the stage: 'Individualism is a calm and considered feeling which disposes each citizen to isolate himself from the mass of his fellows . . . he gladly leaves the greater society to look after itself.' Within recent decades these views have been echoed and amplified by many. Christopher Lasch (1979) has traced linkages between individualist presumptions and cultural tendencies toward narcissism; Bellah and his colleagues (1985) argue that certain forms of individualism work against the possibility for committed relationships and dedication to community; for Edward Sampson (1993a) the presumption of a self-contained individual leads to an insensitivity to minority voices, suppression of the other and social division. Ultimately, the conception of an interior origin of action defines the society in terms of unbreachable isolation. If what is most central to our existence is hidden from the other, and vice versa, we are forever left with a sense of profound isolation, an inability to ever know what lies behind the other's visage. By constituting an interior self we inevitably create the Other from whom we shall forever remain alien.

Techno/community: all against all redux

As we find, there are many reasons for welcoming a decline in attempts to lodge moral action in independent minds. It is not simply the conceptual and political limits inherent in individualism that are at stake here. Rather, for many analysts there is a far superior candidate available for achieving the moral project, namely the community. As Alisdair MacIntyre (1984) has proposed, to be an individual self – that is, one who is identified within a narrative of past, present and future – requires a community. To be a moral self, then, is 'to be accountable for the actions and experiences which compose a narratable life within a community' (p. 202). In this sense, the moral project is achieved by sustaining the best of a community's traditions. In effect, 'The virtues find their point and purpose not only in sustaining those relationships necessary if the variety of goods internal to practices are to be achieved . . . but also in sustaining those traditions which provide both practices and individual lives with their necessary historical context' (p. 207). On the more political level, this view resonates with the communitarian attempt to replace a rights-based orientation to societal life, with one emphasizing duties to community.

Let us again, however, consider the community as moral resources in the age of technology. Again the way is paved for such reflection by an earlier classic, in this case Benedict Anderson's (1983) *Imagined communities*. As Anderson proposed the emergence of nation-states was importantly facilitated by the development of print technology – which not only succeeded in unifying and codifying particular languages, but could be used to generate a sense of common interest and common future. In effect, we cannot separate issues of social organization from the technological context. In light of the contemporary context, then, what are the potentials of community-based morality?

If by community we mean a group of people relating face-to-face across time in a geographically circumscribed habitat, there would appear little hope for success in the moral project. As I attempted to outline in *The saturated self* (1991a), twentieth-century technologies of sociation have everywhere eroded the traditional face-to-face community as a generative matrix for moral action. Mass transportation systems have separated home from workplace, and neighbourhoods from commercial and entertainment centres; families are frequently scattered across continents; and largely owing to career demands families move in and out of neighbourhoods with increasing frequency. Even when neighbours or families are within physical proximity, face-to-face interaction has dramatically diminished. Technologically mediated exchange – through telephone, television, radio, CD players, computers and the like – is steadily reducing dependency on those in the immediate surrounds. In these and many other ways both the geographically circumscribed neighbourhood and the traditional family unit are losing their capacity to generate and sustain moral commitment.[5] Thus, while theoretically more appealing than individualism, the emerging technological ethos poses substantial and ever-intensifying limits to lodging morality in geographically based communities.

Yet, while technological developments are reducing the significance of face-to-face communities within the culture, we are also witnessing a striking increase in the number and importance of *technologically mediated communities*. These are communities whose participants rely largely on communication technologies for sustaining their realities, values and agendas. Television evangelism is an obvious case in point. Several million Americans are linked primarily through mediated communication to a set of beliefs that affect decisions from local school systems to the posture of national political parties (see, for example, Hoover, 1988). Less obvious are the 20,000 non-governmental organizations (NGOs) mentioned in the preceding chapter. Such organizations operate internationally – to combat starvation, overpopulation, AIDS, environmental erosion and other threats to human well-being. Over a million such private organizations advance human welfare within the USA. Such organizations are vitally dependent on existing communication technology for continuing sustenance.

Less public in their moral agenda are also the countless number of computer-mediated or *virtual* communities emerging over the past decade. The sense of community often created within such groups is illustrated in Howard Rheingold's *The virtual community*:

> Finding the WELL [a computer-mediated community] was like discovering a cozy little world . . . hidden within the walls of my house; an entire cast of characters welcomed me to the troupe with great merriment as soon as I found the secret door. . . . A full-scale subculture was growing on the other side of my telephone jack, and they invited me to help create something new. The virtual village of a few hundred people I stumbled upon in 1985 grew to eight thousand by 1993. (p. 7)

The emergence of these communities is now facilitated by the World Wide Web on which virtually any organization can mount a colourful invitation to participate. If moral dispositions are solidified through relationships, one might see great promise in twentieth-century communication technologies. Here we find a mushrooming of new communities, many of them specifically constructed around visions of the good. As Dave Healy (1997) appropriately reflects, 'To the extent that the Internet represents a culture of coherence, it serves as a corrective to the dangers of individualism.' (p. 148)

Yet, the very advantages of technologically based organization may simultaneously pose the greatest danger. On the one hand, the range of moral suppositions represented in the cyberworld is enormous and variegated; it is also suffused with potential conflict. At present there are, for example, highly active web sites inviting membership into religious organizations ranging from all the recognized denominations, to a profusion of small sects (including, for example, Sufism, Shaminism, Jainism, Druidism, and Pantheism).[6] Further, one may join in a host of variegated political movements, ranging from lesbian and gay activists, elderly activists and pro-life groups, to the Klu Klux Klan, militia movements and neo-Nazis. The potential power of these forms of mediated engagement is perhaps most dramatically evidenced in the ability of the techno-generated cult, Heaven's Gate, to precipitate mass suicide. Not only do we find here seeds for pervasive social conflict, but such enclaves can be created and sustained rapidly, inexpensively and with little regard to geographic distance. The ease and efficacy of organization is also accompanied by strong centripetal or inner-directed tendencies. With the flick of a switch the individual enters the totalizing reality of the group. In many cases, the techno-mediated relationships are complemented by printed media (newsletters, newspapers, magazines) and face-to-face meetings (religious services, conferences, demonstrations, picnics). Social and political agendas invite a lifestyle of full engagement. Healy (1997) comments on the tendencies toward cyber-segmentation:

> At my university . . . the IRC addicts are just as segregated as the occupants of my son's high school lunch room. In our computer lab the Vietnamese students hang out on Vietnamese channels, just as at Ben's school they all sit at their own tables at lunch. . . . On the net . . . talk tends not to get 'overheard;' the boundaries separating virtual conversants are less substantial, but their effect is more dramatic. Two virtual places may be 'separated' by only a keystroke, but their inhabitants will never meet. (p. 62)

Accompanying such segmentation is a tendency for moral/ political positions to become polarized and rigidified. The in-group reality becomes increasingly convincing and external realities become increasingly malevolent. When the moral/political agendas become manifest in public action, jarring conflict is almost inevitable. Such ruptures in civil society have become commonplace: in battles over rights to abortion, the environment, gay and lesbian rights, freedom of speech, social justice, school prayer, gun control, and more. I suspect there are few readers who have not joined in advocacy in one or more of these domains, and who have simultaneously nurtured strong antagonism for the opposition. These are all struggles among competing visions of the moral society. However, it is when a commitment to justice, dignity, freedom and moral integrity lends to the bombing of the Federal Building in Oklahoma City that we begin to confront the impasse of community based morality.

Towards relational being

As the preceding analysis suggests, our legacy for pursuing the moral project is severely limited. In light of the emerging technological context, neither individualism nor communalism holds substantial promise for securing an acceptable mode of cultural life. Both traditions are deeply flawed – conceptually, ideologically and practically. Indeed with the emerging clash of global cultures one might view these traditions as potential hazards to our future well-being. Each is deeply divisive. On what conceptual grounds are we thus to proceed; are there significant alternatives to individualism and communalism for pursuing the moral project in the twenty-first century? As outlined in the preceding chapter, there is subtle but significant movement taking place, one that will demand nurturant and creative attention in order to bear fruit. It is movement that works to subvert the self/society binary, and to subsume both self and community within a broader reality of relatedness.

In certain respects the emerging technologies again create the space for a relational imaginary. Of particular relevance is the development of chat rooms, bulletin boards, list serves and other Internet facilities that enable relationships to take place without specific lodgement in individual bodies (Stone, 1995; Turkle, 1995). That is, identities can be put forward that may or may not be linked in any specific way to the concrete existence of the participants and these cyber-identities may carry on active and engaging relationships. Most significant for our purposes, we have here relationships that proceed not on the basis of 'real selves' (originary minds within a body), but on the basis of self-constructions or discursive for-mations. (One 'real self' may indeed generate multiple self-constructions). It is only the coordinated functioning of these discursive formations that enables the cyber 'community' (list serve, chat room, bulletin board, inter-active game) to be achieved. In effect, the cyber community has no geographic locus outside the web of discourse by which it is constituted. We approach here a condition of pure relatedness, without individuals or community in the traditional sense.

Inspirations for an image of relationship without self or community gains further impetus from the techno-sphere. For several decades the computer has served as one of the chief metaphors for human functioning. The cognitive revolution in psychology, along with the artificial intelligence movement and cognitive science, have derived much of their intelligibility from various equations of person and computer. However, with the dramatic expansion of the Internet and the World Wide Web, the computer gradually loses its rhetorical fascination. The Internet is a domain that brings instantaneous relationship to an exponentially increasing popula-tion throughout the globe. It is a domain so vast and so powerful that it can scarcely be controlled by the nation-state. It is legislated by no institution; it functions virtually outside the law. In this context the computer is merely a gateway into a domain without obvious end. The metaphor of the computer – limited and parochial – is gradually placed by the *network* – a world that stretches toward infinity.

In the same way that the technological ethos has previously favoured the realities of self and of community, so does it now function to inspire concern with relationship. This concern has made its way into many pages of the present work. The concern with relational conceptions of the self, and with relational process in therapy, organizations, education and political action, have all been focal. In each case the attempt is to make manifest the reality of human relatedness and the significance of relationship for all we value. Yet, unlike traditional scholarship, such theorizing is not typically devoted to illuminating the truth about human action. Rather, social constructionism generally eschews the warrants of 'truth' and 'objectivity' in favour of a use-based conception of language. Thus, the attempt of relational theorizing is primarily to furnish a range of discursive resources that might enlarge the potentials for human interchange. This aversion to truth posits also brings us face to face with the challenge of the moral project. In what sense can relational accounts, born of a constructionist sensibility, serve as moral resources for the future?

At the outset the constructionist aversion to fundamental or foundational claims (monologic and totalitarian) also works against moral commitment. If so, then constructionism is placed under attack for its lack of moral standpoint – its 'moral relativism'. In effect, there is no moral standpoint here but a vacuum.[7] Yet, it is precisely within its groundlessness that we locate the moral potential of constructionism for the postmodern world. There is no attempt within constructionism to ground its suppositions in a foundation or first philosophy, nor simultaneously to suppress any ethic or ideology. Rather, from the constructionist perspective, all moral discourses are resources for creating meaning – which is to say, resources essential for creating a sense of the good (worth, value, ideals). At the same time, however, when these resources are used in exclusion of all others, when they become hegemonic in their ends, they become destructive. Now, for the constructionist there is no foundational warrant for championing creation over destruction. However, if we value the very process of valuing, then we have a stake in fostering processes of relationship from which values emerge. In embracing a particular moral good there is latent a more fundamental commitment to the process out of which the good can be achieved – essentially a relationship of creation rather than destruction.

If this path seems reasonable, then our attention turns from the attempt to generate a specific moral code to issues of moral difference. It is in the space of difference that we locate the potential for mutual destruction – the end of valuing. In most sectors of life discursive relations proceed without severe obstruction. As we converse with family, friends, neighbours and so on there will emerge implicit (and sometimes explicit) moral codes – agreements on what is proper, appropriate or desirable. In effect, normal human interchange will yield up standards of the good. In this sense, the moral project is always already in motion. No foundational rationality is required for the sense of the good to emerge. However, the major problem at this juncture is not the generation of morality in itself, but the existence of multiple moralities. It is when enclaves of the good come to see their local standards as universal and alterior commitments as inferior or threatening that the stage is set for the dissolution of meaning. It is in the process of mutual annihilation that we confront the destruction of relationship – thus the end of moral meaning.

In conclusion: sustaining the matrix of meaning

It is thus we find our major challenge today is that of conflicting moralities. By what means can we now go on satisfactorily together – living side by side with those whose visions of the good are, for us, a form of hell? We might initially be drawn towards the promulgation of discourse ethics – a set of principles that would help us to adjudicate our differences – as in the case of Habermas's (1993) significant efforts. However, in light of the anti-foundationalist thrust of constructionist reasoning, there is reason to avoid transcendental warrants for particular kinds of conversation. And, given arguments for the use-based character of meaning, there is little desire to generate abstract, context-free 'rules for good conversations'. Rather, for many constructionists, there is more to be gained by turning from scholarship to societal practices. The practices of particular concern to morality are those relevant to sustaining constructive processes of meaning-making in the face of difference.

Practices for sustaining the generative creation of meaning have been focal throughout the present work. We have discussed numerous means of bridging the gaps separating those who occupy disparate and conflicting realities. Indeed, many of the chapters have set a course toward self-demonstration in this respect. As also described, many practitioners and theorists are now engaged in the attempt to replace agonistic relations with productive meaning-making. Such efforts issue from such disparate domains as family therapy, organizational development, communication, counseling, education, social work, community organizing, and more. These explorations are scarcely the private preserve of constructionists; the efforts themselves are communal. Within such explorations, however, lie potentials for what may become significant societal resources for sustaining the moral project. It is thus that the present offering ends not with a blueprint for a promising future, but an invitation to join in the exploration and creation of practical resources for sustaining the process of morality-making itself.

Notes

1 For an extended treatment of this process, see Gergen (1991).

2 Such a conclusion would also be congenial with a rapidly growing body of literature on the historical and cultural construction of the mind. See, for example, Foucault (1978); Lutz (1988); Graumann and Gergen (1996).

3 For a more extended analysis of the 'loss of self' in the media age, see Turkle (1995) and Gergen (1996).

4 These conclusions are surely resonant with other accounts of 'the loss', 'decentring' or 'deconstruction' of the self in recent scholarship. However, where key writings by Foucault, Lacan and Derrida derive their conclusions from theoretical premises, the present analysis attempts to trace the sense of dissolution to particular circumstances of cultural technology. In effect, we might suppose that the very intelligibility of the theoretical analyses may be derived from common discourse in contemporary culture.

5 For further discussion of technology and the erosion of the traditional family, see Meyrowitz (1985) and Gergen (1991).

6 See www.spiritual.com for a listing of several thousand entries into cyberfaith.

7 For further discussion of constructionism and moral relativism, see Gergen (1994a), Chapter 4.

BIBLIOGRAPHY

Addison, R.B., & Packer, J.J. (Eds.). (1989). *Entering the circle: hermeneutic inquiry in psychology.* Albany, NY: SUNY Press.

Albertsen, N. (1988). Postmodernism, post-Fordism, and critical social theory. *Environment and Planning, 6:* 339–365.

Allen, D.B., Miller, E.D., & Raghu, N. (1991). North America. In N. Raghu (Ed.), *Comparative management* (pp. 23–54). Cambridge, MA: Ballinger.

Alvesson, M., & Willmott, H. (1992). On the idea of emancipation in management and organization studies. *The Academy of Management Review, 17:* 432–464.

Amundson, J. (1996). Why pragmatics is probably enough for now. *Family Process, 35:* 473–486.

Andersen, T. (1991). *The reflecting team: dialogues and dialogues about dialogues.* New York: W.W. Norton.

Andersen, T. (1995). Reflecting processes; acts of informing and forming; you can borrow my eyes but you must not take them away from me! In S. Friedman (Ed.), *The reflecting team in action* (pp. 11–38). New York: Guilford Press.

Anderson, B. (1983). *Imagined communities.* London: Verso.

Anderson, H. (1997). *Conversation, language and possibilities, a postmodern approach to psychotherapy.* New York: Basic Books.

Anderson, H., & Goolishian, H. (1992). The client is the expert: a not-knowing approach to therapy. In S. McNamee & K. Gergen (Eds.), *Therapy as social construction* (pp. 25–38). Thousand Oaks, CA: Sage.

Apple, M. (1982). *Education and power.* Boston: Routledge & Kegan Paul.

Apple, M. (1993). *Official knowledge, democratic education in a conservative age.* New York: Routledge.

Arendt, H. (1969). *On violence.* New York: Harcourt Brace Jovanovich.

Argyris, C. (1996). Actionable knowledge: design causality in the service of consequential theory. *The Journal of Applied Behavioral Science, 32:* 390–406.

Argyris, C., Putnam, R., & Smith, D. (1985). *Action science.* San Francisco: Jossey-Bass.

Aries, P. (1962). *Centuries of childhood: a social history of family life.* New York: Vintage.

Aronowitz, S., & Giroux, H.A. (1991). *Postmodern education: politics, culture and social criticism.* Minneapolis: University of Minnesota Press.

Ashbach, C., & Schermer, V.L. (1987). *Object relations, the self, and the group.* London: Routledge & Kegan Paul.

Ashley, D. (1990). Postmodernism and the 'end of the individual': from repressive self-mastery to ecstatic communication. *Current Perspectives in Social Theory, 10:* 195–221.

Astley, G. (1985). Administrative science as socially constructed truth. *Administrative Science Quarterly, 30*: 497–513.

Astley, G., & Zammuto, R. (1992). Organization science, managers, and language games. *Organization Science, 3*: 443–460.

Atkouf, O. (1992). Management and theories of organizations in the 1990s: toward a critical radical humanism? *The Academy of Management Review, 17*: 407–431.

Averill, J.R. (1982). *Anger and aggression: an essay on emotion.* New York: Springer-Verlag.

Averill, J.R., & Nunley, E.P. (1992). *Voyages of the heart.* New York: Free Press.

Ayer, A.J. (1940). *The foundation of empirical knowledge.* New York: Macmillan.

Bacigalupe, G. (1996). Writing in therapy: a participatory approach. *Journal of Family Therapy, 18*: 361–374.

Badinter, E. (1980). *Mother love: myth and reality.* New York: Macmillan.

Bakan, D. (1990). *Sigmund Freud and the Jewish mystical tradition.* London: Free Association Books.

Bakhtin, M.M. (1981). *The dialogic imagination: four essays by M.M. Bakhtin* (M. Holquist, T.C. Emerson, & M. Holquist, Eds.). Austin, TX: University of Texas Press.

Bakhtin, M.M. (1985) *Speech genres and other late essays.* Austin, TX: University of Texas Press.

Barbules, N.C. (1993). *Dialogue in teaching.* New York: Teachers College Press.

Barnes, B. (1974). *Scientific knowledge and sociological theory.* London: Routledge & Kegan Paul.

Baron, J., Forgione, P., Rindone, D., Kruglanski, H., & Davy, B. (1989). *Toward a new generation of student outcome measures: Connecticut's common core of learning assessment.* Presentation at the annual meetings of the American Educational Research Association, San Francisco, CA.

Bartlett, C., & Ghoshal, S. (1991). Global strategic management: impact on the new frontiers of strategy research. *Strategic Management Journal, 12*: 5–16.

Baudrillard, J. (1988). *The ecstasy of communication.* New York: Semiotext(e).

Baudrillard, J. (1994). *Simulacre and simulation.* Ann Arbor, MI: University of Michigan Press.

Bazerman, C. (1988). *Shaping written knowledge: the genre and activity of the experimental article in science* Madison, WI: University of Wisconsin Press.

Becker, C., Chasin, L., Herzog, M., & Roth, S. (1995). 'From stuck debate to new conversation on contraversial issues: a report from the public conversations project.' *Journal of Feminist Family Therapy, 7*: 143–163.

Becker, J. & Varelas, M. (1995). Assisting construction: the role of the teacher in assisting the learner's construction of preexisting cultural knowledge. In L. Steffe & J. Gale (Eds.), *Constructivism in education.* Hillsdale, NJ: Lawrence Erlbaum.

Belenky, M., Clinchy, B.M., Goldberger, N.R., & Tarule, J.M. (1986). *Women's ways of knowing.* New York: Basic Books.

Bell, D. (1960). *The end of ideology.* Glencoe, IL: Free Press.

Bell, D. (1974). *The coming of post-industrial society.* London: Heinemann.

Bellah, R.N. et al. (1985). *Habits of the heart.* Berkeley, CA: University of California Press.

Benhabib, S. (1992). *Situating the self.* Cambridge: Cambridge University Press.

Berg, I.K., & de Shazer, S. (1993). Making numbers talk: language in therapy.

In S. Friedman (Ed.), *The new language of change: constructive collaboration in psychotherapy* (pp. 5–25). New York: Guilford Press.

Berger, P., Berger, B., & Kellner, H. (1973). *The homeless mind*. New York: Vintage.

Berger, P. & Luckmann, T. (1966). *The social construction of reality*. New York: Doubleday/Anchor.

Berman, M. (1982). *All that is solid melts into air: the experience of modernity*. New York: Simon & Schuster.

Berman, R.A. (1989). *Modern culture and critical theory*. Madison, WI: University of Wisconsin Press.

Bernstein, R. (1989). The end of history, explained for a second time. *New York Times*, 10 December, Section 4: 6.

Berquist, W. (1993). *The postmodern organization*. San Francisco: Jossey Bass.

Beyer, L., & Apple, M. (1988). *The curriculum: problems, politics and possibilities*. Albany, NY: State University of New York Press.

Billig, M. (1987). *Arguing and thinking: a rhetorical approach to social psychology*. Cambridge: Cambridge University Press.

Billig, M. (1990). Collective memory, ideology and the British royal family. In D. Middleton & D. Edwards (Eds.), *Collective remembering*. London: Sage.

Billig, M., Condor, S., Edwards, D., Gane, M., Middleton, D., & Radley, A. (1988). *Ideological dilemmas: a social psychology of everyday thinking*. London: Sage.

Bleich, D. (1988). *The double perspective, language, literacy and social relations*. Oxford: Oxford University Press.

Bloom, L.R. (1996). Stories of one's own: nonunitary subjectivity in narrative representation. *Qualitative Inquiry*, 2: 176–197.

Blumenfeld-Jones, D.S. (1995). Dance as a mode of research representation. *Qualitative Inquiry*, 1: 391–401.

Bohan, J., & Russell, G.M. (1999). *Conversations about psychology and sexual orientation*. New York: New York University Press.

Boje, D. (1992). *The university in a panoptic cage: the disciplining of the student and faculty body*. Paper presented at the National Academy of Management Meetings, Las Vegas, Nevada.

Boje, D., Gephart, R., & Thatchenkery, T. (Eds.). (1996). *Postmodern management and organization theory*. Newbury Park, CA: Sage.

Boje, D.M., Gephart, R.P., & Joseph, T. (Eds.). (1997). *Postmodern management and organization theory*. Thousand Oaks, CA: Sage.

Boland, R.J., & Tenkasi, R. (1992). *Post-modernism and its implications for information system design*. Paper presented at the National Academy of Management Meetings, Las Vegas, Nevada.

Botschner, J. (1995). Social constructionism and the pragmatic entente: a reply to Osbeck. *Theory and Psychology*, 5: 145–151.

Bowles, S., & Gintis, H. (1976). *Schooling in capitalist America*. New York: Basic Books.

Boyacigiller, N., & Adler, N. (1991). The parochial dinosaur: organizational science in a global context. *The Academy of Management Review*, 16: 262–290.

Boyatzis, R. (1982). *The competent manager: a model for effective performance*. New York: Wiley.

Boyte, H., & Evans, S. (1986). *Free spaces*. New York: Harper & Row.

Bradley, B.S. (1989). *Visions of infancy, a critical introduction to child psychology*. Cambridge: Polity Press.

Bradshaw-Camball, P., & Murray, V. (1991). Illusions and other games: a trifocal view of organizational politics. *Organizational Science*, 2: 379–398.

Brooks, C., & Warren, R.P. (1970). *Modern rhetoric*. New York: Harcourt Brace and World.

Brown, N. (1959). *Life against death, the psychoanalytical meaning of history*. Middletown, CT: Wesleyan University Press.

Brown, R.H. (1987). *Society as text*, Chicago: University of Chicago Press.

Bruffee, K.A. (1993). *Collaborative learning*. Baltimore: Johns Hopkins University Press.

Bruner, J. (1986). *Actual minds, possible worlds*. Cambridge, MA: Harvard University Press.

Bruner, J. (1990). *Acts of meaning*. Cambridge, MA: Harvard University Press.

Bruner, J.S. (1996). *The culture of education*. Cambridge, MA: Harvard University Press.

Buber, M. (1970). *I and thou*. New York: Scribner.

Budge, G.S., & Katz, B. (1995) Constructing psychological knowledge: reflections on science, scientists and epistemology in the APA Publication Manual. *Theory and Psychology*, 5: 217–232.

Burkitt, I. (1991). *Social selves: theories of the social formation of personality*. London: Sage.

Burkitt, I. (1996). Social and personal constructs. *Theory and Psychology*, 6: 71–77.

Burrell, G., & Morgan, G. (1979). *Sociological paradigms and organizational analysis*. Portsmouth, NH: Heinemann.

Butler, J. (1990). *Gender trouble: feminism and the subversion of identity*. New York: Routledge.

Butler, M.H., Gardner, B.C., & Bird, M.H. (1998). Not just a time-out: change dynamics of prayer for religious couples in conflict situations. *Family Process, 37*: 451–475.

Cabaj, R.P., & Stein, T.S. (Eds.). (1996). *Textbook of homosexuality and mental health*. Washington, DC: American Psychiatric Press.

Calas, M., & Smircich, L. (1991). Voicing seduction to silence leadership. *Organization Studies, 12*: 567–602.

Calhoun, C. (1994) Social theory and the politics of identity. In C. Calhoun (Ed.), *Social theory and the politics of identity*. Oxford: Blackwell.

Carter, S.L. (1991) *Reflections of an affirmative action baby*. New York: Basic Books.

Case, S., Brett, P., & Foster, S.L. (Eds.). (1995) *Cruising the performative*. Bloomington, IN: Indiana University Press.

Cecchin, G., Lane, G., & Ray, W. (1992). *Irreverence: a strategy for therapist's survival*. London: Karnac Books.

Chandler, A. (1962). *Strategy and structure*. Cambridge, MA: MIT Press.

Cheal, D. (1990) Authority and incredulity: sociology between modernism and post-modernism. *Canadian Journal of Sociology, 15*: 129–147.

Chen, C.C., & Meindl, J. (1991). The construction of leadership images in the popular press: the case of Donald Burr and People Express. *Administrative Science Quarterly, 36*: 521–551.

Chia, R. (1996). From modern to postmodern organizational analysis. *Organizational Studies, 16* (4): 579–604.

Chia, R., & King, I.W. (1998). The organizational structuring of novelty. *Organization, 5*: 461–478.

Child, J. (1972). Organizational structure, environment, and performance: the role of strategic choice. *Sociology, 6*: 2–22.

Clark, P., & Wilson, J. (1961). Incentive systems: a theory of organizations. *Administrative Science Quarterly, 6*: 129–166.

Clegg, S.R. (1989). *Frameworks of power*. London: Sage.

Clegg, S.R. (1990). *Modern organizations: organization studies in the postmodern world*. Newbury Park, CA: Sage.

Clegg, S.R. (1992). *Postmodern management?* Paper presented at the National Academy of Management Meetings, Las Vegas, Nevada.

Clifford, J., & Marcus, G. (Eds.) (1986). *Writing culture*. Berkeley, CA: University of California Press.

Cloud, D.L. (1994). Socialism of the mind: the new age of post-Marxism. In H.W. Simons & M. Billig (Eds.), *After postmodernism*. London; Sage.

Cohen, E. (1995). Towards a history of European physical sensibility: pain in the later middle ages. *Science in Context, 8*: 47–74.

Cole, M. (1998). *Cultural psychology*. Cambridge: Harvard University Press.

Collins, P.H. (1990). *Black feminist thought*. New York: Routledge.

Colville, I.D., Waterman, R.H., & Weick, K.E. (1999) Organizing and the search for excellence: making sense of the times in theory and practice. *Organization, 6*: 129–148.

Combs, G. and Freedman, J. (1990). *Symbol, story, and ceremony: using metaphor in individual and family therapy*. New York: W.W. Norton.

Connolly, W. (1991). *Identity/difference: democratic negotiations of political paradox*. Ithaca, NY: Cornell University Press.

Cooper, R. (1989). Modernism, postmodernism and organizational analysis 3: the contribution of Jacques Derrida. *Organization Studies, 10* (4): 479–502.

Cooper, R., & Burrell. G. (1988). Modernism, postmodernism and organizational analysis: an introduction, Part I. *Organization Studies, 9*: 91–112.

Cooperrider, D.L. (1990). Positive imagery, positive action: the affirmative bais of organizing. In S. Srivastva & D.L. Cooperrider (Eds.), *Appreciative management and leadership*. San Francisco: Jossey-Bass.

Cooperrider, D.L., & Dutton, J.E. (Eds.). (1999). *Organizational dimensions of global change*. Thousand Oaks, CA: Sage.

Cooperrider, D., & Srivastva, S. (1990). Appreciative inquiry in organizational life. *Research in Organizational Change and Development, 1*: 129–169.

Cooperrider, D., Sorensen, P.F., Whitney, D., & Yaeger, T.F. (Eds.) (1999). *Appreciative inquiry*. Cleveland: Stipes.

Corbin, A. (1986). *The foul and the fragrant*. Cambridge, MA: Harvard University Press.

Coulter, J. (1979). *The social construction of the mind*. New York: Macmillan.

Coulter, J. (1983). *Rethinking cognitive theory*. New York: St. Martin's Press.

Cousins, M., & Hussain, A. (1984). *Theoretical traditions in the social sciences*. New York: St. Martin's Press.

Covaleski, M., & Dirsmith, M. (1990). Dialectic tension, double reflexivity and the everyday accounting researcher: on using qualitative methods. *Accounting, Organizations and Society, 15*: 543–573.

Crook, S., Pakulski, J., & Waters, M. (1992). *Postmodernization*. London: Sage.

Crouch, S. (1990). *Notes of a hanging judge*. New York: Oxford University Press.

Crozier, M. (1964). *The bureaucratic phenomenon*. London: Tavistock.

Crystal, G. (1991). *In search of excess: the overcompensation of American executives*. New York: Norton.

Csikszentmihalyi, M. (1990). *Flow: the psychology of optimal experience.* New York: Harper & Row.

Cushman, P. (1990). Why is the self empty: toward a historically situated psychology. *American Psychologist, 45:* 599–611.

Cushman, P. (1995) *Constructing the self, constructing America, a cultural history of psychotherapy.* Reading, MA: Addison-Wesley.

Dahl, R.A. (1957). The concept of power. *Behavioural Science, 2:* 201–205.

Dahl, R.A. (1961). *Who governs? democracy and power in an American city.* New Haven, CT: Yale University Press.

Danziger, K. (1997). *Naming the mind: how psychology found its language.* London: Sage.

Darwin, C. (1896). *The expression of the emotions in man and animals.* New York: Appleton: 1885.

Davies, B., & Harré, R. (1990). Positioning: the discursive production of selves. *Journal for the Theory of Social Behaviour, 20:* 43–63.

de Grazia, A. (1960). The sciences and values of administration-I. *Administrative Science Quarterly, 5:* 421–447.

de Man, P. (1986). *The resistance to theory.* Minneapolis: University of Minneapolis Press.

de Shazer, S. (1991). *Putting difference to work.* New York: W.W. Norton.

de Shazer, S. (1994). *Words were originally magic.* New York: W.W. Norton.

Deese, J. (1984). *American freedom and the social sciences.* New York: Columbia University Press.

Deleuze, G., & Guattari, F. (1983). *Anti-Oedipus, capitalism and schizophrenia.* Minneapolis: University of Minnesota Press.

DeMause, L. (1982). *Foundations of psychohistory.* New York: Creative Roots.

Denzin, N., & Lincoln, Y. (2000). *Handbook of qualitative research.* 2nd ed. Thousand Oaks, CA: Sage.

Derrida, J. (1977). *Of grammatology* (G.C. Spivak, Trans.). Baltimore: Johns Hopkins University Press.

Dershowitz, A.M. (1994). *The abuse excuse.* Boston: Little Brown.

Dewey, J. (1916). *Democracy and education: an introduction to the philosophy of education.* New York: Free Press.

Doan, R.E. (1998). The king is dead; long live the king: narrative therapy and practicing what we preach. *Family Process, 37:* 379–385.

Douglas, M. (1986). *How institutions think.* Syracuse, NY: Syracuse University Press.

Driscoll, M., & Brahn, G. (1995). *Prosthetic territories: politics and hyper-technology.* Boulder, CO: Westview.

du Preez, P. (1980). *The politics of identity.* New York: St. Martin's Press.

Eagleton, T. (1996). *The illusions of postmodernism.* Oxford: Blackwell.

Eco, U. (1983). *Postscript to the Name of the Rose.* San Diego: Harcourt Brace Jovanovich.

Edwards, D., Ashmore, M., & Potter, J. (1995). Death and furniture: the rhetoric and politics and theology of bottom line arguments against relativism. *History of the Human Sciences, 8:* 25–49.

Edwards, D., & Mercer, N. (1987). *Common knowledge, the development of understanding in the classroom.* London: Methuen.

Edwards, D., & Potter, J. (1992). *Discursive psychology.* London: Sage.

Egelund, M. (1997). (Ed.) *Enforskel der gor enforskel: Reflekterende proceser hos born, foroeldre og personale pa en d{o}gninstitution.* Kobenhaven: Hans Reitzels Forlag.

Elder, G.H. (1974). *Children of the great depression*. Chicago: University of Chicago Press.

Elias, N. (1978). *The civilizing process*. New York: Urizen Books.

Ellis, C. (1995). *Final negotiations: a story of love, loss, and chronic illness*. Philadelphia: Temple University Press.

Ellis, C., & Bochner, A.P. (Eds.). (1996). *Composing ethnography*. Walnut Creek, CA: Alta Mira.

Epston. D., & White, M. (1995). Termination as a rite of passage: questioning strategies for a therapy of inclusion. In R. Neimeyer & M. Mahoney (Eds.), *Constructivism in psychotherapy* (pp. 339–354). Washington, DC: American Psychological Association.

Epston, D., White, M., & Murray, K. (1992). A proposal for re-authoring therapy: Rosie's revisioning of her life and a commentary. In S. McNamee & K.J. Gergen (Eds.), *Therapy as social construction* (pp. 96–115). London: Sage.

Erikson, E.H. (1975). *Life history and the historical moment*. New York: Norton.

Etzioni, A. (1993). *The spirit of community*. New York: Crown.

Fay, B. (1987). *Critical social science, liberation and its limits*. Ithaca, NY: Cornell University Press.

Featherstone, M., Hepworth, M., & Turner, B. (1991). *The body: social processes and cultural theory*. London: Sage.

Feyerabend, P. (1976). *Against method*. New York: Humanities Press.

Feyerabend, P. (1978). *Science in a free society*. London: Thetford Press.

Fish, S. (1980). *'Is there a text in this class?' The authority of interpretive communities*. Cambridge, MA: Harvard University Press.

Fisher, H. (1995). Whose right is it to define the self? *Theory and Psychology*, 5: 323–352.

Fleck, L. (1979). *Genesis and development of a scientific fact*. Chicago: University of Chicago Press.

Foucault, M. (1978). *The history of sexuality, Vol. 1* (R. Hurley, Trans.) New York: Pantheon.

Foucault, M. (1979a). *Discipline and punish: the birth of the prison*. New York: Random House.

Foucault, M. (1979b). What is an author? In V.H. Josue (Ed.), *Textual strategies: perspectives in post-structuralist criticism*. Ithaca, NY: Cornell University Press.

Foucault, M. (1980). *Power/knowledge*. New York: Pantheon.

Fowers, B.J., & Richardson, F.C. (1996). Individualism, family ideology and family therapy. *Theory and Psychology*, 6: 121–151.

Frank, A.W. (1995). *The wounded storyteller*. Chicago: University of Chicago Press.

Frascina, F., & Harrison, C. (Eds.). (1982). *Modern art and modernism*. London: Open University Press.

Frederick, W. (1963). The next development in management science: a general theory. *Academy of Management Journal*, 6: 212–219.

Freeman, J., Epston, D., & Lobovits, D. (1997). *Playful approaches to serious problems: narrative therapy with children and their families*. New York: W.W. Norton.

Freedman, D.H. (1992). Is management still a science? *Harvard Business Review*, Nov.–Dec.: 626–657.

Freedman, J., & Combs, G. (1996). *Narrative therapy: the social construction of preferred realities*. New York: Guilford Publications.

Freeman, M. (1993). *Rewriting the self: history, memory, narrative*. New York: Routledge.

Freeman, M. (1999). Culture, narrative, and the poetic construction of selfhood. *Journal of Constructivist Psychology*, *12*: 144–161.

Friedman, S. (Ed.). (1993). *The new language of change: constructive collaboration in psychotherapy*. New York: Guilford Press.

Frieire, P. (1972). *Pedagogy of the oppressed*. New York: Herder and Herder.

Friere, P. (1985). *The politics of education*. South Hadley, MA: Bergin and Garvey.

Frisby, D. (1985). *Fragments of modernity*. London: Polity Press.

Fromm, E. (1941). *Escape from freedom*. New York: Rinehart.

Fukuyama, F. (1992). *The end of history and the last man*. New York: Free Press.

Garfinkel, H. (1967). *Studies in ethnomethodology*. Englewood Cliffs, NJ: Prentice-Hall.

Garroutte, E.M. (1992). When scientists saw ghosts and why they stopped: American spiritualism in history. In T. Wuthnow (Ed.), *Vocabularies of public life*. London: Routledge.

Gates, H.L. (1994). *Colored people: a memoir*. New York: Knopf.

Gebser, J. (1985). *The ever-present origin*. Athens, OH: Ohio University Press.

Gee, J.G. (1992). *The social mind*. New York: Bergin and Garvey.

Gephart, R.P. (1992). *Environmental disasters in the postmodern era: theory and methods for organizational change*. Paper presented at the National Academy of Management Meetings, Las Vegas, Nevada.

Gergen, K.J. (1973). Social psychology as history. *Journal of Personality and Social Psychology*, *26*: 309–320.

Gergen, K.J. (1987). The language of psychological understanding. In H.J. Stam, T.B. Rogers, & K.J. Gergen (Eds.) *The analysis of psychological theory* (pp. 15–128). New York: Hemisphere.

Gergen, K.J. (1991). *The saturated self: dilemmas of identity in contemporary life*. New York: Basic Books.

Gergen, K.J. (1992). Organization theory in the postmodern era. In M. Reed & M. Hughes (Eds.), *Rethinking organization: new directions in organization theory and analysis* (pp. 207–226). London. Sage.

Gergen, K.J. (1994a). *Realities and relationships: soundings in social construction*. Cambridge, MA: Harvard University Press.

Gergen, K.J. (1994b). Mind, text, and society: self memory in social context. In U. Neisser & R. Fivush (Eds.), *The remembering self*. New York: Cambridge University Press.

Gergen, K.J. (1994c). *Toward transformation in social knowledge* (2nd ed.). London: Sage.

Gergen, K.J. (1995a). Metaphor and monophony in the twentieth century psychology of emotions. *History of the Human Sciences*, *8*: 1–23.

Gergen, K.J. (1995b). Performative psychology: the play begins. *Psychology and the Arts*, Fall: 8–9.

Gergen, K.J. (1996). Technology and the self: from the essential to the sublime. In D. Grodin & T. Lindlof (Eds.), *Constructing the self in a mediated age* (pp. 127–140). Beverly Hills, CA: Sage.

Gergen, K.J. (1999). *An invitation to social construction*. London: Sage.

Gergen, K.J., & Gergen, M.M. (Eds.). (1984). *Historical social psychology*. Hillsdale, NJ: Erlbaum.

Gergen, K.J., & Gergen, M.M. (1986). Narrative form and the construction of psychological science. In T. Sarbin (Ed.), *Narrative psychology: the storied nature of human conduct*. New York: Praeger.

Gergen, K.J., & Gergen, M.M. (1994). *Sandoz in the new century, an incorporative vision of communication for managerial effectiveness*. Basle: Sandoz Pharma.

Gergen, K.J., Gulerce, A., Lock, A., & Misra, G. (1996). Psychological science in cultural context. *American Psychologist, 51*: 496–503.

Gergen, K.J., & Kaye, J. (1992). Beyond narrative in the negotiation of human meaning. In S. McNamee & K.J. Gergen (Eds.), *Therapy as social construction* (pp. 166–185). London: Sage.

Gergen, K.J., & Walter, R. (1998). Real/izing the relational. *Journal of Social and Personal Relationships. 15*: 110–126.

Gergen, K.J., & Whitney, D. (1997) Technologies of representation in the global organization: power and polyphony. In D.M. Boje, R.P. Gephart, & T. Joseph (Eds.), *Postmodern management and organization theory*. Thousand Oaks, CA: Sage.

Gergen, M.M. (1988). Toward a feminist metatheory and methodology in the social sciences. In M. Gergen (Ed.), *Feminist thought and the structure of knowledge*. New York: New York University Press.

Gergen, M.M. (2001). *Feminist reconstructions in psychology: narrative, gender, and performance*. Thousand Oaks, CA: Sage.

Giddens, A. (1984). *The constitution of society*. Cambridge: Polity.

Giddens, A. (1990). *Consequences of modernity*. Stanford, CA: Stanford University Press.

Gigerenzer, G. (1996). From tools to theories: discovery in cognitive psychology. In C. Graumann & K. Gergen (Eds.), *Historical dimensions of psychological discourse*. New York: Cambridge University Press.

Gilligan, C. (1982). *In a different voice: psychological theory and women's development*. Cambridge, MA: Harvard University Press.

Gilligan, S., & Price, R. (Eds.). (1993). *Therapeutic conversations*. New York: W.W. Norton.

Giroux, H. (1992). *Border crossings*. New York: Routledge, Chapman and Hall.

Gitlin, T. (1993). The rise of 'identity politics'. *Dissent, 40*: 172–177.

Glendon, M.A. (1991). *Rights talk: the impoverishment of political discourse*. New York: Free Press.

Goldberg, D.T. (1993). *Racist culture*. Oxford: Blackwell.

Goldner, V. (1998). The treatment of violence and victimization in intimate relationships. *Family Process, 37*: 263–286.

Goldner, V., Penn, P., Sheinberg, M., & Walker, G. (1990). Love and violence: gender paradoxes in volatile attachments. *Family Process, 29*: 342–364.

Goncalves, O.F. (1995). Cognitive narrative psychotherapy: the hermeneutic construction of alternative meanings. In M.J. Mahoney (Ed.), *Cognitive and constructive psychotherapies*. New York: Springer.

Goodman, N. (1978). *Ways of worldmaking*. New York: Hackett.

Goolishian, H., & Anderson, H. (1987). Language systems and therapy: An evolving idea. *Journal of Psychotherapy, 24*: 529–538.

Graumann, C.F., & Gergen, K.J. (Eds.). (1996). *Historical dimensions of psychological discourse*. New York: Cambridge University Press.

Gray, C.H. (Ed.). (1995). *The cyborg handbook*. New York: Routledge.

Greenberg, D., & Sadofsky, M. (1992). *The Sudbury Valley School experience*. Framingham, MA: Sudbury Valley School Press.

Griffith, J.L., & Griffith, M.E. (1992). Therapeutic change in religious families: working with the God construct. In L.A. Burton (Ed.), *Religion and the family: when God helps* (pp. 63–86). New York: Haworth Press.

Griffith, J.L. & Griffith, M.E. (1994). *The body speaks: therapeutic dialogues for mind-body problems*. New York: Basic Books.

Gross, B., & Levitt, N. (1994). *Higher superstition: the academic left and its quarrels with science*. Baltimore: Johns Hopkins University.

Grossen, M. (1988). *L'interaction sociale en situation de test* (doctoral thesis, University of Neuchatel).

Grosz, E. (1988). The intervention of feminist knowledge. In B. Caine, E.A. Grosz, & M. de Lepervanche (Eds.), *Crossing boundaries, feminisms and the critique of knowledge*. North Sydney: Allen and Unwin Australia.

Gubrium, J., Holstein, J.A., & D. Buckholdt (1994). *Constructing the life course*. Dix Hills, NY: General Hall.

Fox, M. (1993). Personal communication.

Habermas, J. (1971). *Knowledge and human interests*. Boston: Beacon.

Habermas, J. (1993). *Justification and application: remarks on discourse ethics*. Cambridge, MA: MIT Press.

Hacking, I. (1995). *Rewriting the soul*. Cambridge, MA: Harvard University Press.

Hacking, I. (1999). *The social construction of what?* Cambridge, MA: Harvard University Press.

Hackman, R., & Lawler, E. (1971). Employee reactions to job characteristics. *Journal of Applied Psychology*, 60: 159–170.

Hage, J. (1963). An axiomatic theory of organizations. *Administrative Science Quarterly*, 10: 289–320.

Hage, J., & Powers, C.H. (1992). *Post-industrial lives*. Thousand Oaks, CA: Sage.

Haire, M. (Ed.). (1959). *Modern organization theory*. New York: Wiley.

Hammond, S.A. (1996). *Appreciative inquiry*. Chagnin Falls, OH: Taos Institute.

Harding, S. (1986). *Whose science, whose knowledge*? Ithaca, NY: Cornell University Press.

Hare-Mustin, R., & Marecek, J. (1988). The meaning of difference: gender theory, postmodernism, and psychology. *American Psychologist*, 43: 455–464.

Haraway, D. (1985). Manifesto for cyborgs: science, technology and socialist feminism in the 1980s. *Socialist Review*, 80: 65–108.

Harré, R. (Ed.). (1986). *The social construction of emotions*. Oxford: Blackwell.

Harré, R. (1992). What is real psychology: a plea for persons. *Theory and Psychology*, 2: 153–158.

Harré, R., & Finlay-Jones, R (1986). Emotion talk across times. In R. Harré (Ed.), *The social construction of emotions*. Oxford: Blackwell.

Harré, R., & Gillett, G. (1994). *The discursive mind*. Thousand Oaks, CA: Sage.

Harré, R., & Krausz, M. (1996). *Varieties of relativism*. Oxford: Blackwell.

Harvey, D. (1989). *The condition of postmodernity: an inquiry into the origins of cultural change*. Oxford: Blackwell.

Harvey, D. (1993). Class relations, social justice and the politics of difference. In J. Squires (Ed.), *Principled positions, postmodernism and the rediscovery of value*. London: Lawrence and Wishart.

Hassard, J. (1991). Multiple paradigms and organizational analysis: a case study. *Organization Studies*, 12: 275–299.

Healy, D. (1997). Cyberspace and place. In D. Porter (ed.), *Internet culture*. New York: Routledge.

Hebdige, D. (1987). *Subculture, the meaning of style*. London: Routledge.

Heelas, P., & Lock, A. (Eds.). (1981). *Indigenous psychologies: the anthropology of the self*. London: Academic Press.

Held, B. (1996). *Back to reality: a critique of postmodern psychotherapy*. New York: W.W. Norton.

Hepworth, J. (1999). *The social construction of anorexia nervosa*. London: Sage.

Herman, J. (1992). *Trauma and recovery*. New York: Basic Books.

Hermans, H.J.M., & Kempen, H.J.G. (1993). *The dialogical self: meaning as movement*. San Diego, CA: Academic Press.

Hetrick, W., & Lozada, H. (1992) *Postmodernism and anti-theory: the illusion of organizational science*. Paper presented at the National Academy of Management Meetings, Las Vegas, Nevada.

Hirschman, A.O. (1991). *The rhetoric of reaction*. Cambridge, MA: Belknap.

Hobbes, T. (1651). *The Leviathan*. London: Crooke.

Hoffman, L. (1990). Constructing realities: an art of lenses. *Family Process, 29*: 1–12.

Hoffman, L. (1993). *Exchanging voices: a collaborative approach to family therapy*. London: Karnac Books.

Hollinger, R. (1994). *Postmodernism and the social sciences*. Thousand Oaks, CA: Sage.

Hollingsworth, S., & Sockett, H. (1994). Positioning teacher research in educational reform: movement and momentum. In S. Hollingsworth & H. Sockett (Eds.), *Teacher research and educational reform*. Chicago, IL: University of Chicago Press.

Holzman, L. (1997). *Schools for growth*. Mahwah, NJ: Erlbaum.

Hoover, S.M. (1988). *Mass media religion*. Thousand Oaks, CA: Sage.

Horkheimer, M. (1974). *Eclipse of reason*. New York: Seabury.

House, R. (1971). A path goal theory of leadership effectiveness. *Administrative Science Quarterly, 16*: 321–338.

Hoyt, M.F. (Ed.). (1994). *Constructive therapies*. New York: Guilford Press.

Hoyt, M.F. (Ed.). (1996). *Constructive therapies: volume 2*. New York: Guilford Press.

Hoyt, M.F. (Ed.). (1998). *The handbook of constructive therapies: innovative approaches from leading practitioners*. San Francisco: Jossey-Bass.

Hume, D. (1977). *Treatise on human nature*. New York: Dutton. (First published in 1739).

Hunt, N.M. (1959). *The natural history of love*. New York: Knopf.

Hunter, J.D. (1991). *Culture wars*. New York: Basic Books.

Izard, C.E. (1977). *Human emotions*. New York: Plenum.

Jackson, P. (1968). *Life in classrooms*. New York: Holt, Rinehart and Winston.

Jacques, R. (1992). Critique and theory building: producing knowledge from the kitchen. *The Academy of Management Review, 17*: 582–606.

Jameson, F. (1984). Postmodernism, or the cultural logic late capitalism. *New Left Review, 146*: 53–92.

Johnson D.W., & Johnson, R.T. (1989). *Leading the cooperative school*. Edina, MN: Interaction Books.

Joseph, T. (1994). Organizations as texts: hermeneutics as a model for understanding organizational change. Unpublished doctoral dissertation, Case Western Reserve University.

Jung, C.G. (1973). *Four archetypes*. Princeton, NJ: Bollingen. (Originally published in 1945).

Kaslow, F.W. (Ed.) (1996). *Handbook of relational diagnosis and dysfunctional family patterns*. New York: John Wiley and Sons.

Kelly, G. (1955). *The psychology of personal constructs*. New York: W.W. Norton.

Kern, S. (1992). *The culture of love, Victorians to moderns*. Cambridge, MA: Harvard University Press.

Kesey, K. (1989). *Caverns*. Harmondsworth: Penguin.

Kessen, W. (1990). *The rise and fall of development*. Worcester, MA: Clark University Press.

Kessler, S.J., & McKenna, W. (1978). *Gender: an ethnomethodological approach*. New York: Wiley.

Kilduf, M. (1993). Deconstructing organizations. *The Academy of Management Review*, 18: 13–3.

Kilmann, R., Thomas, K., Slevin, D., Nath, R., & Jerrell, L. (Eds.). (1983). *Producing useful knowledge for organizations*. New York: Praeger.

Kirschner, S.R. (1996). *The religious and romantic origins of psychoanalysis*. New York: Cambridge University Press.

Kleinman, A. (1988). *The illness narratives*. New York: Basic Books.

Knorr-Cetina, K.D. (1981). *The manufacture of knowledge*. Oxford: Pergamon.

Kogan, S., & Brown, A.C. (1998). Reading against the lines: resisting foreclosure in therapy discourse. *Family Process*, 37: 495–512.

Kohlberg, L. (1981). *Philosophy of moral development: moral stages and the idea of justice*. San Francisco: Harper & Row.

Kostera, M. (1997). Personal performatives: collecting poetical definitions of management. *Organization*, 4: 345–353.

Kozulin, A. (1998). *Psychological tools, a sociocultural approach to education*. Cambridge, MA: Harvard University Press.

Kuhn, T. (1962). *The structure of scientific revolutions*. Chicago: University of Chicago Press.

Kuhn, T.S. (1970). *The structure of scientific revolutions*. 2nd rev. (ed.). Chicago: University of Chicago Press.

Kutchins, H., & Kirk, S.A. (1997). *Making us crazy: DSM the psychiatric bible and the creation of mental disorders*. New York: Free Press.

Kvale, S. (1987). Examinations – a psychometric test or a censorship of knowledge? *Nordisk Pedagogik*, 4: 221–234.

Kvale, S. (Ed.). (1992). *Psychology and postmodernism*. London: Sage.

Lacan, J. (1953). Actes due Congress du Rome. *La Psychoanalyze*, I.

Laclau, E., & Mouffe, C. (1985). *Hegemony and socialist strategy*. London: Verso.

Laing, R.D. (1967). *The politics of experience*. New York: Ballantine Books.

Laing, R.D. (1967). *The politics of experience*. Harmondsworth, Penguin.

Lakoff, G., & Johnson, M. (1980). *Metaphors we live by*. Chicago: University of Chicago Press.

Landau, M. (1991). *Narratives of human evolution*. New Haven, CT: Yale University Press.

Lange, A. (1996). Using writing assignments with families managing legacies of extreme traumas. *Journal of Family Therapy*, 18: 375–388.

Lannamann, J.W. (1998). Social construction and materiality: the limits of indeterminancy in therapeutic settings. *Family Process*, 47: 393–413.

Larner, G. (1996). Narrative child family therapy. *Family Process*, 35: 423–440.

Larochelle, M., Bednarz, N., & Garrison, J. (Eds.). (1998). *Constructivism and education*. Cambridge: Cambridge University Press.

Lasch, C. (1979). *The culture of narcissism*. New York: Norton.

Lasch, C. (1991). *The true and only heaven, progress and its critics*. New York: Norton.

Lather, P. (1991). *Getting smart*. New York: Routledge.

Latour, B., & Woolgar, S. (1979). *Laboratory life, the social construction of scientific fact*. Beverly Hills, CA: Sage.

Lavipour, F.G., & Sauvant, K. (Eds.). (1976). *Controlling multinational enterprises: problems, strategies, counterstrategies.* Boulder, CO: Westview.

Lawrence, P.R., & Lorsch, J. (1967). *Organization and environment.* Cambridge, MA: Harvard School of Business.

Layder, D. (1987). Key issues in structuration theory: some critical remarks. *Current Perspectives in Social Theory,* 8: 25–46.

Leary, D. (Ed.). (1990). *Metaphors in the history of psychology.* New York: Cambridge University Press.

Lee, A. (1991). Integrating positivist and interpretive approaches to organizational research. *Organization Science,* 2: 342–365.

Leo, J. (1991). The lingo of entitlement. *U.S. News and World Report,* 14 October: 22.

Levenson, M. (1984). *A geneology of modernism.* Cambridge: Cambridge University Press.

Levin, G.H. (1982). *Writing and logic.* New York: Harcourt Brace Jovanovich.

Levinas, E. (1981). *Otherwise than being or beyond essence.* The Hague: Martinus Nijhof.

Levitt, K. (1970). *Silent surrender: the multinational corporation in Canada.* Toronto: Macmillan.

Levy, R.I. (1989). The quest for mind in different times and different places. In A.E. Barnes & P.N. Stearns (Eds.), *Social history and issues in human consciousness.* New York: New York University Press.

Lieblich, A. (1993). Looking at change. In R. Josselson & A. Lieblich (Eds.), *The narrative study of lives.* Newbury Park, CA: Sage.

Lifton, R.J. (1993). *The protean self: human resilience in an age of fragmentation.* New York: Basic Books.

Lipman-Blumen, J. (1984). *Gender roles and power.* Englewood Cliffs, NJ: Prentice-Hall.

Lobel, S.A. (1990). Global leadership competencies: managing to a different drumbeat. *Human Resource Management,* 29: 39–47.

Locke, E.A. (1968). Toward a theory of task motivation and incentives. *Organizational Behavior and Human Performance,* 3: 157–189.

Locke, J. (1959). *An essay concerning human understanding.* New York: Dover.

Loewenberg, P. (1983). *Decoding the past: the psychohistorical approach.* New York: Knopf.

Lopes, L.L. (1991). The rhetoric of irrationality. *Theory and Psychology,* 1: 65–82.

Luhmann, N. (1976). A general theory of organized social systems. In G. Hofstede & S. Kassem (Eds.), *European contributions of organization theory* (pp. 96–113). Amsterdam: Van Gocum.

Luhmann, N. (1987). *Love as Passion.* Harvard, MA: Harvard University Press.

Lukes, S. (1974). *Power: a radical view.* London: Macmillan.

Lukes, S. (1977). *Essays in social theory.* London: Macmillan.

Lutz, C. (1988). *Unnatural emotions.* Chicago: University of Chicago Press.

Lyons, W. (1986). *The disappearance of introspection.* Cambridge, MA: MIT Press.

Lyotard, J. (1984). *The postmodern condition: a report on knowledge* (G. Bennington & B. Massouri, Trans.). Minneapolis: University of Minnesota Press.

Lyotard, J., & Thebaud, J. (1985). *Just gaming.* Minneapolis: University of Minneapolis Press.

MacIntyre, A. (1984). *After virtue* (2nd ed.). Notre Dame, IN: University of Notre Dame Press.

MacKinnon, L., & Miller, D. (1987). The new epistemology and the Milan approach:

feminist and sociopolitical considerations. *Journal of Marital and Family Therapy*, 13: 139–155.

Madigan, S., & Epston, D. (1995). From 'spy-chiatric' gaze to communities of concern: from professional monologue to dialogue. In S. Friedman (Ed.), *The reflecting team in action*. New York: Guilford Press.

Mancuso, J.C. (1996). Constructionism, personal construct psychology and narrative psychology. *Theory and Psychology, 6*: 47–70.

Mannheim, K. (1951). *Ideology and utopia*. New York: Harcourt Brace.

March, J.G., & Simon, H.A. (1958). *Organizations*. New York: John Wiley.

Marcus, G.E., & Fisher, M. (1986). *Anthropology as cultural critique: an experimental moment in the human sciences*. Chicago: University of Chicago Press.

Marcuse, H. (1964). *One dimensional man*. Boston: Beacon.

Martin, E. (1994). *Flexible bodies: tracking immunity in American culture from the days of polio to the age of AIDS*. Boston: Beacon Press.

Martin, J. (1990) Deconstructing organizational taboos: the suppression of gender conflict in organizations. *Organizational Science*, 1: 339–359.

Martin, J. and Sugarman, J. (1999). *The psychology of human possibility and constraint*. Albany: State University of New York Press.

Martindale, C. (1975). *The romantic progression: the psychology of literary history*. Washington, DC: Hemisphere.

Martindale, C. (1990). *The clockwork muse: the predictability of artistic change*. New York: Basic Books.

McCloskey, D.N. (1985). *The rhetoric of economics*. Madison, WI: University of Wisconsin Press.

McLaren, P. (Ed.). (1994). *Post-modernism, post-colonialism, and pedagogy*. Albert Park, Australia: James Nicholas.

McLeod, J. (1997). *Narrative and psychotherapy*. London: Sage.

McLibben, B. (1989). *The end of nature*. New York: Random House.

McNamee, S., & Gergen, K.J. (Eds.). (1992). *Therapy as social construction*. London: Sage.

McNamee, S., & Gergen, K.J. (1999). *Relational responsibility: resources for sustainable dialogue*. Thousand Oaks, CA: Sage.

Mehan, H. (1979). *Learning lessons, social organization in the classroom*. Cambridge, MA: Harvard University Press.

Merttens, R. (1998). What is to be done (with apologies to Lenin). In I. Parker (Ed.), *Social constructionism, discourse, and realism*. (pp. 59–74). London: Sage.

Messer, S.B., Sass, L.A., & Woolfolk, R.L. (Eds.). (1988). *Hermeneutics and psychological theory*. New Brunswick, NJ: Rutgers University Press.

Meyrowitz, J. (1985). *No sense of place*. New York: Oxford University Press.

Michael, M. (1996). *Constructing identities*. London: Sage.

Miles, R.E., & Snow C.C. (1978). *Organizational strategy, structure and process*. New York: McGraw-Hill.

Miller, G., & de Shazer, S. (1998). Have you heard the latest rumor about solution-focused therapy as a rumor? *Family Process, 37*: 363–377.

Minuchin, S. (1991). The seductions of constructivism. *The Family Therapy Networker*, 15: 47–50.

Mitchell, S. (1993). *Hope and dread in psychoanalysis*. New York: Basic Books.

Modell, J. (1989). A note on scholarly caution in a period of revisionism and interdisciplinarity. In A.E. Barnes & P.N. Stearns (Eds.), *Social history and issues in human consciousness*. New York: New York University Press.

Morawski, J.G. (1985). The measurement of masculinity and femininity: engendering categorical realities. *Journal of Personality*, 53: 171–197.

Morawski, J.G. (Ed.). (1988). *The rise of experimentation in American psychology*. New Haven, CT: Yale University Press.

Morawski, J.G. (1994). *Practicing feminisms, reconstructing psychology: notes on a liminal science*. Ann Arbor, MI: University of Michigan Press.

Morgan, G. (Ed.). (1983). *Beyond method: strategies for social research*. Beverly Hills, CA: Sage.

Morgan, G. (1990). Paradigm diversity of organizational research. In N. Hassard & D. Pym (Eds.). *The theory and philosophy of organizations*. London: Routledge.

Morgan, G. (1993). *Images of organization* (2nd ed.). London: Sage.

Morgan, R.E. (1984). *Disabling America: the 'rights industry' in our time*. New York: Basic Books.

Moscovici, S. (1984). The phenomenon of social representations. In R. Farr & S. Moscovici (Eds.), *Social representations*. London: Cambridge University Press.

Mulkay, M. (1985). *The word and the world: explorations in the form of sociological analysis*. London: Allen & Unwin.

Mumby, D.K., & Putnam, L. (1992). The politics of emotions: a feminist reading of bounded rationality. *The Academy of Management Review*, 17: 465–486.

Mustin, R.T. (1994). Discourse in the mirrored room: A postmodern analysis of therapy. *Family Process*, 33: 199–236.

Myerson, G. (1994). *Rhetoric, reason and society*. London: Sage.

Natter, W., Schatzki, T.R., & Jones, J.P. (Eds.). (1995) *Objectivity and its other*. New York: Guilford.

Neimeyer, G.J., & Neimeyer, R.A. (1985). Relational trajectories: a personal construct contribution. *Journal of Social and Personal Relationships*, 2: 325–349.

Neimeyer, R.A. (1999). Narrative strategies in grief therapy. *Journal of Constructivist Psychology*, 12: 65–86.

Neimeyer, R., & Mahoney, M. (Eds.). (1995). *Constructivism in psychotherapy*. Washington, DC: American Psychological Association.

Nielsen, Eric H. (1992). *Modernism, postmodernism and managerial competences*. Paper presented at the National Academy of Management Meetings, Las Vegas, Nevada.

Newman, F., & Holzman, L. (1996). *Unscientific psychology: a cultural-performatory approach to understanding human life*. Westport, CT: Praeger.

Newman, F., & Holzman, L. (1997). *The end of knowing: a new developmental way of learning*. London: Routledge.

Newman, F., & Holzman, L. (1999). Beyond narrative to performed conversation. *Journal of Constructivist Psychology*, 12: 23–41.

Nkomo, S. (1992). The emperor has no clothes: rewriting race in organizations. *The Academy of Management Review*, 17: 487–513.

Norris, C. (1983). *The deconstructive turn*. London: Methuen.

Norris, C. (1990). *What's wrong with postmodernism?* Baltimore: Johns Hopkins University Press.

Novick, P. (1989). *That noble dream*. New York: Cambridge University Press.

Ogilvy, J. (1990). This postmodern business. *Marketing and Research Today*, 18: 4–21.

O'Hanlon, W.H. (1993). Possibility therapy: from iatrogenic injury to iatrogenic healing. In S. Gilligan & R. Price (Eds.), *Therapeutic conversations*. New York: W.W. Norton.

O'Hanlon, W., & Weiner-Davis, M. (1988). *In search of solutions: a new direction in psychotherapy*. New York: W.W. Norton.

Olssen, M. (1996). Radical constructivism and its failings: anti-realism and individualism. *British Journal of Educational Studies, 44*: 275–296.

O'Neill, P. (1998). *Negotiating consent*. New York: New York University Press.

Ong, W.J. (1982). *Orality and literacy*. London: Methuen.

Osbeck, L. (1993). Social constructionism and the pragmatic standard. *Theory and Psychology, 3*: 337–349.

Osborne, J.F. (1996). Beyond constructivism. *Science and Education, 80*: 53–83.

Paranjpe, A. (1998). *Self and identity in modern psychology and Indian thought*. New York: Plenum.

Parker, I. (1998). Against postmodernism: psychology in cultural context. *Theory and Psychology, 9*: 601–627.

Parker, I., Georgas, E., Harper, D., McLaughlin, T., & Stowall-Smith, M. (1995). *Deconstructing psychopathology*. London: Sage.

Parker, I., & Shotter, J. (Eds.). (1990). *Deconstructing social psychology*. London: Routledge & Kegan Paul.

Parker, M. (1992) Post-modern organizations or postmodern organization theory? *Organization Studies, 13*: 1–17.

Parré, D.A., & Sawatzky, D.D. (1999). *Discursive wisdom: reflections on ethics and therapeutic knowledge*. Unpublished paper, Lousage Institute.

Parry, A., & Doan, R.E. (1994). *Story re-visions: narrative therapy in the postmodern world*. New York: Guilford Press.

Parsons, T. (1956). Suggestions for a sociological approach to the theory of organizations. *Administrative Science Quarterly, 1*: 63–85.

Parsons, T. (1969). On the concept of political power. In R. Bell, D. Edwards, & R. Wagner (Eds.), *Political power: a reader in theory and research* (pp. 251–284). New York: Free Press.

Pearce, W.B., & Littlejohn, S.W. (1997). *Moral conflict: when social worlds collide*. Thousand Oaks, CA: Sage.

Peck, S. (1992). *A world waiting to be born*. New York: Bantam.

Penn, P. (1988). Rape flashbacks: Constructing a new narrative. *Family Process, 37*, 299–310.

Penn, P., & Frankfurt, M. (1994). Creating a participant text: writing, multiple voices, narrative multiplicity. *Family Process, 33*: 217–231.

Pepper, W.C. (1942). *World hypotheses*. Berkeley: University of California Press.

Peters, T. (1992). *Liberation management: necessary disorganization for the nanosecond Nineties*. New York: A.A. Knopf.

Pettigrew, T.F., & Martin, J. (1987) Shaping the organizational context for black American inclusion. *Journal of Social Forces, 43*: 41–78.

Pfeffer. J. (1982). *Organizations and organization theory*. Boston: Pitman.

Pfohl, S. (1992). *Death at the parasite cafe*. New York: St. Martins Press.

Phelan, S. (1989). *Identity politics*. Philadephia, PA: Temple University Press.

Phillips, D.C. (1997). How, why, what, when and were: perspectives on constructivism in psychology and education. *Issues in Education, 3*: 151–194.

Piaget, J. (1954). *The construction of reality in the child*. New York: Basic Books.

Pitkin, H. (1972). *Wittgenstein and justice*. Berkeley, CA: University of California Press.

Polkinghorne, D.E. (1988). *Narrative knowing and the human sciences*. Albany, NY: State University of New York Press.

Potter, J., & Wetherell. (1987). *Discourse and social psychology: beyond attitudes and behavior.* London: Sage.

Pugh, D.S., Hickson, D.J., Hinings, C.R., Macdonald, K.M., Turner, C., & Lupton, T. (1963). A conceptual scheme of organizational analysis. *Administrative Science Quarterly, 8:* 289–315.

Ramirez, M. (1983). *Psychology of the Americas: Mestizo perspectives on personality and mental health.* Elmsford, NY: Pergamon.

Randall, J.H. (1940). *The making of the modern mind.* Boston: Houghton Mifflin.

Rawlins, W.K. (2000). Teaching as a mode of friendship. *Communication Theory, 10:* 5–26.

Reason, P., & Bradbury, H. (Eds.) (2001). *Handbook of action research.* London: Sage.

Reed, M., & Hughes (Eds.). *Rethinking organization.* London: Sage.

Rheingold, H. (1993). *The virtual community: homesteading on the electronic frontier.* Reading, MA: Addison-Wesley.

Richards, J. & von Glasersfeld, E. (1979). The control of perception and the construction of reality. *Dialectica, 33:* 37–58.

Richards, P.S., & Bergin, A.E. (1997). *A spiritual strategy for counseling and psychotherapy.* Washington, DC: American Psychological Association.

Riesman, D. (1953). *The lonely crowd.* New Haven, CT: Yale University Press.

Riikonen, E., & Smith, G.M. (1997). *Re-imagining therapy: living conversation and relational knowing.* London: Sage.

Rogoff, B. (1990). *Apprenticeship in thinking.* New York: Oxford University Press.

Rorty, R. (1979). *Philosophy and the mirror of nature.* Princeton, NJ: Princeton University Press.

Rorty, R. (1982). *Consequences of pragmatism.* Minneapolis: University of Minneapolis Press.

Rose, N. (1985). *The psychological complex: psychology, politics and society in England, 1869–1939.* London: Routledge & Kegan Paul.

Rose, N. (1990). *Governing the soul: the shaping of the private self.* London: Routledge.

Rosen, H., & Kuehlwein, K.T. (Eds.). (1996). *Constructing realities: meaning-making perspectives for psychotherapists.* San Francisco: Jossey-Bass Publishers.

Rosenau, P.M. (1992). *Postmodernism and the social sciences.* Princeton, NJ: Princeton University Press.

Rosengren, W. (1967). Structure, policy and style: strategies of organizational control. *Administrative Science Quarterly, 12:* 140–164.

Rumelt, R. (1974). *Strategy, structure, and economic performance.* Boston: Harvard Business School.

Rushing, W. (1967). The effects of industry size and division of labor on administration. *Administrative Science Quarterly, 12:* 273–295.

Rychlak, J.F. (1988). *The psychology of rigorous humanism* (2nd ed.). New York: New York University Press.

Salomon, G. (Ed.). (1996). *Distributed cognitions: psychological and educational considerations.* New York: Cambridge University Press.

Sampson, E.E. (1977). Psychology and the American ideal. *Journal of Personality and Social Psychology, 35:* 767–782.

Sampson, E.E. (1978). Scientific paradigms and social values: Wanted – a scientific revolution. *Journal of Personality and Social Psychology, 36:* 730–743.

Sampson, E.E. (1988). The debate on individualism. *American Psychologist, 43:* 15–22.

Sampson, E.E. (1989). The challenges of social change for psychology: globalization and psychology's theory of the person. *American Psychologist, 44:* 914–921.

Sampson, E.E. (1993a). *Celebrating the other, a dialogic account of human nature.* Boulder, CO: Westview.

Sampson, E.E. (1993b). Identity politics: challenges to psychology's understanding. *American Psychologist, 48*: 1219–1230.

Sandel, M.J. (1982). *Liberalism and the limits of justice.* Cambridge: Cambridge University Press.

Sarbin, T.R. (Ed.). (1986). *Narrative psychology: the storied nature of human conduct.* New York: Praeger.

Sarbin, T.R., & Mancuso, J.C. (1980). *Schizophrenia: medical diagnosis or verdict.* Elmsford, NY: Pergamon.

Sass, L.A. (1992a). *Madness and modernism.* New York: Basic Books.

Sass, L.A. (1992b). The epic of disbelief: the postmodern turn in contemporary psychoanalysis. In S. Kvale (Ed.), *Psychology and postmodernism* (pp. 166–182). London: Sage.

Schein, E. (1993). On dialogue, culture, and organizational learning. *Organizational Dynamics, 22*: 40–51.

Schnitman, D.F. (1996). Between the extant and the possible. *Journal of Constructivist Psychology, 9*: 263–282.

Schon, D.A. (1983). *The reflective practitioner: how professionals think in action.* New York: Basic Books.

Schwartz, B. (1986). *The battle for human nature.* New York: Norton.

Seeger, F. Voigt, J., & Waschescio, U. (1998). *The culture of the mathematics classroom.* New York: Cambridge University Press.

Seikkula, J., Aaltonen, J., & Alakare, B. (1995). Treating psychosis in western Lapland: reflective processes and open dialogue instead of hospitalization and heavy medication. In S. Friedman (Ed.), *The reflecting team in action* (pp. 62–81). New York: Guilford Press.

Selvini-Palazzoli, M., Boscolo, L., Cecchin, G., & Prata, G. (1980). Hypothesizing, circularity, neutrality: three guidelines for the conduct of the session. *Family Process, 19*: 3–12.

Semin, G., & Chassein, J. (1985). The relationship between higher order models and everyday conceptions of personality. *European Journal of Social Psychology, 15*: 1–16.

Senge, P. (1990). *The fifth discipline: the art and practice of the learning organization.* New York: Currency Doubleday.

Shafritz, J.M., & Ott, S. (1987). *Classics of organization theory.* Chicago: Dorsey Press.

Shapin, S. (1994). *A social history of truth.* Chicago: University of Chicago Press.

Shapin, S. (1996). *The scientific revolution.* Chicago: University of Chicago Press.

Sharan, S. (1990). *Cooperative learning.* New York: Praeger.

Sheinberg, M., & Penn, P. (1991). Gender dilemmas, gender questions and the gender mantra. *Journal of Marital and Family Therapy, 17*: 33–44.

Shorter, E. (1992). *From paralysis to fatigue, a history of psychosomatic illness in the modern era.* New York: Free Press.

Shotter, J. (1980). Action, joint action and intentionality. In M. Brenner (Ed.), *The structure of action.* Oxford: Blackwell.

Shotter, J. (1984). *Social accountability and selfhood.* Oxford: Blackwell.

Shotter, J. (1990). The social construction of remembering and forgetting. In D. Middleton & D. Edwards (Eds.), *Collective remembering.* London: Sage.

Shotter, J. (1993a). *Cultural politics of everyday life*. Toronto: University of Toronto Press.

Shotter, J. (1993b). *Conversational realities*. London: Sage.

Shotter, J. (1995). In dialogue: social constructionism and radical constructivism. In L.P. Steffe & J. Gale (Eds.), *Constructivsm in education*. Hillsdale, NJ: Erlbaum.

Shweder, R.I. (1991). *Thinking through cultures*. Cambridge, MA: Harvard University Press.

Simon, H. (1957). *Administrative behavior* (2nd ed.). New York: Macmillan.

Simonds, R.H. (1959). Toward a science of business administration. *The Journal of the Academy of the Management*, 2: 135–138.

Simons, H.W. (Ed.). (1989). *Rhetoric in the human sciences*. London: Sage.

Simons, H. (Ed.). (1990). *Case studies in the rhetoric of the human sciences*. Chicago: University of Chicago Press.

Simonton, D.K. (1984). *Genius, creativity, and leadership*. Cambridge, MA: Harvard University Press.

Simonton, D.K. (1990). *Psychology, science and history: an introduction to historiometry*. New Haven, CT: Yale University Press.

Sloterdijk, P. (1987). *Critique of cynical reason*. Minneapolis: University of Minnesotta Press.

Sluzki, C.E. (1992). Transformations: a blueprint for narrative changes in therapy. *Family Process*, 31: 217–230.

Smedslund, J. (1978). Bandura's theory of self-efficacy, a set of common sense theorems. *Scandinavian Journal of Psychology*, 19: 1–14.

Smedslund, J. (1988). *Psycho-logic*. New York: Springer-Verlag.

Smith, B.H. (1997). *Belief and resistance*. Cambridge, MA: Harvard University Press.

Smith, D.E. (1987). Women's perspective as a radical critique of sociology. In S. Harding (Ed.), *Feminism and methodology*. Bloomingon, IN: Indiana University Press.

Snyder, M. (1996). Our 'other history': poetry as a metaphor for narrative therapy. *Journal of Family Therapy*, 18: 337–359.

Soyland, A.J. (1994). *Psychology as metaphor*. London: Sage.

Spacks, P.M. (1995). *Boredom, the literary history of a state of mind*. Chicago: University of Chicago Press.

Spector, M., & Kitsuse, J.I. (Eds.) (1977). *Constructing social problems*. Menlo Park, CA: Cummings.

Spence, D. (1982). *Narrative truth and historical truth*. New York: W.W. Norton.

Spencer, H. (1885). *Principles of psychology*. New York: Appleton.

Srivastva, S., & Barrett, F.J. (1988). The transforming nature of metaphors in group development: a study in group theory. *Human Relations*, 41: 31–63.

Srivastva, S., Cooperrider, D.L., & Associates (1990). *Appreciative management and leadership: the power of positive thought and action in organizations*. San Francisco: Jossey-Bass.

Stearns, C.Z., & Stearns, P.N. (1986). *Anger: the struggle for emotional control in America's history*. Chicago: University of Chicago Press.

Stearns, P. (1989). *Jealousy: the evolution of an emotion in American history*. New York: New York University Press.

Stearns, P. (1994). *American cool*. New York: New York University Press.

Steffe, L., & Gale, J. (Eds.). (1995). *Constructivism in education*. Hillsdale, NJ: Lawrence Erlbaum.

Steffe, L., & Gale, J. (Eds.). (1996). *Alternative epistemologies in education*. Hillsdale, NJ: Erlbaum.

Stenner, P., & Eccleston, C. (1994). On the textuality of being. *Theory and Psychology*, 4: 85–103.

Sternberg, R.J. (1989). *The ethnic myth*. Boston: Beacon.

Sternberg, R.J. (Ed.). (1990). *Wisdom, its nature, origin and development*. New York: Cambridge University Press.

Stewart, E.C. (1972). *American cultural patterns: a cross-cultural perspective*. Chicago: Intercultural Press.

Stone, A.R. (1995). *The war of desire and technology at the close of the mechanical age*. Cambridge: MIT Press.

Strati, A. (1992). Aesthetic understanding of organizational life. *The Academy of Management Review*, 17: 568–581.

Suddaby, K., & Landau, J. (1998). Positive and negative timelines: a technique for restorying. *Family Process*, 37: 287–298.

Sugiman, R., Karasawa, M., Liu, J.H., & Ward, C. (Eds.) (1999). *Progress in Asian social psychology* (Vol. 2) Seoul: Kyoyook-Kwahak-Sa.

Suleiman, S.R. (1986). *The female body in western culture: contemporary perspectives*. Cambridge, MA: Harvard University Press.

Sykes, C.J. (1992). *A nation of victims, the decay of the American character*. New York: St. Martins.

Szasz, T.S. (1997). *The manufacture of madness: a comparative study of the inquisition and the mental health movement*. New York: Syracuse University Press. (Originally published in 1970)

Taggart, M. (1985). The feminist critique in epistemological perspective: questions of context in family therapy. *Journal of Marital and Family Therapy*, 11: 113–126.

Tavris, L.A. (Ed.). (1982). *Multinational managers and poverty in the Third World*. South Bend, IN: Notre Dame University Press.

Tavris, C. (1982). *Anger, the misunderstood emotion*. New York: Simon & Schuster.

Taylor, C. (1989). *Sources of the self*. Cambridge, MA: Harvard University Press.

Taylor, T. (1992). *Mutual misunderstanding*. Durham, NC: Duke University Press.

Thatchenkery, T. (1992). Organizations as texts: hermeneutics as a model for understanding organizational change. *Research in Organizational Change and Development*, 6: 197–233.

Thatchenkery, T.J., & Pasmore, W.A. (1992). *Postmodernism and the learning organization: implications for the academy*. Paper presented at the National Academy of Management Meeting, Las Vegas, Nevada.

Thompson, A.A., & Strickland, A.J. (1992). *Strategic management*. Homewood, IL: Irwin.

Thompson, C.J. (1993). Modern truth and postmodern incredulity: a hermeneutic deconstruction of the metanarrative of 'scientific truth' in marketing research. *International Journal of Research in Marketing*. 10: 32–338.

Thompson, J.D. (1956). On building an administrative science. *Administrative Science Quarterly*, 1: 102–111.

Thompson, V.A. (1960). Hierarchy, specialization, and organizational conflict. *Administrative Science Quarterly*, 5: 485–521.

Tiefer, L. (1992). Social constructionism and the study of human sexuality. In E. Stein (Ed.), *Forms of desire*. New York: Routledge.

Tocqueville, A. de (1969). *Democracy in America*. New York: Doubleday.

Tomkins, S. (1962). *Affect, imagery and consciousness*, (Vol. 1). New York: Springer.

Tomm, K. (1999). Co-constructing responsibility. In S. McNamee & K.J. Gergen (Eds.), *Relational responsibility: resources for sustainable dialogue* (pp. 129–138). Thousand Oaks, CA: Sage.

Torbert, W.R. (1991). *The power of balance: transforming self, society, and scientific inquiry*. Newbury Park, CA: Sage.

Tu Wei-ming (1985). Selfhood and otherness in Confucian thought. In A.J. Marsella, G. Devos, & F.L.K. Hsu, (Eds.), *Culture and self: Asian and western perspectives*. New York: Tavistock.

Tugendhat, C. (1972). *The multinationals*. New York: Random House.

Turkle, S. (1995). *Life on the screen, identity in the age of the internet*. New York: Simon & Schuster.

Turner, B.S. (Ed.). (1990). *Theories of modernity and postmodernity*. London: Sage.

Tyler, S. (1987). *The unspeakable: discourse, dialogue, and rhetoric in the postmodern world*. Madison, WI: University of Wisconsin Press.

Ulmer, G. (1987). *Applied grammatology. poste(e)-pedagogy from Jacuqes Derrida to Joseph Beuys*. Baltimore: Johns Hopkins University Press.

Ulmer, G. (1989). *Teletheory/grammatology in the age of video*. London: Routledge.

Usher, R., & Edwards, R. (1994). *Postmodernism and education*, London: Routledge.

Ussher, J.M. (1992). *Women's madness: misogyny or mental illness?* Amherst: University of Massachusetts Press.

van den Berg, J.H. (1961). *The changing nature of man*. New York: Norton.

van Dijk, T.A. (1989). *Elite discourse and racism*. Newbury Park, CA: Sage.

van Eemeren, F.H., & Grootendorst, R. (1983). *Speech acts in argumentative discussions*, Dordrecht: Foris.

van Maanen. J. (1988). *Tales of the field*. Chicago: University of Chicago Press.

Vernon, R. (1977). *Storm over the multinationals: the real issues*. Cambridge, MA: Harvard University Press.

von Glasersfeld, E. (1979). The control of perception and the construction of reality. *Dialectica, 33*: 37–50.

von Glasersfeld, E. (1988). The reluctance to change a way of thinking. *Irish Journal of Psychology, 9*: 83–90.

Vroom, V.H. (1964). *Work and motivation*. New York: Wiley.

Vygotsky, L.S. (1978). *Mind in society: the development of higher psychological processes*. Cambridge, MA: Harvard University Press.

Walkerdine, V. (1997). *Ethnomathematics: challenging eurocentrism in mathematics education*. Albany, NY: State University of New York Press.

Walkerdine, V. (1998). *Counting girls out: girls and mathematics*. London: Falmer.

Wallach, L., & Wallach, M.A. (1994). Gergen versus the mainstream: are hypotheses in social psychology subject to empirical test? *Journal of Personality and Social Psychology, 67*: 223–242.

Wallach, M., & Wallach, L. (1983). *Psychology's sanction for selfishness*. San Francisco: W.H. Freeman.

Warriner, C.K., Hall, R., & McKelvey, B. (1981). The comparative description of organizations: a research note and invitation. *Organization Studies, 2*: 173–175.

Wartenberg, T. (1990). *The forms of power*. Philadelphia, PA: Temple University Press.

Watzlawick, P., Beavin, J., & Jackson, D. (1967). *Pragmatics of human communication*. New York: W.W. Norton.

Weber, M. (1958). *The Protestant ethic and the spirit of capitalism*. New York: Scribner.

Weick, K. (1995). *Sensemaking in organizations*. Thousand Oaks, CA: Sage.

Weick, K.E., & Van Orden, P.W. (1990). Organizing on a global scale: a research and teaching agenda. *Human Resource Management*, 29: 49–61.

Weingarten, K. (1991). The discourse of intimacy: adding a social constructionist and feminist view. *Family Process*, 30: 285–305.

Weingarten, K. (1998). The small and the ordinary in the daily practice of a postmodern narrative therapy. *Family Process*, 37: 3–15.

Wells, G. (1999). *Dialogic inquiry, towards a sociocultural practice and theory of education*. Cambridge: Cambridge University Press.

Wertsch, J.V. (1991). *Voices of the mind: a sociocultural approach to mediated action*. Cambridge, MA: Harvard University Press.

Wertsch, J.V., & Toma, C. (1995). Discourse and learning in the classroom: A sociocultural approach. In L.P. Steffe & J. Gale (Eds.), *Constructivism in education*. Hillsdale, NJ. Erlbaum.

West, C. (1993). *Race matters*. New York: Vintage.

White, M., & Epston, D. (1990). *Narrative means to therapeutic ends*. New York: W.W. Norton.

Whitley, R. (1992) The social construction of organizations and markets: the comparative analysis of business recipes. In M. Reed & M. Hughes (Eds.), *Rethinking organization*. London: Sage.

Wiener, M., & Marcus, D. (1994). A sociohistorical construction of depression. In T.A. Sarbin & J.I. Kitsuse (Eds.), *Constructing the social*. London: Sage.

Willmott, H. (1997). Managment and organization studies as science? *Organization*, 4: 309–344.

Wise, A. (1979). *Legislated learning*. Berkeley, CA: University of California Press.

Wittgenstein, L. (1953). *Philosophical investigations*. (G. Anscombe, Trans.). New York: Macmillan.

Wittington, E. (1985). *Sometimes a shining moment: the Foxfire experience*. New York: Anchor Press.

Wolf, W. (1958). Organizational constructs: an approach to understanding organizations. *The Journal of the Academy of Management*, 1: 7–15.

Wood, G.H. (1988). Democracy and the curriculum. In L.E. Beyer & M.W. Apple (Eds.), *The curriculum, problems, politics and possibilities*. Albany, NY: State University of New York Press.

Wood, T., Cobb, P., & Yackel, E. (1995). Reflections on learning and teaching mathematics in elementary school. In L. Steffe & J. Gale (Eds.), *Constructivism in education*. Hillsdale, NJ: Lawrence Erlbaum.

Wortham, S.F. (1994). *Acting out participant examples in the classroom*. Amsterdam: John Benjamins.

Wortham, S. (1996). Are constructs personal? *Theory and Psychology*, 6: 79–84.

Wykoff, G.S. (1969). *Harper handbook of college composition*. New York: Harper & Row.

Yakkhlef, A. (1981). Outsourcing and the construction of accountable worlds. *Organization*, 5: 425–446.

Yakkhlef, A. (1992). Call for special research forum: configurational approaches to organization. *Academy of Management Journal*, 35: 685–692.

Young, K. (1997). *Presence in the flesh*. Cambridge, MA: Harvard University Press.

Zimmerman, J.L., & Dickerson, V.C. (1996). *If problems talked: narrative therapy in action*. New York: Guilford Press.

INDEX

U.W.E.L. LEARNING RESOURCES